Indians Illustrated

THE HISTORY OF COMMUNICATION

Robert W. McChesney and
John C. Nerone, editors

*A list of books in the series appears
at the end of this book.*

INDIANS
ILLUSTRATED

*The Image of Native Americans
in the Pictorial Press*

JOHN M. COWARD

University of Illinois Press

URBANA, CHICAGO, AND SPRINGFIELD

Library of Congress Cataloging-in-Publication Data
Names: Coward, John M.
Title: Indians illustrated: the image of Native Americans in the
    pictorial press / John M. Coward.
Description: Urbana : University of Illinois Press, 2016. | Series:
    The history of communication | Includes bibliographical
    references and index.
Identifiers: LCCN 2015046831 (print) | LCCN 2016011529
    (ebook) | ISBN 9780252040269 (cloth : acid-free paper) |
    ISBN 9780252081712 (paperback : acid-free paper) | ISBN
    9780252098529 | ISBN 9780252098529 (ebook)
Subjects: LCSH: Indians of North America—Press coverage—
    History. | Indians of North America—Public opinion—
    History. | Illustrated periodicals—United States—History.
    | Journalism, Pictorial—Social aspects—United States—
    History. | Visual communication—United States—History. |
    Stereotypes (Social psychology)—United States—History. |
    Indians in popular culture—United States—History. | Public
    opinion—United States—History. | Popular culture—United
    States—History. | United States—Race relations—History.
Classification: LCC PN4888.I52 C67 2016 (print) | LCC PN4888.I52
    (ebook) | DDC 070.4/4997000497—dc23
LC record available at http://lccn.loc.gov/2015046831

Contents

Acknowledgments

This book took shape over many years of reading, researching, and writing—as well as a great deal of rewriting and revision. I was assisted along this path by friends and colleagues at the University of Tulsa and in the larger community of journalism and media historians I have been fortunate to know. First, I want to acknowledge the support of my colleagues at the TU Faculty of Communication, Joli Jensen, Mark Brewin, and Ben Peters. I have also been encouraged over the years by TU colleagues in other departments, including Brian Hosmer from history and Garrick Bailey from anthropology. My work as a journalism historian has been enriched by my friends in the American Journalism Historians Association (AJHA) and the History Division of the Association for Education in Journalism and Mass Communication (AEJMC). In particular, I thank William E. Huntzicker for his generous spirit and long-standing support of my research on Native Americans and the nineteenth-century press. I also want to thank the editors and reviewers of scholarly journals where parts of this book were first published, including Pat Washburn of *Journalism History*, Barbara Friedman and Kathy Roberts Ford of *American Journalism*, and Berkley Hudson of *Visual Communication Quarterly*.

For research support and access to collections, I am grateful to American Antiquarian Society and The American Historical Print Collectors Society Fellowship for research time in the AAS collection. Paul Erickson, director of academic programs at AAS, was especially helpful in making me feel at home at that outstanding research library. I also received generous support from the American Journalism Historians Association through the Joseph McKerns Award, which supported research in the collections of at the New-York Historical Society. In support of the publication of this book, I thank the Office of Research and Sponsored Programs at the University of Tulsa for their generous assistance. I also want to thank the staff at the University of Illinois Press, especially Daniel Nasset, for their support of this project.

On a more personal note, I am grateful for the love and support of my children, Ian and Rachel, and my life-long partner and best friend, Linda, without whom I could not have completed this project. Finally, I dedicate this book to my mother,

Loretta Mason Coward (Carson-Newman College, Class of 1948), who grew up in an old Cherokee town in the southeast corner of Tennessee known today as Ducktown. She provided the example of hard work and stick-to-itiveness that shaped me during my childhood and adolescence, lessons that carried over into my scholarly life. I am a better person because of her love.

Introduction

Illustrating Indians in the Pictorial Press

The cover of *Harper's Weekly* on December 7, 1878, featured an extraordinarily dramatic Indian illustration. The full-page engraving, "A Battle in the Clouds," showed a resolute, bare-chested warrior battling an enraged eagle lured to a mountaintop using a rabbit as bait[1] (figure 0.1). The warrior held one of the eagle's legs with his left hand, swinging a coup stick in his right hand to fend off the bird's talons, which were dangerously close to his body. The field of contest was a lofty mountain summit and the prize for which the warrior struggled was the rich spoil of magnificent feathers "so dear to the heart of every Indian," *Harper's Weekly* explained. "He uses them for many purposes—to decorate his head-dress, his robes, his leggins, and to give accuracy to the deadly flight of his arrows. For the latter purpose they are split lengthwise. They are rarely used whole in decoration, the Indians displaying considerable skill in combining portions of differently colored feathers so as to produce an effect pleasing to the barbaric taste."[2]

This illustration was cover material in *Harper's Weekly* because it presented—in a visually exciting way—a powerful Indian warrior in the midst of a violent quest, a battle between a proud but uncivilized American savage and a wild and dangerous predator. In other words, this illustration was published on the cover because it represented a remarkable encounter in the American wilderness, a mythic scene of untamed Western life that the editors hoped would capture the public's imagination and, if they were lucky, draw a few more readers to the weekly.

This striking scene was largely imaginary, however, its details most likely based on a thrilling but secondhand tale of Indian adventure in the American West.[3] The artist was William de la Montagne Cary, a veteran *Harper's* staff artist who had traveled widely and spent time with Indians in their villages. Despite such experiences, neither Cary nor *Harper's* claimed that the artist witnessed this event. Moreover, *Harper's* included no place or time of this encounter and provided no attribution to a witness or photograph, only a line at the bottom of the page explaining that the scene was "Drawn by W. M. Cary." In fact, the engraving did not portray a specific individual at a particular place or time but a generic Indian warrior, a man unidentified by name or tribe. All of this signals the allegorical nature of this en-

FIGURE O.I. W. M. Cary's 1878 cover illustration for *Harper's Weekly* was more imagination than reality, an idealized Noble Savage created for popular consumption.

graving, an illustration published more for its visual appeal than for its news value. The imaginary nature of this illustration was not a problem for Cary, the editors, or the paper's readers. After all, this was a bold and wildly romantic scene, true in a symbolic, if not literal, sense. This illustration also carried a particular set of Indian meanings because it represented some of the qualities that made the Noble Savage actually noble and, for that matter, savage. Again, there were clues in the published explanation: "Attacking the king of birds with his 'coup' stick, instead of with the rifle or the bow, is probably an act of bravado, to display his prowess for the admiration of some dusky coquette of the forest." This warrior's dangerous encounter with the eagle, then, was not about feathers at all, or at least not entirely. It was a feat of Indian derring-do meant to catch the eye of a certain "dusky" woman.

This example of Native American male bravery—romanticized in Cary's imagination to attract white, middle- and upper-class class readers from across the United States—reveals a number of important ideas surrounding the popular image of the American Indian in the last half of the nineteenth century. Cary's valiant warrior was a nineteenth-century representation of a "good" Indian, a popular and aesthetically pleasing Noble Savage. This idealized figure gave *Harper's* and its readers a way to see and appreciate—at a superficial level—this aboriginal American man, an extraordinary warrior rising from savagery to become a heroic (and virile) American symbol. This book is a study of such Indian images—romantic, violent, racist, peaceful, and otherwise—in the nineteenth-century illustrated press. More specifically, this research offers a social and cultural history of Indian illustrations during the heyday of the illustrated press. This era—the pictorial press era—was marked by a proliferation of detailed, realistic woodblock engravings, pictures of newsworthy people and interesting events from across the nation and the world. These pictures formed the basis for a new product in American journalism, the illustrated press, picture-packed weekly newspapers that prospered in the last half of the nineteenth century. "The time was ripe for pictorial journalism," historian Joshua Brown has noted. "By the mid-1850s the transportation revolution, innovations in printing technology, and an expanded literary and pictorial market came together to provide almost all the conditions necessary for a commercially viable illustrated press."[4] These papers were part of a visual revolution in nineteenth-century journalism that brought images—including hundreds of news and feature pictures of Native Americans—into the lives and imaginations of ordinary American readers.

This book argues that these Indian illustrations were an important source of visual information about Indians and Indian life in the second half of the nineteenth century, pictures influential enough that traces of these images can be found in American popular culture to this day. Indeed, I argue that these pictures—along with news stories, editorials, advertisements, dime novels, photography, popular entertainment, and the like—helped create and sustain a host of popular ideas and attitudes about Indians, especially ideas about the way Indians were supposed to look and act. Indian illustrations in the pictorial press, I maintain, were part of the social and cultural machinery that produced and reinforced an enduring set of Indian stereotypes and visual tropes in the American popular imagination, reinforcing the ways that white Americans understood Native Americans and their place in U.S. society. As I argue in the following pages, such pictures were a significant part of this meaning-making process because they frequently depicted Indians and Indian life in popular but narrowly conceived ways. In pictures, Indians could be—and were—simplified and presented in familiar and easily understood categories, usually as variations on the "good" Indian/"bad" Indian stereotypes long established in Euro-American culture.[5] Thus, when the occasion presented itself, Indians could be pictured as Noble Savages: proud, brave, strong, and unsullied by the evils of the civilized world. On other occasions, they could be represented as treacherous and bloodthirsty savages, primitive people on the wrong side of history and a menace to civilized, honest, God-fearing whites. In still other cases, Native Americans could be ridiculed or praised in pictures and words that reflected a superficial and sometimes contradictory set of ideas about their virtues and deficiencies as a race. By describing and analyzing the various themes and visual tropes across the years of the illustrated press, this book provides a deeper understanding of the racial codes and visual signs that white Americans used to represent Native Americans in an era of western expansion and Manifest Destiny.

Visualizing the Indian "Other"

For decades—centuries, actually—American Indians have been victims of the Euro-American racial imagination. In popular culture and the mass media, Indians have been portrayed by a set of racial stereotypes and visual clichés, forces so powerful that they have shaped ideas about Indians and their lives for generations of white Americans. As historian Robert Berkhofer put it in his now-classic 1978 study *The White Man's Indian,* "Native Americans were and are real, but the *Indian* was a White invention and still remains largely a White image, if not stereotype."[6] In recent years Native Americans have become increasingly vocal in identifying and pushing back against Indian stereotypes in words and pictures. Writing about the representation of Indian soldiers and sailors in World War II, for example, Ojibwe scholar Selene Phillips pinpointed the problem: "After centuries in which the word 'Indian' has been part of our written and spoken languages, it is almost impossible to encounter the word without envisioning specific mental images."[7] Devon Mihesuah, a Choctaw scholar, framed the problem this way: "No other ethnic group in the United States has endured greater and more varied distortions of its cultural identity than American Indians."[8] In addition, Mihesuah noted, most Americans—indeed, most people around the globe—"appear to have definite expectations of what Indians should look like." Indian men are "tall and copper-colored, with braided hair, clothed in buckskin, and moccasins, and adorned in headdresses, beadwork and/or turquoise." Indian women, Mihesuah continued, are beautiful and exotic, like the Disney version of Pocahontas, who "sings with the forest animals" and is "blessed with a Barbie doll figure."[9] The major purpose of this book is to describe and analyze Indian images in the nineteenth-century illustrated press and to explain the origins and meanings of these representations in American popular culture.

At the foundational level, this study builds on the cultural approach to communication, an idea advanced by the late communication scholar James Carey. The cultural approach looks at communication not simply as the transmission of information, but as "the maintenance of society in time" and, importantly, as the "the representation of shared beliefs."[10] The news, that is, does something more than convey information or facts; it allows for the construction of community and common understandings, the underlying beliefs that hold a society together and shape its ideology. Following this view, the act of reading a newspaper—and viewing its images—works in ways that ritually reassure the reader, who is participating, Carey writes, in "a situation . . . in which a particular view of the world is portrayed and confirmed."[11]

Applying Carey's approach to Indian imagery in the illustrated press, I argue that these representations helped sustain and reinforce a number of powerful ideas and beliefs about Indians and Indian life in the last half of the nineteenth century. Indian images in the pictorial press were products of the racial ideology of nineteenth-century Euro-American life and these images functioned in ways that confirmed a set of ideas about what it meant to be an American—that is, a white Euro-American—and what it meant to be an outsider, an Indian "other." The ideas and beliefs embedded in the illustrated press, then, were manifestations of an ideology that was largely Anglo-American, Protestant, and capitalist, categories that automatically set Native Americans apart from the political and cultural mainstream of nineteenth-century American life. In short, American Indians were almost always perceived as outsiders, a category of people different from "normal" Americans. This position ensured that they would be represented in the illustrated press most often in ways that simplified and accentuated those differences. Even when Indians and Indian cultures were represented more or less accurately or sympathetically, the images in the pictorial press functioned in ways that maintained racial boundaries and emphasized cultural differences.

In a similar way, my analysis treats Indian representations in the pictorial press as constructed artifacts—"something people make," as media historian and sociologist Michael Schudson has written.[12] Journalists make the news, Schudson writes, through a complex process "of selecting, highlighting, framing, shading and shaping what they report."[13] Moreover, this news-making process is constrained by a variety of social forces, including such matters as "what counts as a fact in journalism."[14] More often than not, the forces that shape journalistic choices work in ways that support mainstream society and the status quo and, in the words of press historians Juan Gonzalez and Joseph Torres, marginalizes minorities and outsiders as "an array of backward and violent non-white peoples."[15] In the case of

Native Americans, as Gonzalez and Torres suggest, this news-making process was not neutral or balanced but socially determined and ethnocentric, shaped by the dominant standards and values of Euro-American life. Thus Indian illustrations, as well as the captions and stories that explained them, were circumscribed by the fact that Native Americans were routinely identified as racially and culturally different, a category of uncivilized people who could be visually distinguished from "normal" Euro-Americans. In other words, Indian representations in the illustrated press were always subject to specific cultural, sociological, and journalistic practices as an inevitable part of the process of making illustrated news. This sociological view of news production, along with Carey's cultural approach, provides a basis for an examination of Indian images at a broad ideological level, as illustrations that—whatever else they may communicate—represent a number of powerful and deeply held ideas about the nature of American Indians and their place and meaning in the American experience.

In short, Indians were represented in the final decades of the nineteenth century in ways that diminished their cultural values and political power. As Gonzalez and Torres make clear in *News for All the People,* the American media have long been guided by an all-encompassing white racial narrative.[16] The U.S. media, they write, were part of an ideological system that "played a pivotal role in perpetuating racist views among the general population." This process affected outsiders, including Native Americans, "by routinely portraying non-white minorities as threats to white society and by reinforcing racial ignorance, group hatred, and discriminatory government policies."[17] As I argue in the following chapters, this was often the case with Indian illustrations, though the idea and image of the Indian varied across the decades in ways that sometimes blurred or contradicted this racial narrative.

This book is an extension of my previous work on Native American representations in the nineteenth-century press. In *The Newspaper Indian,* I examined news stories and editorials about Indians, arguing that mainstream newspapers were "a significant force in the creation and promotion of a powerful set of Indian representations that dominated the nineteenth-century imagination."[18] That study was focused on written texts and made only passing references to Indian imagery or the illustrated press. Yet even as I completed that research I was aware of the influence of Indian imagery on popular perceptions of Native Americans. This book is my attempt to fill the scholarly gap surrounding the meaning and significance of Indian images in the illustrated press.

The study and significance of popular imagery has often been an afterthought in the study of history. Writing in the 1950s, historian Robert Taft pointed out that images have been misused or overlooked by American historians. While historians are "meticulous about documenting their written manuscripts with source notes and arguments," Taft wrote, "[they] use illustrations without the least attempt at documenting the source or the authenticity of the illustrations used."[19] In the 1990s, historian Louis P. Masur made a similar argument regarding history textbooks, noting that most publishers "do not provide students with even a superficial understanding of the place and meaning of images in American history."[20] In addition, Masur noted, "Authors do not situate the images in their historical context or locate those images within the history of visual production and reproduction; they do not discuss the images within the narrative, thereby reinforcing the notion that pictures may illustrate but not shape historical events."[21] More recently, historian Joshua Brown has argued that the illustrated press and its wealth of imagery deserve a more central place in the history of nineteenth-century life. For the most part, Brown writes, scholarship on the illustrated press has been reduced to "a scholarly form of decoration," a development that "ignores news images as evidence of a social practice in its own right."[22] As these comments suggest, popular imagery can be a powerful way of investigating the past and understanding the forces at work at a particular historical moment. Like photographs, as Annette Kuhn has argued, illustrations "cannot be taken at face value, nor as a 'mirror of the real.'" Instead, she argues, they are "material for interpretation, evidence in that sense: to be solved, like a riddle; read and decoded, like clues left behind at the scene of a crime."[23] In the case of Indians in the pictorial press, a study of popular imagery reveals some of the principal ways that Americans made sense of Native Americans at a time when Indian lives and cultures were threatened by western emigration, violence, and a host of other social and political forces in U.S. society.

Although a number of illustrated papers came and went during the nineteenth century, this study focuses primarily on the two most popular and significant illustrated weeklies, *Frank Leslie's Illustrated Newspaper,* founded at the end of 1855, and *Harper's Weekly,* founded in 1857. From the start, these papers brought pictures of important people and news events to a wide range of American readers. This was no small accomplishment. Indeed, it was a major shift in the nature of news, the beginning of a visual revolution in journalism. With the rise of *Leslie's* and *Harper's* and other illustrated papers, a broad range of American readers could see printed images of newsworthy people and places every week and at a relatively modest price. These pictures were realistic-appearing illustrations, engraved drawings sometimes based on photographs but frequently based on artist sketches from the scene or, in a great many cases, imaginative re-creations of news events based on interviews or written accounts. Whatever their source or fidelity to the truth, these pictures ushered in a new age of visual journalism and a new profession, the "special artist," a visual reporter who could provide vivid sketches of important news makers and news events, including portraits of notable Indians, scenes of Indian life, cartoons, action-oriented pictures of Indian-white violence, and thousands of other pictures, which, taken together, made a difference in the popular perception of Indians and Indian-white relations well into the twentieth century.

One of the first scholars to investigate the artists and illustrators who depicted Indians was Robert Taft, a professor at the University of Kansas who began his studies in the 1930s. Taft was trained as a chemist, not a historian, but his work in chemistry led to his wide-ranging history of U.S. photography, *Photography and the American Scene,* published in 1938. His interest in imagery, in turn, led Taft to Western art and illustration, which resulted in his second major book, *Artists and Illustrators of the Old West, 1850–1900.* Published in 1953, Taft provided rich and deeply researched biographical accounts of Western artists, including such well-known figures as John Mix Stanley and Frederic Remington. Taft also investigated the lives and careers of many lesser-known illustrators and artists who worked for the illustrated papers. These include such men as A. R. Waud and Theodore Davis, both of whom became famous for their Civil War illustrations, as well as a host of other illustrators who produced pictures of Indians and the American West, such as W. M. Cary, Alfred E. Mathews, Joseph Becker, Jules Tavernier and Paul Frenzeny, William A. Rogers, Rufus Zogbaum, Henry Farny, and many others. Although most of these men were dead before Taft began his research, he interviewed and corresponded with as many artists and their relatives as he could, gathering an impressive amount of first- and secondhand information about drawing and painting the American West and the Indians who lived there. "Thousands of notes have been made, thousands of letters have been written, and thousands of miles have been traveled in collecting this source material," Taft declared.[24]

Taft's accomplishment was significant, yet his study was largely biographical and descriptive, information that fleshed out the lives and achievements of Western illustrators. Taft's purpose was celebratory; he sought to create interest in these artists and illustrators for future generations of Western historians, artists, and collectors, noting "the increasing number of individuals who have an intense interest and admiration for the Old West."[25] As this quote suggests, Taft's history was largely positive, more concerned with documenting the accomplishments of Western illustrators than criticizing them or interpreting their images within a larger ideological context. Taft has almost nothing to say, for example, about the political, social, and cultural consequences of Manifest Destiny or the uses and significance of racial stereotypes in Indian illustrations. For Taft the West was a place of American triumph and the artists and illustrators who worked there were part of the success of western expansion and conquest. Although I too examine the lives and work of a number of Western illustrators—Cary, Theodore Davis, Frederic Remington, and others—my study raises important questions about race, representation, and culture that have been largely ignored in the study of Indian imagery in the pictorial press. Indeed, the purpose of my research is to offer a critical analysis of the assumptions, ideas, and meanings associated with these illustrations.

The Rise of the Pictorial Press

With *Frank Leslie's Illustrated Newspaper* and *Harper's Weekly* leading the way, illustrated newspapers and magazines thrived in the last half of the nineteenth century. As early as 1857, the *Cosmopolitan Art Journal* declared, "The 'illustration' mania is upon our people."[26] Press historian Frederic Hudson, writing in 1873, also remarked on the ubiquity of the illustrated papers. "Every newspaper stand is covered with them," he wrote. Hudson pointed out that the pictures in these papers were "object-teaching" the reading public. "[The illustrated papers] make the battlefields, the coronations, the corruptions of politicians, the balls, the race-course, the yacht race, military heroes . . . Farragut and Porter, Grant and Sherman, familiar to everyone," Hudson wrote. "They are, in brief, the art gallery to the world," he concluded.[27] Notwithstanding Hudson's grandiose claim, the illustrated papers were one of the primary ways that ordinary American readers came to know what important people and famous places looked like. One purpose of the illustrated press, in fact, was to give readers a visual sense of the news in a timely fashion.[28] Writing in 1880, Richard Kimball noted that Frank Leslie's goal was to provide "exact illustrations of the current events of the day, and in this way to make them a prime agent in the instruction of the people."[29] Leslie's plan worked, especially in his own estimation. Writing a year after the paper's founding, Leslie claimed that he had already succeeded in "giving to the American public an illustrated paper worthy of the country, equal to its intelligence." Moreover, he boasted, "Not a picture has been given that did not possess some interest; not an event of importance has occurred that has not been noticed."[30] American readers liked what they saw. Readers were, in the words of historian Richard West, "fascinated by pictures."[31] In *Leslie's* third year of publication, journalism historian Frank Luther Mott noted, "subscriptions began flooding the office," and Leslie was claiming a circulation of more than 100,000.[32] Frank Leslie's success did not go unnoticed. In early 1857, he inspired a serious competitor, *Harper's Weekly,* founded by Fletcher Harper and his brothers, owners of their own publishing firm. Like *Leslie's,* it prospered quickly, reaching a circulation of 90,000 by October 1859.[33]

Pictorial journalism, as it came to be known, solved a major technological problem in picturing the news: nineteenth-century printing technology could not reproduce photographs, a process that would have to await the perfection of the halftone in the 1890s.[34] Some fifty years earlier, British publisher Herbert Ingram developed a way of printing detailed newspaper illustrations from engraved wooden blocks, an innovation that promised a new visual world for readers.[35] Enterprising young artists like Henry Carter soon began to exploit this visual form. Born in England in 1821, Carter was interested in wood engraving from an early age. His father disapproved of his artistic interests, however, so the teenage Carter submitted sketches to a London publisher signed with a pseudonym, "Frank Leslie," which became his professional name. Leslie's interest in picturing the news was honed during his six years at the *Illustrated London News,* where he worked his way up from novice engraver to manager of the engraving department. Leslie was good at his job. "He distinguished himself by displaying, in his youthful zeal, the kind of speed, dexterity, inventiveness, and self-exploitation that were indispensible in running an illustrated newspaper," historian Joshua Brown wrote.[36]

Ambitious to start his own illustrated newspaper, Leslie immigrated to the United States in 1848. By 1852, he had become the chief engraver for the first American pictorial paper, *Gleason's Pictorial Drawing-Room Companion,* published in Boston. *Gleason's* quickly developed a following, but publisher Frederick Gleason was more interested in illustrated features than news, prompting Leslie to move to New York and establish his own publishing house. In late 1855 Leslie founded *Frank Leslie's Illustrated Newspaper,* a weekly aimed at a growing audience of urban readers, especially working-class readers.[37] Toward that end, the newspaper was copiously illustrated, often sensational, and sometimes lurid—with an emphasis on crime, violence, and crusades against corruption.[38] In his inaugural issue, Leslie made his mission clear; he wanted to impart "to the journal all the rapidity and freshness essential to the efficiency of a newspaper." Using the talents of his network of skilled wood engravers, Leslie crowed, "we shall have pictorial delineations of every remarkable event that occurs . . . with almost the same promptness as the written intelligence of the fact itself."[39] Yet it was Leslie's emphasis on sensational pictures that sparked public interest and made the weekly prosper. One observer summed up Leslie's over-the-top formula in bold terms: "Murder and horror, executions and assassinations, prize fights and wars, every *cause celebre,* every sensation, every exposure made grist for a mill that ground out the flaming double-page engravings that made his name a household word."[40]

Leslie's also succeeded because of speed, an innovation in the production of woodblock prints pioneered by Leslie himself. The key was cutting large blocks of wood—usually Turkish boxwood—into a number of pieces, a division of labor that put several engravers to work on a single illustration. Starting with a photograph or an artist's sketch from the field, a *Leslie's* staff artist copied the illustration on the large wooden block, which was then cut into a number of separate pieces. Different engravers carved their parts of the illustration on their piece of wood. Next the engraved pieces were reassembled and bolted back together to produce the completed engraving. This process allowed wood engravings to be completed overnight, reducing the production process by weeks.[41] Mott summed up the rise of *Leslie's* by noting its speed: "The news stories were illustrated by large, striking pictures which usually followed the events they portrayed by about two weeks—a promptitude in news illustration never known in America and not matched by any competitor until after the Civil War."[42]

Leslie also learned the power of news illustrations when his paper launched a crusade against tainted milk in New York City in 1858. As Andrea Pearson has pointed out, *Leslie's* swill milk campaign included the extensive use of pictures, which *Leslie's* took great pains to produce and promote. Leslie sent his chief artist, Albert Berghaus, along with two staff artists, Sol Eytinge and the young and not-yet-famous Thomas Nast, to the city's stables to document sick cows. *Leslie's* published eight pictures of Berghaus "working in the field as an investigative reporter," Pearson noted.[43] Leslie also promoted his investigative artists in the columns of the paper, referring to the pictures as "accurate," "correct," and "authentic." In addition, Pearson noted, Leslie learned the value of pictures in selling the news: "He must have learned that written news seemed far more accurate, concrete, and marketable when accompanied by an appropriate illustration."[44] Leslie continued his pictorial crusade when the New York state senate passed a bill to prevent the adulteration of milk in April 1861.[45] In this crusade, Pearson found, Leslie affirmed the power of the image and helped establish a journalistic legend that flourished during the Civil War and extended to the post–Civil War West and Indian wars: the myth of the "on-the-spot" journalist, witnessing history as it was being made.

Fletcher Harper launched his illustrated weekly on January 1, 1857. Like Leslie, Harper wanted to create a national market for illustrated news, though with more refined content for genteel middle- and upper-class readers.[46] *Harper's Weekly* made its uplifting mission clear, boldly announcing itself on its cover as "A Journal of Civilization." The weekly also promoted itself as "a first-class newspaper," as Mott noted.[47] Indeed, *Harper's* was edited with an eye to the entire family. "Like television today," Fiona Halloran notes, "*Harper's Weekly* was a staple of home life, read not only by husbands and fathers but also by wives, mothers, and older children."[48] Fletcher, the youngest of the four Harper brothers, was devoted to his new weekly, "his pet enterprise," his grandson said.[49] Following his brothers, Fletcher was trained as a printer. He was also "a shrewd and enterprising businessman, and a good Methodist," according to Mott. Harper had a keen eye for talent as well, hiring George William Curtis as political editor and twenty-two-year-old (and former *Leslie's* artist) Thomas Nast as cartoonist, both of whom went on to lead a campaign against the corrupt Tweed ring in New York City in the 1870s.[50] Unlike Leslie, Harper had no background in news and at the beginning was more interested in publishing quality literature than pictures of news events. "The pictures in the first few issues were neither numerous nor important," Mott found, "but the number increased rapidly."[51] Reviewing the early years of *Harper's Weekly*, art historian Andrea Pearson made the same assessment. "Harper generally used images to supplement weekly serial novellas or travel pieces," Pearson discovered.[52]

This focus changed during the Civil War, when news interest was high and images from the battlefield were much in demand.[53] "During the Civil War," one historian concluded, "*Harper's Weekly* out-Leslied *Leslie's Newspaper*, bringing into America's drawing rooms descriptions and scenes of battle within days of their occurrence."[54] The war circulation of *Harper's Weekly* climbed to "120,000 by the end of 1861, and stayed at a figure above the 100,000 mark throughout most of the conflict—a very unusual circulation for that time," Mott noted.[55] In fact, both *Leslie's* and *Harper's* were well positioned to benefit from the Civil War. Leslie once claimed to have more than eighty artists covering the war and, by war's end, claimed to have published some 3,000 war illustrations.[56] "It is not too much to say that no important expedition, during the last four years, has left the scene of action with Frank Leslie's Illustrated Newspaper being represented in it by an Artist of acknowledged ability and experience," *Leslie's* boasted. *Harper's Weekly* employed some of the most famous Civil War artists, including Theodore Davis and Alfred Waud, both of whom made hundreds of war drawings.[57] Illustrations were the only practical way to represent the fighting because photographs of battlefield action were nearly impossible given the slow exposure times and other limitations of photographic technology in the 1860s.[58] The illustrated papers met the demand for action by publishing seemingly realistic illustrations of combat alongside stories from their correspondents, satisfying their readers' need for war news and turning a tidy profit for themselves. Even when the battlefield scenes were mostly imaginary, vivid, action-oriented war illustrations were good for business. In short, *Leslie's* and *Harper's* attracted readers—and profits—when they provided apparently realistic illustrations of violent action and battlefield excitement.

After 1865, much of the national narrative shifted west, to the adventures of settlers, soldiers, cowboys, and Indians on the plains and in the mountains West. In New York, editors wanted frontier illustrations that would recapture the excitement of the Civil War and dramatize the Indian wars and the American frontier.[59] *Harper's* artist Theodore Davis, for example, reported an impromptu meeting in April 1867 with Fletcher Harper, who was walking along Broadway. "Why are you not with General Hancock's Indian Expedition?" Harper asked his artist.[60] Davis was eager to return to the field. Only three days later, Davis had made his way to Kansas, ready to supply pictures from the frontier. As we shall see, the desire for action-oriented news and images from the Indian frontier and around the American West became a significant part of the success of the pictorial press, even when the illustrator was not on the scene and the fidelity of the illustration was highly dubious.

Pictorial Journalism and Its Limits

Using wood engravings and other nineteenth-century imaging technologies, pictorial journalists could—for the first time in mass media history—quickly and routinely present images of news makers and national events to a vast popular audience.[61] In the United States, the illustrated papers made the nation and the world visually accessible in a way that had not been possible before. Political leaders, exotic peoples, and faraway places could be represented visually in the homes and parlors of the reading public. In this way, illustrated journalism revolutionized the way that ordinary citizens understood and engaged Native Americans, the prairies and mountains of the American West, and other people and places beyond their immediate experience.

Yet the promoters of pictorial journalism promised more visual "reality" than they could deliver. In 1852, Frederick Gleason, publisher of *Gleason's Pictorial Drawing-Room Companion*, boasted that his woodcuts would offer Boston readers a "faithful delineation of men and manner, all over the world, its perfect transcript of ancient and modern cities, its likeness of eminent characters, its geographical illustrations of scenery and localities, and, in short, its illustrations of every notable current event."[62] This goal was vastly overstated. Nevertheless, *Leslie's* and *Harper's* promoted their illustrations as accurate and truthful. They did this whenever possible by stressing that their images were based on direct observations by artists in the field. A scene of Arctic exploration in the inaugural issue of *Leslie's* emphasized this point: "From a Sketch Made on the Spot."[63] Similarly, a *Harper's Weekly* battlefield scene from the 1863 Sioux war was labeled for authenticity: "Sketched by an Officer Engaged," the caption read.[64] Unfortunately, as Robert Taft has noted, "the artist occasionally made a slip and was somewhere else—probably in the home office—rather than on the spot."[65] Even if the artist (or officer) was at the right spot at the right time, his drawing was likely to be incomplete, "shaped by the limitations of time and the chaos of circumstance," in the words of historian Joshua Brown.[66] Nevertheless, "seeing was believing" for many nineteenth-century readers. Over time, as Michael Carlebach concluded, "the public began to trust the information contained in the illustrations that filled each issue."[67]

The fidelity of the pictorial press, in short, was always suspect to one degree or another, leading critics to accuse offending illustrators of inventing scenes out of whole cloth. According to Taft, rivals accused some artists of picturing a scene "before it occurred, or, more frequently of having pictured a scene that never occurred."[68] In addition, the production process was complicated, passing through several hands as it went from a rough paper sketch to a finished drawing on wood to a divided and reassembled block and finally a printed engraving.[69] Along the way, staff artists and engravers sometimes "improved" the original sketch or photograph to add excitement, follow convention, or tell the story they wanted to tell. In other words, both illustrators in the field and engravers in the back shop had the ability—and often the incentive—to change a scene or photographic image to suit their own aesthetic or ideological ends. Photo historian Martha Sandweiss has documented an early but telling example of this kind of editorial deception. In May 1858, Sandweiss found, photographer Humphrey Lloyd Hime photographed a group of European and Indian voyageurs making a portage on a Canadian expedition. When the scene was illustrated in the *Illustrated London News* several months later, the engraver changed the Iroquois boatmen into Europeans. This change, Sandweiss concluded, was explicitly racial, reaffirming in imagery "the broadly perceived connections between the heroism of the exploration and the racial identity of the explorers."[70] In a similar vein, Carlebach discovered two versions of a portrait of the Seminole leader Och-Lochta Micco, popularly known as Billy Bowlegs. In the original photograph, Carlebach found, Och-Lochta Micco was unarmed, but a lithograph based on the photo included a rifle, added by an unidentified publisher.[71] One specific effect of this addition was to reinforce the hostility of a notorious Seminole warrior. Another effect was more mercenary: to meet the expectations of middle-class customers and sell more lithographs.[72]

Despite such deceptions, the illustrated papers used the rise of photography to promote the accuracy and realism of their images.[73] Again, this promise exceeded the facts even when the published engraving closely resembled the original photograph. Nineteenth-century photography could capture some aspects of the real world, to be sure, and a great many illustrations were faithful reproductions of original photographic images. But photographs could not render "reality" itself for a host of reasons, including the obvious but sometimes overlooked fact that photographs have finite temporal and visual boundaries, unlike actual lived experience. That is, photographs represent reality at a single moment in time, not the continuous unfolding of actual time. In addition, photographic subjects were routinely posed, dressed, manipulated, or altered in ways that changed or misrepresented what they purported to depict, even on the battlefield.[74] Finally, as noted previously, nineteenth-century photography suffered from a number of technical limitations that restricted the kinds of events and activities that could be photographed. Wet-plate collodion equipment, long exposure times, and heavy equipment, for instance, limited much early photography to portraits, landscapes, and other static subjects.[75] For much of the nineteenth century, action photography was beyond the capability of even the best photographers and their equipment. As we shall see, none of these limitations hindered the energy or determination of the pictorial press to capture pictures of important people and vivid images of news events from across the continent. With dozens of artists and photographers in the field and staff artists and engravers in the home office, Frank Leslie and Fletcher Harper spent their professional lives providing American readers with appealing and seemingly accurate illustrations, no matter the picture's limited perspective or questionable fidelity to people and events of the actual world. As Brown has pointed out, whatever the accuracy or fidelity of these pictures, these "engravings were the images the public viewed and it was their representation of events to which readers responded."[76]

The illustrations included in this study were analyzed for the subjects and themes they included and, on occasion, for what they did not. That is, I attempted to describe and interpret the specific content of the images themselves, including both major and minor themes within the pictures and, not least, those details in the images that carried social or cultural significance regarding Indians and Indian life. I also sought to interpret these images within the larger context of the publication itself, especially the story or occasion that brought these pictures into the pages of the illustrated press at particular historical moments. In this way, I endeavored to look beyond the content of the illustrations themselves in order to provide more complete understandings of the images and their meanings within the larger stream of illustrated Indian news in the last half of the nineteenth century.

I also examined the captions and stories that accompanied these Indian illustrations. As Sandweiss reminds us, images can't always speak for themselves; they often need captions to be understood. Regarding historic images from the American West, Sandweiss notes, the text often reinforces the theme of the picture. In other cases, however, the text and the image send ambiguous, even contradictory, messages. In still other cases, Sandweiss adds, "the photographic captions call the reader's attention to what is impossible to see in the photographs themselves."[77] Although Sandweiss was writing about Western photography, these shifts of meaning between the image and the text are true as well for Indian illustrations in the pictorial press. Following Sandweiss, my analysis of Indian illustrations includes the captions and stories that accompanied these illustrations, information that provides additional context for a deeper and more nuanced explanation of these pictures and their meanings.

Scope of the Study

This study describes and analyzes a range of Indian illustrations published during the most active years of the illustrated press, beginning in the mid-1850s and extending into the 1890s. Within this period, I have examined hundreds of Indian illustrations covering a variety of Indian subjects and themes, although I am well aware that I have not analyzed every Indian illustration in the pictorial press. Nevertheless, I have worked to include a range of Indian images on a variety of topics over a period of several decades as a way of identifying the principal themes as well as significant variations and permutations of these pictures. I would note too that Indian illustrations and the captions and stories that explain them include a number of ambiguities and contradictions that render absolute conclusions about their meanings and significance difficult and sometimes confounding. This uncertainty should not be a surprise, however, given the span of years under consideration, the large number of Indian illustrations produced, and the complex and fraught relations between Euro-Americans and Native Americans in the final decades of the nineteenth century. Considered from this perspective, the variations and ambiguities associated with illustrated Indians reflect the richness of these representations as well as the shifting nature of ideas and beliefs about Indians over time and in various contexts.

It is important to note here that the ideas and themes attached to Indian images in the pictorial press were not conjured out of thin air; they were based on centuries of written texts. As I argued *The Newspaper Indian,* Columbus and other European explorers used the power of written language to organize and make sense of America, a process that helped domesticate the wilderness and subdue its native people.[78] In letters, journals, decrees, and other documents, Europeans represented Indians and Indian life in language that identified their differences and accentuated their deficiencies. Columbus himself noted that the first people he encountered were naked, primitive, and "very poor in everything," all signs of their lack of civilization and thus their savagery.[79] Indians were also portrayed as the "other" in the colonial press, including the first English-language newspaper published in North America, Benjamin Harris's *Publick Occurrences Both Forreign and Domestick.* The one and only edition of *Publick Occurrences* (it was quickly suppressed by colonial authorities) included references to both "Christianized Indians," who were good, and "barbarous Indians," who were not.[80] This division expressed the existing classification of Indians into two general categories: romantic Noble Savages and brutal, bloodthirsty killers. Both categories cast Indians as the American Other, uncivilized people "perceived and understood as fundamentally different from and opposed to American life and its ideals."[81]

The "good" Indian/"bad" Indian division evolved across the decades and flourished in nineteenth-century print culture. Both types turned up, for example, in the popular *Leatherstocking Tales* of James Fenimore Cooper. Cooper had little experience with actual Indians but he did as much as any American writer of the antebellum era to advance the idea of the bloodthirsty warrior and romantic Noble Savage. "In war," Cooper wrote in 1850, "[the Indian] is daring, boastful, cunning, ruthless, self-denying, and self-devoted; in peace, just, generous, hospitable, revengeful, superstitious, modest, and commonly chaste."[82] Henry Wadsworth Longfellow made the romantic Indian the star attraction of his epic poem, *The Song of Hiawatha,* published in 1855.[83] The romantic Indian turned up in antebellum newspapers as well. In 1834, for example, a Tennessee weekly described an Indian woman mourning over the twin graves of her husband and child. "The father of Life and Light has taken from me the apple of my eye, and core of my heart, and hid him in these two graves," the Indian woman said. "I will moisten one with my tears, and the other with the milk of my breast, till I meet them in that country where the sun never sets."[84] This was "Indian Eloquence," as the paper's headline put it. It was also romantic fiction, it seems, an Indian stereotype based on a white writer's imagination, not an incident witnessed by any newspaper correspondent.[85] In the same vein, an 1838 *Washington Telegraph* report on the Seminole war recounted the story of a white captive rescued by a seventeen-year-old girl just before his execution. The incident, the *Telegraph* declared, was "a singular development of noble feeling and humanity upon the part of the Indians."[86] Singular development or not, the story is suspiciously similar to the rescue of Captain John Smith by Pocahontas in colonial Virginia, a similarity that suggests its fictional—and romantic—origins. Good Indian stories, it seems, lived long on the printed page.

Good and bad Indians also turned up in European and American imagery and art. A 1505 German woodcut, for example, offered a vivid scene of Native American cannibalism, reinforcing the savagery of the Caribbean Indians.[87] In 1590, a Theodor de Bry engraving of an exotic, well-muscled "Great Lorde of Virginia" was published in London, evidence of the regal American savage.[88] In colonial America, Indian murderers turned up in the crude woodcuts published in various editions of Mary Rowlandson's popular captivity story, *A Narrative of the Captivity and Restoration of Mrs. Mary Rowlandson,* which first appeared in 1682.[89] In antebellum America, artists such as George Catlin traveled up the Missouri River to paint Indians, who were, he believed, "an interesting race of people, who are rapidly passing away from the face of the earth."[90] Catlin produced hundreds of portraits and scenes of Indian life, romantic pictures he displayed at exhibitions he called *Catlin's Indian Gallery* beginning in 1837. Catlin's 1841 book, *Letters and Notes on the Manners, Customs, and Conditions of the North American Indians,* featured black and white engravings of many of these paintings, becoming, as Alan Trachtenberg writes, "the most widely circulated Indian images available at the time."[91] Artist Charles Deas, active in the 1840s, painted both Noble Savages and more sinister Indians, including a terrified warrior fighting for his life in *The Death Struggle.* This painting, completed in 1845, focused on what art historian Carol Clark called a "blood-spilling, eye-popping" fight between an Indian hunter and a white trapper.[92] Violence, of course, was a familiar story in the conquest of America; it was also a popular aspect of early American visual culture. Like the language of discovery and conquest, the ideas and themes in Indian paintings and popular imagery played a significant role in shaping the illustrated Indian.

I should also add a word about *presentism,* the tendency of historians (and the public) to judge the ideas and activities of the past by the values of today. This is an easy trap to fall into, especially when the topic involves complex issues of race, conquest, dispossession, misrepresentation, and the like. Although I have tried to avoid presentism in this study, I recognize that I am a product of my own time, education, and experience, factors that account for the nature and limitations of this analysis. Nevertheless, I have attempted throughout the book to keep my conclusions within the context of nineteenth-century American culture and ideology, recognizing that nineteenth-century ideas were often very different from today's ideas and that historical actors lived in a different time and place.

The chapters that follow investigate Indian illustrations in several pictorial papers during an era marked by the rise of popular imagery. The topics are loosely chronological and organized around a number of prominent Indian themes found in the pictorial press. The analysis begins in chapter 1 with an examination of Indian portraits, one of the earliest and most common ways that Indian faces and bodies came to the pages of the illustrated press. Indian portraits, in fact, appeared in both *Gleason's Pictorial* and *Ballou's Pictorial,* early but short-lived illustrated papers published in Boston.[93] In chapter 2, I review the work of William de la Montagne Cary and other artists who drew pictures of Indians living their lives, pictures of peaceful Indians that often drew less attention than more action-oriented pictures of war and conflict. This chapter examines illustrations of activities such as dancing and hunting, as well as burial rituals, male-female relations, and Indians engaged in work and play, topics often overlooked in studies of Indian illustrations. In chapter 3, I consider the representation of Indian women—also overlooked in most previous studies of the pictorial press—contrasting the romantic "Indian princess" stereotype with a harsher set of qualities often associated with Indian women in the pictorial press. In chapter 4, I explore some of the most important Indian illustrations of Theodore Davis, one of the first illustrators to travel west following the Civil War. His pictures of a Kansas stage attack and arrow-pierced skeletons of soldiers helped popularize images of Indian violence as an important—and sensational—visual trope in an era of Western expansion. Chapter 5 investigates illustrations of the Indian wars more broadly. Looking at Indian-white violence in the 1860s, I argue that Indian war coverage and related images of Indian-white violence were considerably more imaginary than real, functioning in ways that supported the ideology of Manifest Destiny. Although some illustrations depicted scenes of actual battles by "on the spot" artists, reality was less important than the creation of white heroes and Indian demons, images that reinforced the necessity of military conquest. Other violent illustrations were purely allegorical, invented scenes meant to symbolize the continuing—and, from the nineteenth-century point of view, *necessary*—struggle between civilization and savagery. Chapter 6 expands the range of the research to include Indian cartoons in another illustrated publication, the *Daily Graphic,* a New York paper that became the nation's first illustrated daily paper. This chapter compares cartoon Indians before and after the Battle of the Little Bighorn, the fight that captured the public's imagination and quickly became the most famous battle between plains Indians and the U.S. Army. Like much of the press, the *Graphic* demonized the Sioux in the weeks following the battle, though it soon moderated its tone and published more tempered Indian images. Chapter 7 reviews the Indian illustrations of Frederic Remington, widely acclaimed today as the most famous Western illustrator and painter. Remington, who was too young to cover the major Indian wars, nevertheless created a number of significant Indian war images, including important but highly fictionalized *Last Stand* illustrations that shaped ideas about Indian fighting for several generations of Americans. In chapter 8, I examine racial imagery in *Frank Leslie's Illustrated Newspaper* in the final years of the nineteenth century, comparing the illustrations of Indians and African Americans as a way of explaining the shifting nature of race and representation as Western expansion ran its course. In the conclusion, I review the major findings of the research and offer some ideas about the significance and meaning of Indian images in the pictorial press.

As noted earlier, this book is part of my ongoing scholarly project to describe and analyze the role of the nineteenth-century press as it represented Native Americans. One question animates much of this inquiry: Why did pictorial press artists and editors depict Indians in the ways that they did? One answer to this question is the complicated and persistent love-hate relationship between Indians and white Americans that shaped Indian imagery as far back as the colonial era. This relationship, in turn, regularly reduced Indian representations to "good" Indian/"bad" Indian stereotypes and clichés, which helps explain why the artists, illustrators, and editors of the pictorial press rarely managed to portray Indians in humane, empathetic, or fully developed ways. Even when illustrators and their papers were sympathetic to Indians and Indian issues, the differences between Indians and whites in the illustrated press were often simplified or misunderstood—or both.

In general, the "understanding gap" concerning Indians in the illustrated press persisted because white, mainstream artists and editors almost always believed in the superiority of Euro-American life, especially in the brutal struggle over land and resources, and even when they found some sympathetic Indians who displayed "Indian qualities" they could admire. I offer a number of explanations for this long misunderstanding, some practical and journalistic, others tied to the overarching ideology of American progress and Manifest Destiny. These ideas, in combination with the ordinary processes of representation in the illustrated press, ensured that Indians and Indian life would be routinely—if not consistently—portrayed as different from, and deficient to, "normal" America and Americans. There were, of course, very real differences between Indians and whites, differences that were certain to be portrayed in the illustrated papers. Nevertheless, the illustrated papers routinely emphasized Indian differences and deficiencies and, in that way, reduced them to symbols or caricatures, actions that had major consequences on the lives of Indians in America. This was also a telling example of the media's continued inability—or unwillingness—to deal with race and culture in a fair, balanced, or nuanced manner. In the words of media historians Juan Gonzalez and Joseph Torres, the U.S. media from the beginning "assumed primary authorship of a deeply flawed national narrative: the creation myth of heroic European settlers battling an array of backward and violent non-white peoples to forge the world's greatest democratic republic."[94] In the following pages, I describe and analyze a number of telling and dramatic examples of Indian pictures and stories that support this flawed national narrative.

CHAPTER 1

Posing the Indian

*Native American Portraits
in the Illustrated Press*

On September 10, 1881, *Frank Leslie's Illustrated Newspaper* published a half-page illustration of a sketch by artist A. B. Shults. The artist captured a scene rarely shown in the illustrated press: a blanket-clad Indian posing for a photographic portrait in front of a crowd of onlookers as well as the photographer himself, Charles Milton Bell, whose head was under a black cloth[1] (figure 1.1). The occasion for the portrait, *Leslie's* explained, was a meeting between interior secretary Samuel J. Kirkwood and a delegation of Western chiefs, an effort to settle a land dispute between the government, the Sioux, and the beleaguered Ponca tribe. Some months earlier, the Poncas had fled their reservation in Indian Territory and returned to their homeland in Nebraska, now part of the Great Sioux Reservation. At the Washington, DC, meeting, Secretary Kirkwood sought—and received—Sioux permission to cede 25,000 acres of their reservation to the Poncas, a decision that surprised Kirkwood. "The Secretary was so pleased with the liberality of the Sioux," *Leslie's* reported, "that he had the entire body of delegates escorted to the photographic studio of C. M. Bell, where photographs of each were taken at the expense of the department."[2] This was the scene that artist Shults had captured, an event that evidently pleased the Indians as well. As *Leslie's* put it, "[The Indians] watched every movement of the operators with great interest, and were profuse in thanks when informed that each one would be given copies of his photograph to take with him to his people."[3]

Artist Shults's illustration was unusual because it offered a glimpse of the elaborate process of making an Indian portrait in a photographic studio, a scene that included a stone-faced Indian and an anxious photographer's assistant. The *Leslie's* caption also offered a set of meanings for this illustration and the portraits that photographer Bell produced. As an agent of the government, Secretary Kirkwood's photographic gift not only provided the Indian leaders with mementos of their trip, but it also provided official documentation of the Indian delegation's visit to Washington and reified the success of the negotiation, a symbolic process furthered

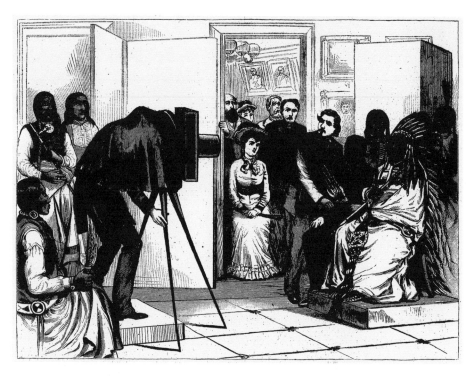

FIGURE I.I. Photographer C. M. Bell took portraits of Sioux leaders in Washington, DC, in 1881. *Leslie's* reported that the Indians "watched every movement of the [camera] operators with great interest."

by the appearance of this *Leslie's* illustration. All of this suggests that Indian portraits in the illustrated press were more than simple pictures of Indians faces and bodies; they were complex cultural productions laden with multiple meanings and open to various interpretations. Moreover, the rise of the illustrated papers meant that Indian portraits—for the first time in U.S. history—could be circulated to a mass audience in a cheap, popular, and convenient form. This fact amplified the significance of these illustrated portraits among the reading public, many of whom had limited exposure to painted Indian portraits and little or no experience with actual Indians.

This chapter examines posed photographic portraits of Indian delegations and individuals in the illustrated press. The research focuses on the two most important pictorial papers, *Frank Leslie's Illustrated Newspaper* and *Harper's Weekly,* as well as two earlier and lesser-known papers, *Gleason's Pictorial* and *Ballou's Pictorial.* The research covers the rise and prime years of the pictorial press, from the early 1850s, when *Gleason's* was founded, to the 1890s, when the rise of the halftone signaled the beginning of the end for the nineteenth-century illustrated press. Although the research is selective rather than exhaustive, the portraits analyzed here represent the most common types of Indian portraits published in the pictorial press.[4] In contrast to studies that focus on Indian violence and battle imagery,[5] this study analyzes nonviolent Indian imagery—portraits—and seeks to explain how these images helped construct and maintain particular racial meanings and Indian stereotypes. Following Stuart Hall's work on race and representation, the study describes and analyzes the signs of racial classification and difference in Indian portraits and discusses how these signs limit and define the "ethnic other."[6] Accordingly, the chapter raises questions about the nature and meaning of Indian portraits. Who were the Indians represented in these illustrations and, more importantly, when and why did the papers publish these portraits? How and under what conditions were these portraits made? What qualities did these portraits emphasize or ignore? Finally, what did these portraits mean to readers of the pictorial press? These and other questions are addressed in the following pages.

Making Indian Portraits

The creation, publication, and meaning of Indian portraits in the illustrated press is complicated by a number of cultural and technical factors, including the history and characteristics of portrait painting, the conventions and limitations of early photography, and the editorial process of turning photographs into illustrations. In other words, making Indian portraits was tied to a set of larger ideas about technology, race, and representation that existed in mid-nineteenth-century visual culture, a process that was often ambiguous, even contradictory, and whose practices predated the creation of the pictorial press. In fact, painted portraits of Indian chiefs—dignified "Noble Savages"—were a well-established genre well before the invention of photography in the late 1830s.[7] Artist George Catlin, for example, painted hundreds of Indian portraits in order to document and preserve, in Catlin's words, "an interesting race of people, who are rapidly passing away from the face of the earth."[8] By the 1850s, photography became the basis for most of the illustrated portraits in the pictorial press, though early photography was subject to a great many technical limitations. Lee Clark Mitchell has noted, for instance, that early photography required subjects to remain absolutely still, a process aided by headrests and body clamps.[9] In addition, the conventions of portrait photography called for a serious "public" face, a practice that can be traced back to classical sculpture.[10] Moreover, studio portraits were controlled situations usually meant to reveal subjects at their best, a fact that added an air of dignity to many of these encounters.[11] In short, as photographic historian Frank Goodyear writes, "Photographic sessions were a highly formalized ritual that effectively made it impossible to create a spontaneous or 'natural' image."[12]

All of these factors ensured that early photographic portraits of Indians—as well as whites—were notably artificial. Although Indians sometimes had their own interests in sitting for a portrait,[13] portrait photography was subject to manipulation by the photographer, who could set up poses, select clothing, and choose backgrounds to create particular effects. Washington photographer Bell, for example, used the same studio setting for dozens of individual Indian portraits.[14] "Bell was particularly successful at manipulating his [Indian] subjects to meet his often sensational ends," Goodyear writes, "frequently posing them in front of painted backdrops and outfitting them in elaborate Native costumes."[15] An 1880 studio portrait of Red Cloud, Goodyear noted, puts the Lakota chief in "a completely fictionalized setting," including a papier-mâché rock in front of a painted seascape.[16]

Importantly—and in contrast to the beliefs of mid-nineteenth-century photographic enthusiasts—photography was hardly a neutral recorder of factual reality. As historian Martha Sandweiss writes, photographs should not be taken at face value. "They need to be understood as constructions of the human imagination, as the result of selective attention to a particular subject," she notes.[17] Photographs also have the tendency to "usurp reality," as Mitchell puts it, causing viewers to "mistakenly assume that photographs reproduce scenes as they are, and dismiss too readily the way the camera shapes [the] experiences it records."[18] In other words, photographs and the photographic process—as well as those illustrations based on photographs—both disclose and conceal, shaping the image and obscuring the relations between the photographer and the subject. In the case of Indians this was often a complicated relationship affected by the actions and desires of both parties. Mitchell notes, for example, that Indians "repeatedly posed for the camera in ways they assumed were expected, even as photographers have just as persistently set scenes they envisioned as natively apt."[19] Additionally, photographers had particular goals in mind when they made Indian portraits, as Joanna Cohan Scherer has noted. Official photographers aimed to document Indian leaders and tribal delegations, which promoted, but did not guarantee, more straightforward and ethnographically accurate photographs.[20] Commercial photographers, on the other hand, had no such interest. "These men often attempted to make their subjects look exotic, savage, or romantic to create more interest in their product—the Indian prints they sold," Scherer writes.[21] The results, more often than not, were portraits that met the commercial needs of photographers who controlled and manipulated their Indian subjects through the portrait-making process. The process of turning photographs into engravings also changed Indian portraits. Engravers sometimes altered details or removed backgrounds, settings, or even people to make Indian portraits appear "more Indian." In one instance, discussed later, engravers removed studio props and added a prairie background so that Sitting Bull would appear in his expected habitat—outdoors.

Significantly, too, Indian photographic portraits almost always included clear and meaningful signs of racial difference. In the illustrated press, Indians had to meet the public's expectations and *look like Indians*—or at least look like what most whites thought Indians were supposed to look like. Accordingly, Indian portraits in the illustrated press almost always included racial and cultural stereotypes and visual clichés, casting Indians as "primitive" and "savage." Physiognomic and cultural characteristics were crucial in this process; in fact, these qualities were tied to "Indian" character and behavior.[22] As Mitchell noted, "Dark skin, long hair, odd costumes, and a variety of weapons confirm the Indian's allegorization as the 'other'—counter to all that had come to mark civilized life."[23] In this way Indians were racially identified by their appearance and dress, details that had major social, cultural, and political implications. Mitchell notes, for instance, that Indians were living on land desired by increasing numbers of white settlers. Thus the very appearance of Indians marked them as "unfit for residency" and worked to undermine Indian claims to a legitimate place in the expanding nation.[24] In addition, as Western historian Richard White has pointed out, some photographic portraits of nineteenth-century westerners—including well-known Indians such as Sitting Bull and Geronimo—"turned individuals into symbols." In this way, White concludes, "complicated human beings vanished into representations."[25]

It is important to point out, however, that Indians were not always pawns in the portrait-making process. Many Indians wanted portraits for themselves and their families, willingly posing for portrait photographers. But the private use of photographic portraits soon gave way to more public uses, including use by the illustrated press.[26] In addition, as the *Leslie's* example discussed earlier shows, Indians sometimes collaborated with the photographer for political reasons. Red Cloud, for example, was photographed 128 times in the last forty years of his life, becoming the most photographed Indian in the nineteenth century.[27] Red Cloud's willingness to be photographed, Goodyear argues, was a way for him "to speak to both the dominant culture and his own people."[28] In other words, Red Cloud recognized the power of imagery and its usefulness in carving out "an independent space for [the Lakota] during the second half of the nineteenth century."[29] Red Cloud used photography as "a means of simultaneously paying deference to and resisting those Euro-Americans who sought to subjugate the Lakotas," Goodyear writes.[30] This point—that Indians successfully used the portrait-making process for their own ends—complicates the conventional notion that Native Americans were always victims of the camera.[31]

Photographic Portraits and the Illustrated Press

The development of the pictorial press brought a growing public interest in pictures of famous people—"illustrious Americans," as photographer Mathew Brady put it.[32] Showing society's movers and shakers, after all, was a major advantage of the illustrated press, which employed a corps of skilled engravers to turn photographic portraits of newsworthy people into realistic-appearing illustrations.[33] Using this process, formal portraits of great men—and they were almost all men—were common in the pages of the pictorial press, appearing in virtually every issue of *Leslie's* and *Harper's*. In the Civil War era, these portraits often focused on military leaders, as when *Leslie's* published full-page, official portraits of Union generals such as William T. Sherman[34] and Philip Sheridan[35] decked out in their finest dress uniforms. Less-prominent figures also turned up in the pages of the pictorial press, as in 1868 when *Leslie's* ran a series of head-and-shoulder illustrations of state judges in New York and other states.[36]

Indian portraits, by contrast, were much less common in the pictorial press. Yet some Indians—again, mostly men—became objects of attention and curiosity, though on an episodic basis. As racial and cultural outsiders, Indians did not make news routinely; there was, for example, no Indian equivalent of a state judge who warranted a portrait in the illustrated press. Nevertheless, Indian chiefs and other headmen did become worthy of illustrated portraits when they became known for their violence or when they turned up as members of official delegations in Washington and other cities. Occasionally even ordinary, nonnewsworthy Indians, including some Indian women and children, were deemed interesting enough to be photographed and their portraits published in the illustrated press.[37]

The rise of the photographic portrait in the mid-nineteenth century fostered a public discussion over the meaning of such pictures. In 1857, for instance, portrait painter Rembrandt Peale argued that daguerreotypes might serve as reasonable "memorials" of the sitter, but, as mechanical reproductions, photographs lacked the "skill, taste, mind and judgment" supplied by a skilled portrait painter.[38] In response, early portrait photographers argued that their images—which harnessed the scientific precision of the camera and its unblinking lens—captured the essence of the sitter, the person's true character. Thus, portrait photographers, as Alan Trachtenberg has noted, "developed a rationale which held that the true daguerrean artist looked through surfaces to depths, treated the exterior surface of persons as signs or expressions of inner truths, of interior reality."[39] Barnhurst and Nerone make a similar point, noting that the "fixity" of the illustrated portrait and its accompanying text "was supposed to present the essence, the distilled character, of the personage."[40] Following this logic, Indian portraits represented more than simple documentation of famous leaders and their visits to Washington; these portraits were seen as "windows" into the Indian character and disposition. Thus, Indian faces in the pictorial press could be read for signs of essential Indian racial characteristics, especially savagery and treachery, and, in other cases, nascent civilizing influences. Commenting on three front-page Indian portraits in 1871, for instance, *Leslie's* claimed that its illustrations "preserve much of the native dignity of the aboriginal man." Two of these men, Little Robe and Little Raven, revealed "even something of the benevolence and reasonableness that have marked their latter careers," while the third Indian, Bird Chief, *Leslie's* claimed, "resembles a meditative Dante of the West."[41]

Finally, but significantly, photographic portraits—as well as the illustrations based on those portraits—took on new and unintended meanings once they found their way into the public arena. Sandweiss writes that early photographic processes, such as the daguerreotype, produced one-of-a-kind images, portraits usually reserved for private use.[42] As the photographic technology improved and multiple copies became more easily available, photographers realized the commercial possibilities of portrait photography, including the publication and sale of Indian portraits. When portraits ceased to be private, Sandweiss writes, they lost their biographical specificity. Moreover, Indians had no control over public images, which could now "be used to tell or illustrate any number of stories."[43] This loss of control had important consequences when Indian portraits turned up in *Leslie's* and *Harper's Weekly*. Importantly, too, Indian portraits were routinely explained by captions or accompanying stories, texts by the artists or their editors that reflected Euro-American views and perspectives. Thus illustrated Indians were rarely allowed to speak for themselves in the pictorial press, another loss of control that affected the meaning of Indian portraits.

Official delegation portraits also took on larger meanings, especially political meanings. Mitchell points out that Washington delegation photographs were meant as "simple record shots, of interest primarily in identifying individuals, not as pictorial compositions." And yet, he notes, "photographers seized the opportunity to read implications into the occasion."[44] Indeed they did. Mitchell cites a photograph by noted Washington photographer Alexander Gardner that featured government negotiator Lewis Bogy with a raised right arm, his finger dramatically pointing toward a new home in the West for his Kaw and Sac and Fox visitors. The relocation of these Indians was reinforced in the photograph's caption, which referred to the commissioner "advising them to go to a new home."[45] Such poses were not-too-subtle reminders of Washington's intentions, as well as its power over Indian imagery. As we shall see, similar demonstrations of visual power turned up in many Indian portraits.

The Indian Group Portrait

One of the staples of the illustrated Indian was the group or delegation portrait. These illustrations were based on official photographs that were a routine part of many Indian visits to eastern cities. This was the case in 1852 when *Gleason's Pictorial*, the first U.S. illustrated paper, published a front-page group portrait of several Seminole men, illustrating their visit to New York (figure 1.2). This illustration showed six men, five Seminoles and Abram, their African American interpreter.[46] Although the United States had been at war with the Seminoles some years earlier, these Seminole leaders were shown sitting and lounging peacefully, apparently at ease in a studio. The most famous of the Seminoles was Billy Bowlegs, shown, like the other men in the drawing, in elaborate clothing. Bowlegs, the article explained, was wearing "a calico frock, leggins, a belt or two, and a sort of short cloak."[47] His head was covered by a turban, "enclosed in a broad silver band, and surmounted by a profusion of black ostrich feathers." Yet the portrait was at odds with at least some parts of the article. Bowlegs, for example, was described in the text as a "surly, and

BILLY BOWLEGS.   CHOCOTE TUSTENUGGEE.   ABRAM.   JOHN JUMPER.   PASATCHEE EMANTHLA.   SARPARKEE YOHOLA.

BILLY BOWLEGS AND CHIEFS OF THE SEMINOLE INDIANS.

FIGURE 1.2. The Seminole leader known as Billy Bowlegs *(far left)* was described in *Gleason's Pictorial* as "surly" and a "dangerous foe of the white man," a description unsupported by his complacent pose.

at all times cross and unmanageable"—a description unsupported by the portrait. Perhaps, the article suggested, this was a false pose from a "wily, dangerous foe of the white man." The article offered this explanation: "He now pretends that he is willing, and, in fact, desirous, to emigrate; he says that game is getting scarce in Florida, and he thinks he can do much better at the West." Finally, *Gleason's* noted, even an unruly Indian like Bowlegs seemed to know that "the Great Seminole nation itself must yield before the white man."[48]

   This representation is interesting because it reveals Bowlegs and the Seminoles in contradictory ways on the same page. Bowlegs is identified in the text as a "treacherous and cruel Indian," yet the portrait shows him unarmed and at rest, seemingly harmless. The message here is that Bowlegs and his companions remain Indians—they can't change that, of course—but they were Indians who might submit to the advance of civilization. In this circumstance, the Seminoles were suitable Indians for the front cover of an illustrated paper—colorful, exotic men who, if not fully civilized, were safe enough to sit for their portrait.

   Another band of "safe" Indians appeared in a group portrait on the cover of *Ballou's Pictorial* in 1856 (figure 1.3). These six Chippewa men had been photographed in Boston, where they had visited the statehouse and met with Governor

BALLOU'S PICTORIAL

M. M. BALLOU, | CORNER OF TREMONT | AND BROMFIELD STS.   BOSTON, SATURDAY, JANUARY 19, 1856. $3.00 PER ANNUM. | 6 CENTS SINGLE. | VOL. X., No. 3.—WHOLE No. 227.

THE CHIPPEWA INDIANS.

The recent visit of a party of full-blooded Chippewa Indians to our city has afforded us the opportunity of presenting to our readers a group of red men as they appear in their native dignity, contrasted with the miserable and degenerate specimens of the race we see in our streets at rare intervals, peddling baskets and moccasins. It is very rarely that we meet, on our seaboard, with a fair representation of the lords of the forest. Some eighteen years since, a delegation of Sacs and Foxes were here, among whom were Keokuk and Black Hawk's son, and the visit was something more than a nine days' wonder. They visited the State House, where they were received and addressed by Governor Everett, and afterwards exhibited some of their war dances and ceremonials on the Common, in the presence of a vast concourse of spectators. The group of red men here depicted were drawn for us by Mr. Barry from a photograph by Masury & Silsbee, and each head is an accurate likeness. The artist has done himself great credit by this spirited representation. The Indians of this party rejoice in names which, though they may appear musical to Indian ears, do not strike us as being particularly dulcet, and we doubt whether even Mr. Longfellow, notwithstanding his most skillful management of Indian nomenclature in Hiawatha, could manage to weave them into melodious rhythm. We have numbered the individuals composing the group [See page 37.

1. MAH-YAH-CHE-WA-WE-TONG.   2. WAB-BE-DE-YAH.   3. NAH-NAH-AUG-A-YASH.
   A-YAH-BE-DWA-WE-TONG.   5. KE-BE-DWA-KE-YHICK.   4. NE-SHE-KA-O-GE-MAH.

THE CHIPPEWA INDIANS.

FIGURE 1.3. *Ballou's Pictorial* featured a rather somber portrait of a Chippewa delegation visiting Boston in 1856, commenting that their names "do not strike us as particularly dulcet."

Everett. *Ballou's* also reported that the men "exhibited some of their war dances and ceremonials on the Common" for a group of spectators.[49] The story drew a pointed contrast between the "native dignity" of these Chippewa—"lords of the forest"—and the "degenerate" Indians who sometimes turned up in Boston. But the illustration created a more ambiguous impression. It showed two rows of dark-haired men wrapped in blankets, several of whom wore European-style clothing. These were "good" Indians, presented formally in a studio and without weapons. But the illustration left no doubt that these men were different from ordinary Bostonians. The most prominent man in the picture was Ke-Be-Dwa-Ke-Yhick, a notably dour-faced man sitting in the middle of the front row. On his left sat Ne-She-Ka-O-Ge-Mah, who was also frowning—a sign, perhaps, of his unhappiness about the portrait-making process. Although two of the men in the back row were smiling and appeared friendly, this image makes plain that these Chippewa were different from whites and, despite their dignity, an odd and unhappy band. Even their names were troublesome, *Ballou's* remarked. "The Indians of this party rejoice in names which, though they may appear musical to Indian ears, do not strike us as particularly dulcet."[50] Like *Gleason's* depiction of Billy Bowlegs and the Seminoles, the meaning of this Indian portrait was mixed.

In early 1866, *Harper's Weekly* published a front-page group portrait of four men, "Iowas, Sacs, and Foxes," in Washington for an official visit (figure 1.4). The image was based on a photograph by Washington photographer Alexander Gardner.[51] The photograph and the *Harper's* illustration based on the photo showed four men, each identified with phonetic transcriptions of his name.[52] All were serious—grim, in fact—as if any hint of mirth or humor would undercut their official mission. They were dressed in decorative ceremonial clothes and moccasins. They wore ornate headgear; two had impressive bear-claw necklaces. As photographed and illustrated, this was an impressive Indian delegation of important and self-contained tribal leaders. The story describing these Indians offered both criticism and praise. Lag-er-Lash, for example, was described as "half-civilized."[53] The story criticized another Indian in the delegation, Moless, for failing to take advantage of "a very liberal English education." But these tribes were "quiet and peaceful" and the "Iowas are the most thrifty; [they] cultivate their lands, and carry on extensive dealings in wood."[54] The purpose of the visit was to renew an 1861 treaty, *Harper's* reported, but the visit also stroked the egos of the visitors:

> An Indian considers it one of the greatest events of his life to visit Washington and see his "Great Father"; and nothing gives him more pleasure, or makes him think himself, or be esteemed by others of his tribe, a great man, than when he can rehearse to a listening audience what he had seen and heard on his travels.[55]

Despite this assertion of pleasure, this *Harper's* cover did not appear to be a happy occasion. Indeed, the men had been posed in a studio setting to suit the

HARPER'S WEEKLY.
A JOURNAL OF CIVILIZATION.

VOL. X.—No. 474.] NEW YORK, SATURDAY, JANUARY 27, 1866. [SINGLE COPIES TEN CENTS.
[$4.00 PER YEAR IN ADVANCE.

Entered according to Act of Congress, in the Year 1866, by Harper & Brothers, in the Clerk's Office of the District Court for the Southern District of New York.

Ta-ra-kee.   Pe-ti-o-ki-ma.   Lug-er-lash.   Too-hi.

INDIAN DELEGATION OF IOWAS, SACS, AND FOXES FROM NEBRASKA TO WASHINGTON.—PHOTOGRAPHED BY A. GARDNER, WASHINGTON, D. C.—[SEE PAGE 56.]

FIGURE 1.4. Based on a photograph by Alexander Gardner, this group portrait presented Indian leaders in a rigid and formal pose, an artifact of studio photography in the 1860s.

formal demands of the photographer and his technology. The slowness of the exposure, in fact, helps explain the stiffness of the image. In addition, Gardner most likely directed the gaze of each man, which in each case is distant and unfocused. Such direction explains why the man on the left, Tar-a-kee, is facing right, while the other three men are turned and looking slightly left. They are not looking at or engaged with each other, nor are they looking at the camera. All of this suggests Gardner's power over the image and the relative powerlessness of the Indians in this process. This is evident in the solemnity of their expressions, the stiffness of their poses, and their arrangement in front of the camera. These Indian leaders may have been pleased about the prospect of receiving photographs to take back to Nebraska, but it seems unlikely that they knew that their likenesses would appear on the cover of a major weekly newspaper. It seems even more unlikely that they would understand the effect of their likenesses on thousands of *Harper's Weekly* readers, most of whom were middle-class Americans with little direct experience with actual Indians, much less four Iowa and Sac and Fox chiefs. For these viewers, this *Harper's* image served to mark the "otherness" of these Indians, presenting them as strange and exotic people. This official portrait, then, reinforced the idea of Indians as outsiders, different from and opposed to the civilized society represented by *Harper's* and its readers. The cover of the publication made its editorial mission perfectly clear; this was a "Journal of Civilization," a motto that appeared only an inch or two above the head of the standing chief, Lag-er-lash.

Harper's Weekly published another official group portrait of Indians in October 1877[56] (figure 1.5). The occasion was a Washington visit by a group of Sioux and Arapaho chiefs. The *Harper's* illustration was a copy of a Mathew Brady photograph, although the engraver omitted four men in "white" clothing who were pictured in the original photograph. The engraver also removed some faux columns and arches that were part of Brady's studio backdrop.[57] These changes simplified the illustration and kept the focus on the Indians. It showed two rows of ornately dressed Indian men, five sitting and four standing. Several of the men held pipes, including Red Cloud, who was seated on the left side of the image. Brady had arranged the men in something of a semicircle, with Red Cloud and Little Bigman turned to the right. Three Bears, standing in the middle of the illustration, was turned left toward Red Cloud, while Young-man-afraid-of-his-horses and Iron Crow, seated on the right, faced directly ahead. Both the photograph and the illustration showed an impressive—but expressionless—group of Indian men. The blank faces of these Indians are worth exploring in some detail. The faces are serious, following the convention of portrait photography. Meetings between Indians and federal officials were serious matters, after all. Moreover, smiling Indians might be misunderstood because Indians were not ordinarily believed to be happy. Following the stereotype, Indians were supposed to be stoic and a picture of smiling Indians would run counter to prevailing ideas about the nature of the Indian character.[58] In addition, smiling Indians might be interpreted as a sign of weakness

FIGURE 1.5. Red Cloud and Spotted Tail were among the Sioux and Arapaho leaders who posed for photographer Mathew Brady. The engraver altered the original photograph, simplifying the background and removing four men in "white" clothing.

on the part of government negotiators. The article explaining the illustration supports the gravity of the negotiations, referring to the "wants and grievances" of the chiefs, including their desire for "supplies of wagons, seeds, mowing machines, schools and teachers, etc."[59] These desires were not from ordinary citizens, but from Indians, people who—try as they might—were always different. "At the last interview they were dressed in the garb of civilized men, having laid aside that of their native wilds," the article stated. It also singled out one Indian's bad attitude: "Chief Spotted Tail was the most persistent mendicant of all. He wanted 'forty dollars apiece to buy things for their women and children, and a trunk to carry their clothing in.'" Spotted Tail's request, apparently, was not granted, but the article noted that "some of their requests were granted" and that the Indians "departed in a happy frame of mind."

All of this demonstrates the limitations of the official delegation portrait. Indian leaders came to Washington routinely and they routinely agreed to sit for photographs. But the photographs and the illustrations based on these photographs were highly orchestrated productions and their meanings were often prescribed by the practices of their production. These group portraits showed Indian leaders working on behalf of their people under extremely trying conditions. In fact, continued U.S. expansion and settlement of the West meant that traditional Indian cultures were disrupted and threatened with extinction. Red Cloud, Spotted Tail, and other Indian leaders were fully aware of these threats and they negotiated as best they could, trying against overwhelming odds to find a way to remain on their land and, in many cases, avoid conflict.

Almost none of this was revealed in this or other delegation illustrations, which brought these Indians to the attention of American readers in a formal and highly structured way. In the pictorial press, these powerful Indians were pictured but silenced, reduced to serious faces and well-dressed bodies. In addition, the process of staging the photograph and making the exposure served the government's interest, impressing upon these Indian leaders the significance of the negotiation process and the technological and recording powers associated with Euro-American civilization. In all these ways, the production, composition, and publication of Indian delegation portraits in the illustrated press was a highly unequal encounter that reinforced Euro-American ideas about the need for civilization to triumph over savagery for a wide range of American readers.

Illustrating Newsworthy Indians

"Names make news" is an old journalistic practice and the illustrated press routinely followed the "names" rule, publishing portraits of notorious—and thus newsworthy—Indians from its earliest days. Some of these illustrations depicted Indians as dark and brooding savages, angry warriors eager to scalp, rape, and kill. This was the case for many Indian war illustrations, of course.[60] It was also the case in many of the hyperbolic anti-Indian cartoons of the era.[61] But formal portraits were another matter. Because these portraits were posed and required at least the tacit consent of the subject, these portraits often showed men who were less hostile than might be expected. In fact, many such portraits showed Indians apparently at peace, even when the newsworthiness of these Indians was based on violence.

In 1858, for instance, *Harper's Weekly* took a peaceful approach when it reported on the end of the third Seminole war. The paper published individual portraits of several Seminole leaders, Indians who had been enemies of the United States only months earlier. One portrait depicted No-Rush-Adjo, described as a Seminole "Inspector-General"[62] (figure 1.6). No-Rush-Adjo was staring calmly but directly at the viewer, elaborately dressed in a ceremonial shirt with a decorated sash, unfeathered hat, and large jewelry. No-Rush-Adjo was, by these details, clearly identified as an Indian. But he was not presented as an enemy nor was he particularly savage. He was not armed either, which might well be expected in a portrait of a man with a military title at the end of a bitter war with the United States. Another Seminole on the same page, Long Jack, was shown holding a bow and arrow, though more as a prop than as a threat. Long Jack was, *Harper's* explained, "Billy Bowlegs' Lieutenant," which made him an enemy Indian, subject to vilification.[63] Like No-Rush-Adjo, however, Long Jack was posing calmly for the photographer, looking directly at the

NO-KUSH-ADJO, INSPECTOR-GENERAL.   YOUNG WIFE OF BILLY BOWLEGS.   LONG JACK, BILLY BOWLEGS'S LIEUTENANT.

FIGURE 1.6. After the end of the third Seminole war in 1858, *Harper's Weekly* published individual portraits of three Seminoles—two men and an unidentified woman—without rancor or hostility.

viewer. Despite the recent end of the war and the weapon in his hand, this portrait did not present Long Jack as a killer. The final Indian on the page[64] was a rarity, a woman. She was given no name, however, identified only by her relationship to the Seminole leader: "Young Wife of Billy Bowlegs."[65] Like the Seminole men on the page, she was dark-skinned and dressed for the occasion. The portrait showed her in a flowing dress with rows of beads and a scarf around her neck. She was not smiling—smiling Indians were rare in the illustrated press—but she was not frowning either. There was some sadness in her eyes, perhaps a reflection of her feelings about the Seminole losses in the war. Whatever her feelings, she too was presented without evident rancor. In this case, *Harper's* published illustrations of three Seminoles in a relatively neutral light, especially given the recent violence.

Leslie's offered a somewhat different approach to Indian representations in 1863 when it published portraits of three Indian men who had been involved in the notorious 1862 "Minnesota Massacre"[66] (figure 1.7). The portraits, all based on photographs, were placed atop a story about the prison that housed dozens of Sioux Indians who had been arrested in connection with the violence. The center portrait, and the largest, showed Ampetu Tokeca, or Other Day, described as a "good Indian" and a "noble Indian." He was good, *Leslie's* explained, because he rescued sixty-two whites at Yellow Medicine, Minnesota, during the Sioux raids. He was dressed in "white" clothing and his hair was cut short, apparent signs of his civilized nature. On the right side of the page, *Leslie's* published a portrait of Little Crow, described as the leader of the uprising. Little Crow was shown in a

FIGURE 1.7. *Leslie's* portraits of the "Sioux murderers" in Minnesota in 1863 presented "the good Indian," Other Day *(center),* as the most civilized, while the worst Indian, Cut Nose *(left),* appeared the most savage.

white shirt with a dark jacket and tie, not his Indian clothing. The formal clothing may have been a sign of his status as a leader, or perhaps his relative sophistication. Yet Little Crow's hair was a sign of something else. It was long and unkempt, more suitable for a savage than a gentleman. The portrait on the left showed the worst of the trio, a man described as "a perfect monster," a man who "had murdered 18 women and children." This was Mah-pe-oke-na-jin, or Who Stands in the Cloud, *Leslie's* explained, better known as Cut Nose. He too was shown in a European-style jacket, but, unlike the other two men, he was wearing a traditional feathered headdress and thus was marked as the most "Indian" of the three portraits. It is not clear in *Leslie's* who made these portraits or when the photos were taken,[67] but it is notable that the illustrations revealed three types of Indians. The good Indian, Ampetu Tokeca, was presented as the most civilized. The Indian leader, Little Crow, appeared to be partially civilized, while the Indian murderer, Mah-pe-oke-na-jin, was shown with feathers, marked as the *least* civilized and the *most* Indian.

More "good" and "bad" Indians turned up on the cover of *Leslie's* when the paper published eleven Indian portraits on its cover in 1873[68] (figure 1.8). These were Modoc Indians from Northern California and their newsworthiness sprang from an infamous incident in the Modoc war in which General Edward R. S. Canby and several others were killed during a peace negotiation. The attack was a shock to many Americans and it was widely seen as evidence of Indian treachery. The Modocs were swiftly demonized, especially their leader, Kintpuash, known as Captain

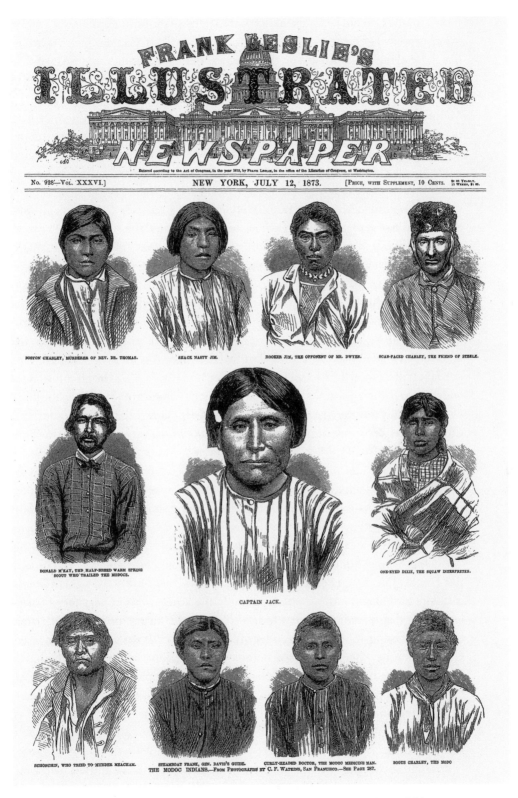

FIGURE 1.8. The Modoc leader known as Captain Jack was the centerpiece of this *Leslie's* cover in 1873, a page that reinforced the belief that all Modocs were treacherous criminals.

Jack.[69] In fact, Captain Jack's likeness was the largest of the portraits on *Leslie's* cover, visual evidence of his role as the principal Modoc villain. Captain Jack's portrait, like those of the other Indians on the page, was based on photographs taken by the German-born photographer Louis Heller.[70] In contrast to Indian portraits made in Washington, which usually showed proud men dressed in fine native clothing, the Modocs were unadorned. They stared grimly back at the camera, without feathers or bear-claw necklaces. Most were dressed in collarless cloth shirts buttoned at the neck. Most had thick black hair, cut short. One portrait showed a dark-skinned woman with a blanket around her shoulders. She was identified by her nickname, "One-Eyed Dixie, the Squaw Interpreter." In fact, long before the murder of General Canby at the peace negotiation, Modoc leaders had been assigned colorful—and sometimes derogatory—English names. *Leslie's* listed these names below each man's image. There was "Boston Charley" and "Steamboat Frank." More tellingly, there was "Shack Nasty Jim," "Hooker Jim," "Scar-faced Charley," and "Bogus Charley." Two of the Modocs escaped such labels. One was "Schonchin," which may have been his Modoc name, and the other was "Donald M'Kay," described as a half-breed who was not actually Modoc at all, but an army scout from the Warm Springs band. Significantly, M'Kay was dressed in the most civilized manner, his white collar held in place by a kind of ruffled tie. Taken together, these illustrations and labels presented the Modocs as dangerous Indians. Indeed, the circumstances and context of these portraits was well known in the summer of 1873, when the furor over the Canby murder was at its peak. With Captain Jack at the center of the page, these Indians were presented as criminals, Indians who in appearance and in name personified that role.

But this theme was only partially true. Some of these Heller portraits were involuntary mug shots, photographs taken after the Modocs were captured and awaiting trial.[71] Yet the situation was complicated and at least some of the photos actually represented something different. As the text inside explained, some of these Indians were not criminals at all. The article began with Captain Jack, describing him as the "principal captive," but refraining from any overheated commentary.[72] It reported that Hooker Jim chased Peace Commissioner Leroy Dyer, "but at the sight of Dyer's pistol he turned and ran." Most surprisingly, the article praised Scar-faced Charley, noting that he had protected Judge Elijah Steele during the attack and, later, had helped bring about the surrender of Captain Jack. "It is said that [Scar-faced Charley] was never guilty of a treacherous act, and that he was brave and faithful," *Leslie's* reported. The story also praised Donald M'Kay, the half-breed scout, as "an intelligent-looking fellow, and in this instance true to the special confidence bestowed upon himself and warriors." Likewise, Steamboat Frank was praised as the man who "performed signal service by conducting the scouting party to Jack's second retreat."[73]

In all these ways, the *Leslie's* article provided a more positive and detailed view of the Modoc men than the portraits on the cover. A careful *Leslie's* reader would learn that not all of these Indians were hostiles; in fact, they were not all Modocs. Nor were all the pictured Indians responsible for the murders; some were army allies. These distinctions were not clear on the cover, however, which labeled all of these Indians as Modoc Indians—a label that was highly prejudicial in 1873. Scar-faced Charley might well have been a "good" Indian—a friend of whites who saved Judge Steele—but he was depicted on the same page as Captain Jack, the notorious Modoc leader who would later be executed. For middle-class readers in Albany, Baltimore, or Cincinnati, the distinction between good and bad Indians in the wilds of Northern California could easily be lost. Moreover, this group of illustrated portraits offered little insight into the Indian character. Captain Jack was shown with an appropriately glum expression—he was a murderer likely to be hanged, after all—but the portraits of the friendly Indians were equally glum. In this case, *Leslie's* Indian portraits misled readers by blurring the distinctions between these Indians, depicting all of them as hostile Modocs when, in point of fact, there were important differences between these individuals and their actions in 1873.

Even Sitting Bull, a warrior once demonized as "Custer's killer," could be made safe for public viewing in an illustrated press portrait. In 1890, when the Hunkpapa Lakota leader was linked to the Ghost Dance movement and the hysteria it generated among whites, *Leslie's* published a relatively benign illustration of Sitting Bull.[74] This picture, taken from a studio photograph by David F. Barry, was a full-length portrait of Sitting Bull dressed in a ceremonial feathered headdress and carrying a club. In the original photo, Sitting Bull was clearly indoors, posed in front of props and furniture.[75] In *Leslie's* engraving, Sitting Bull had been moved to the prairie, a nod perhaps to his infamy as, in the language of the caption, "the So-Called High Priest of the Indian Messiah Craze." Sitting Bull's expression in the engraving was serious and determined—maybe "fierce," as one scholar put it[76]—but the illustration showed him standing tall in a static, rather stately pose. He was an armed Indian, to be sure, and possibly dangerous in his (fake) natural habitat. But as with other once-fierce warriors who posed for the pictorial press, Sitting Bull was not presented as a crazed savage ready to scalp or kill the next settler he found on the northern plains. Those sorts of depictions were published in the illustrated papers mostly in Indian cartoons, which were freed from the limitations of fact and which relied on exaggeration and hyperbole to make larger cultural and political points.[77]

Although Sitting Bull and other Indian warriors were not depicted in overtly hostile portraits, there was one notable exception to this rule. The Chiricahua Apache war chief Goyahkla or Goyathlay, known as Geronimo, did pose for field portraits that showed him as an armed and dangerous Indian. In the most famous of these photographs, a kneeling Geronimo is shown scowling at the camera, holding a rifle diagonally across his body. At the time it was taken, this was an unambiguous Indian portrait, one that appeared to reveal the Apache leader exactly as white readers expected him to be—angry, armed, and violent. This photo, cropped to remove the rifle, was the basis for a Geronimo portrait in *Harper's Weekly* when he and his band surrendered in 1886[78] (figure 1.9). Well into the twentieth century, Geronimo's famous face turned up in the daily press and other popular publications with some frequency.[79]

The circumstances surrounding this Geronimo portrait are unclear, but they are crucial to understanding Geronimo's angry pose. The photograph was taken by A. Frank Randall, an Arizona photographer who produced a number of field portraits of Apache warriors. Western historian Robert Utley says the portrait was taken at the San Carlos reservation in 1884.[80] Other scholars date the portrait to 1887,[81] although that claim is contradicted by its publication in the summer of 1885.[82] The date of the portrait makes a difference because in 1884 Geronimo was

FIGURE 1.9. Goyathlay, known as Geronimo, was depicted in 1886 as a scowling warrior, exactly the image readers expected of this Apache fighter.

continuing his protracted negotiations with General Crook, which meant he was in and out of various reservations and army posts, where he was peaceful but wary. This fact may account for Geronimo's determined demeanor and the fact that he was armed with a rifle. In other words, Randall's field portrait captured Geronimo at a particular moment in his relations with the army and the U.S. government, a time when he was neither fully free nor fully surrendered. Given the withering campaign against him, his family, and his people, Geronimo had plenty of reasons to show his anger—and his rifle—in front of the photographer. Moreover, as anthropologist William M. Clements has suggested, Geronimo may have had previous experience with the camera as well as his own motives for posing the way that he did, projecting an unmistakable look of defiance. "Most likely, Geronimo sensed what photography could do and attempted to have it do what he wanted when he posed for the camera," Clements concluded.[83] These facts help explain the unusualness of this portrait, one of the few illustrated Indian portraits to show an Indian leader as an overtly hostile warrior. There was another explanation as well—profit. Photographer Randall had an economic incentive to capture an angry Apache chief, and a photograph of Geronimo, the most famous and notorious Apache, was likely to sell well on the souvenir market. Indeed, Randall produced a series of Apache portraits, a way of exploiting public interest in Indian warfare in the Southwest.[84] In the 1880s, at a time when the Indian threat in the West was fading, photographs of Indians—especially angry or hostile Indians—became interesting to many Americans as vivid emblems of the "vanishing race." In the popular imagination, as Martha Sandweiss has noted, these sorts of Indian photographs "came to be viewed through the haze of romantic sentimentalism."[85] As a Western photographer, Randall was prepared to cash in on Geronimo's continuing appeal.

The Meaning of Indian Portraits

This chapter confirms the unremarkable fact that most of the Indians whose portraits appeared in the pictorial press were notable leaders and other headmen. Typically, these men were chiefs and political figures and they were photographed (and then illustrated) when they became newsworthy, especially when they were involved in conflicts with whites or when they met with government officials in Washington. Stereotyping was a routine part of this representational process. As we have seen, Indian portraits emphasized Indian physiognomy, especially facial features that marked the subjects as Indians—dark skin, dark hair, prominent noses, and high cheekbones. These illustrations also highlighted cultural signs such as feathers, necklaces and beads, blankets, and buckskin clothing. In some cases, photographs were altered to remove non-Indians or to shift the subject from the studio to the plains. In all these ways the illustrated press portraits staged Indians for public scrutiny with little ambiguity about their racial identity. This sort of representation—or, in some cases, *mis*representation—reinforced racial differences, placing Indians in an inferior racial category and making distinctions between civilized whites and "savage" Indians that no nineteenth-century reader was likely to miss.

Another finding of this chapter is the power of the camera over nineteenth-century illustrated portraits. Because these portraits were based on posed photographs, the elaborate process of making a photographic portrait meant that Indians who agreed to be photographed were routinely presented as mute and "pacified" Indians, savages who were more acceptable and less threatening to working- and middle-class white readers. With the notable exception of Geronimo, portraits of even hostile chiefs revealed relatively benign and stereotypically "stoic" Indian faces, not illustrations of fierce-looking "red devils." In many cases, these highly controlled portraits were at odds with accompanying stories, which sometimes described these same Indians in hyperbolic and racist terms.

More broadly, this chapter also documents the pictorial press's—and the nation's—shifting attitude toward Indians, an ambivalence that manifested itself in a variety of ways. Some Indians were presented as "good" Indians, seemingly peaceful and sometimes almost—but not quite—civilized. On occasion, even "bad" Indians were depicted in peaceful, rather bland portraits, in part because of the processes and conventions of studio photography. Thus, one popular portrait of Sitting Bull, once perceived as the most "evil" Indian of them all, was not illustrated as a wild-eyed killer, but as a dignified Indian man. On the other hand, some Indian portraits revealed dour and apparently hostile Indians, themes that were sometimes contradicted by the written reports they were meant to illustrate. When *Leslie's* published portraits of the notorious Modocs on its cover, for example, the copy explained that some of these Indians were actually allies of the whites and not "bad" Indians at all.

This ambivalence made a certain kind of sense in the changing racial currents of late nineteenth-century America. Most Western settlers and their supporters had little use for Indians or Indian ways, a racial hostility that was sometimes reflected in *Leslie's* and *Harper's*. But there was a more sympathetic strand of American thought that also turned up in the press, especially in the eastern press, where the Indian threat was much less compelling. Following this logic, the editors and artists of the illustrated papers often demonstrated a kind of "double-mindedness" toward Indians, a visual ambiguity that can be charted in the variations of Indian portraits in the illustrated press.

On the larger, ideological level, a major function of the illustrated Indian portrait was cultural containment, a journalistic form of racial control. That is, the practice and nature of the portrait-making process allowed Indians to be cast as stereotypical "good" and "bad" Indians in the studio, where even the "worst" Indians could be presented in nonthreatening ways. This process, after all, suggested the Indians' deference to white authority. Indians who sat for a photographer could be seen as more civilized and less savage than Indians in the field. In addition, most Indians in portraits were made in the city, before or after meetings with government officials. For the readers of the pictorial press, these Indians were obviously Indians but not especially threatening Indians. Indeed, many of these Indians were less of a threat than a colorful and exotic American curiosity, one tamed by the photographer and his equipment and rendered safe on the pages of the illustrated papers.

The notion of symbolic social control follows an idea of historian Alan Trachtenberg, who has pointed out that substituting English names for aboriginal names on the land and on the map was a way of taming an unexplored territory. "The new names brought the alien and unfamiliar into a familiar system of knowledge," he writes. "Naming and viewing complement each other."[86] So it was with Indian portraits. These illustrations, bounded by the practices and procedures of nineteenth-century photography and illustration, represented Indians in narrow but familiar ways, making them visible, accessible, and, in some superficial sense, knowable. Yet these Indians were silent on the page, their faces and bodies available for inspection but their place in society made for them by the artists and editors of the pictorial press.

CHAPTER 2

Illustrating Indian Lives

Difference and Deficiency in
Native American Imagery

William de la Montagne Cary—known to the public as W. M. Cary—was one of the most active and popular artists working in the American West in the last half of the nineteenth century. Born in 1840 in Tappen, New York, Cary first went west in 1861, traveling up the Missouri River from St. Louis to Fort Union by steamboat.[1] Cary and his traveling companions, W. H. Schieffelin and E. N. Lawrence, made the most of their journey to the northern plains. "They remained at Fort Union for six delightful weeks," historian Robert Taft reported, "hunting, visiting the Indians encamped about the Fort, and making friends with them, and taking side excursions of several days out on the prairie with their newfound friends."[2] Continuing west with a wagon train, Cary and his party were captured by a band of Crows. Fortunately, a Crow chief recognized a fur company official in the group and the travelers were freed, making their way to Fort Benton. After two weeks there, Cary and his friends continued west, eventually reaching Portland and the Pacific.[3] Over the next three decades, Cary drew on this and later western journeys to create hundreds of sketches, drawings, and paintings of Western scenes, including many scenes of Indians and Indian life. Cary's drawings were published in *Frank Leslie's Illustrated Newspaper, Harper's Weekly, Scribner's Magazine,* and other publications.[4] Although he is probably best known as an illustrator for his imaginary but influential drawing of Custer's Last Stand published in the *Daily Graphic* in July 1876, Cary produced many examples of Indians in less violent, more ordinary situations. Just a few months before his Last Stand illustration, for example, *Harper's Weekly* featured six Cary drawings on a single page, a showcase of illustrated journalism enclosed by a border of Indian lances and necklaces, topped by arrows[5] (figure 2.1). The drawings showed Indians trading with whites, a routine but significant activity in the frontier West. The largest drawing, located in the center of the page, showed an Indian camp outside "a United States fort," probably Fort Union. Several tepees were in the foreground and a number of Indians

Traders Store.

En Route.

Preparing for Trade

The Trading Post and Fort

Return from Trading

Dissatisfaction

INDIAN TRADING.—Drawn by W. M. Cary.—[See Page 267.]

FIGURE 2.1. W. M. Cary documented Native American economic activity in the West, including the hard lot of Indian women.

were shown milling about the camp. In the three small scenes across the top, Cary depicted several Indians in various stages of the trading process. The most striking element of the three drawings was the relationship between the man and the woman in the center drawing. The man was tall and finely dressed, a pipe in one hand, ceremonial feathers in the other. The woman walked behind the man, stooped by a large bundle on her back. The *Harper's* story focused not on trading but on the disparity between the sexes: the man was "strutting in advance, self-important and overbearing," while the woman was "bending under the weight of a heavy load."[6] The scene inside the trading post showed a woman facing a trader behind the counter, but the article added this detail: the store, it said, was filled with "every thing (including whiskey) which can attract the peculiar class of customers whose wants he supplies." Cary's drawings at the bottom of the page showed the woman returning with a bundle of trade goods and, in the final scene, the man beating her for her poor trades. "It is evident from the concluding sketch that in this instance the lord and master of the wigwam is highly displeased with the results of the poor woman's dealings, and is giving her a severe lesson," *Harper's* explained.

Cary's illustrations, and the story that explained them, shed light on popular ideas and attitudes about Indians and Indian life in the post–Civil War era. Cary was a careful observer who had considerable experience in Indian country, and his *Harper's Weekly* drawings told a simple but dramatic story, one that reinforced existing ideas about Indians and their place in U.S. society. In this issue of the weekly, readers would be reminded that some Indians had a fondness for alcohol. Moreover, Indian men were magnificent but vain creatures, far too proud to work. They also abused and beat their women, treating them as little more than beasts of burden, as Cary depicted in his dramatic scenes. Cary biographer Mildred Ladner, in fact, argues that these pictures "leave no doubt about Cary's sentiments concerning the role of women in Plains Indian society."[7]

Beyond documenting the mistreatment of Indian women, these Cary illustrations highlighted important social and cultural differences between Indians and whites. In combination with their captions and stories, these pictures revealed Indians by their deficiencies, casting them as strange, uncivilized people. It is notable, too, that these trading encounters were presented as generic Indian activities, unconnected to an actual place, time, or specific tribe. Cary's illustrations were, *Harper's* explained, "interesting phases of life among the Indians on the Western plains."[8] In other words, *Harper's Weekly* published these drawings not as illustrations of particular people and specific incidents—though Cary presumably witnessed such scenes—but as interesting pictures meant to give readers a broad idea about the look and nature of Indians and their lives.[9] This simplified view of generic Indian life marked much of nonviolent Indian imagery in the pictorial press in the second half of the nineteenth century, ensuring that American Indians and their ways would be seen as markedly different from—and often inferior to—Euro-Americans and the norms of Euro-American life.

This chapter examines a range of ceremonial, domestic, and nonviolent Indian images in the nineteenth-century illustrated press. These illustrations show Native Americans engaged in a variety of activities associated with Indians—trading, dancing, hunting, grooming, working, playing, and other routine activities. The chapter examines a small but varied set of such Indian illustrations by Cary and other artists, pictures taken from a larger survey of images in *Frank Leslie's Illustrated Newspaper* and *Harper's Weekly* in the last half of the nineteenth century. The research identifies and describes several significant themes in these illustrations and raises questions about the meaning and significance of these Indian images. Why were these illustrations published? What patterns or visual tropes shaped these illustrations? Which themes or topics were emphasized and which were downplayed or ignored? What did these domestic Indian illustrations reveal about the popular understanding of Indians in the last half of the nineteenth century? These and other questions are addressed in the following pages.

Indian Life in the Popular Imagination

Europeans began drawing pictures of Native Americans and Native American life early in the discovery era. An illustrated broadside produced in Augsburg, Germany, in 1505, for example, depicted an unspecified group of Caribbean Indians wearing leafy skirts and necklaces. Not surprisingly, the broadside emphasized the differences between Europeans and Indians, explaining that Indian men take any women they please as wives, "whether it is their mother or sister or friend." They fight with each other, and even worse, they also "eat one another and they hang and smoke the flesh of those killed." The engraving, in fact, showed the top half of a human torso—a head and arms—hanging from the log structure in the village. Another Indian was shown eating a human forearm like an ear of corn. The broadside also claimed that these Indians "live to be 150 and have no government."[10] From the start, it seems clear, Europeans made crucial distinctions between themselves and the odd, unknown, and uncivilized people of the New World. In colonial North America, Englishman John White produced a series of watercolors depicting Virginia Indians, again highlighting the differences between the civilized and the savage. In 1590, Flemish engraver Theodor de Bry used White's paintings as a basis for a series of American pictures, one of which depicted an idealized "Great Lorde of Virginia" dressed in fringed skins and beads—and sporting a long tail. Significantly, de Bry changed White's original image, making the warrior's features "much more muscular, poised and fierce," as one scholar put it.[11] De Bry also engraved White's paintings of the well-ordered village of Secota on the Carolina coast, a settlement complete with pole houses covered in skins; gardens of tobacco, corn, and pumpkins; prayer and ceremonial grounds; and a chief's tomb.[12] These American scenes surely fascinated many European viewers; they were produced, in fact, to encourage interest in the colonies, downplaying the Indian threat in favor of an intriguing new land of peaceful people. As Wendy Shadwell has noted, "Too vivid a depiction of savage and possibly threatening natives could have been counterproductive."[13] In short, these and other early Indian images revealed a way of imagining Indians and Indian life that focused on their more exotic differences with Europeans, and these differences, in turn, were made useful to particular European causes.

The creation of the Indian image in America was a complex and ambiguous process, however, shaped by competing ideas about the nature of Indians and their societies. Although violence and deviance were depicted in some early imagery (as noted previously), other depictions were influenced by romantic notions of American Indians and the European concept of the Noble Savage.[14] These ideas were prominent in the antebellum era, when Charles Bird King, George Catlin, and other artists traveled west to paint Indians. In search of the Noble Savage, these artists sought to depict Indians in their natural, precontact condition, uncorrupted by the temptations of civilization. In 1822, for instance, King produced a group portrait of Pawnee warriors as idealized Roman nobles, "men to be admired for physical prowess as well as reason," as one scholar put it.[15] For his part, Catlin explained that his Indian paintings were a way of preserving "an interesting race of people, who are rapidly passing away from the face of the earth.[16] Toward that end, Catlin documented the daily activities and cultural practices of the Indians he painted, illustrating and writing about Mandan lodges and funeral customs, to cite just two examples.[17] Like Bird's Pawnees, Catlin's Indians were gloriously noble, but they remained savage, their images shaped by the social norms and cultural assumptions of Euro-American life. Antebellum Indian imagery, in Schimmel's words, rendered Indians "in terms of what they might become or what they were not—white Christians."[18] To put it another way, many antebellum Indian paintings owe as much to artists'—and the public's—deeply seated, ethnocentric assumptions and ideas about Indians and their lives as they do to the artists' real-world observations of Indians. As I argue in this chapter, these assumptions and ideas influenced the nature and style of domestic, peaceful Indian imagery published in the illustrated press in the second half of the nineteenth century.

None of this is especially surprising. Indeed, because Indians existed outside the established social and cultural norms of Euro-Americans, they were necessarily represented by their differences. The process of representing the cultural other was rarely straightforward or neutral, however, because the recognition and representation of differences was also an act of cultural assessment, a process of evaluating Native Americans and Native American life by the standards of Western civilization. Looking across the cultural divide, nineteenth-century Americans often interpreted these differences in one of two ways: as evidence of the "natural" and exotic lives of Noble Savages, or as evidence of Indian savagery and deficiency. Historian Robert Berkhofer Jr. calls this second category the "deficient Indian" theme. Thus, Native Americans, Berkhofer writes, "were described not as they were in their own eyes but from the viewpoint of outsiders, who often failed to understand their ideas or customs."[19] Mainstream society—that is, white, Euro-American society—used Indian differences to make moral evaluations of Indians, which meant that Indians and their customs and activities were routinely portrayed as deviant, sometimes exotic, and occasionally praiseworthy, but more often than not, inferior. For the pictorial press, the various ceremonial and domestic aspects of Indian life were ideal occasions for depicting Indians as colorful curiosities, people worthy of attention because they lived, looked, and acted in strange but alluring ways.

In the pages of the illustrated weeklies, in fact, domestic Indian illustrations were also notable because they were strikingly different from the domestic illustrations of white society. *Leslie's* and *Harper's Weekly* published political news as well as reports about crime and various disasters, frequently illustrated by realistic-appearing engravings of people and places. These papers also published stories and pictures of business and industry, domestic and home life, and more genteel topics such as fashion and leisure activities. Literature, art, and religion were also staples in the pictorial press. This content was meant to inform and entertain a broad range of American readers. It is significant, too, that both *Leslie's* and *Harper's* sought a mass audience, including readers from the expanding middle class. While *Leslie's* was aimed more toward the working class, *Harper's* sought a wealthier and more sophisticated audience, going so far as to call itself "A Journal of Civilization."[20] Given this emphasis, illustrations of Indian rituals and habits offered a glimpse into a "primitive" or "savage" world outside the experience of ordinary (white) readers; that is, these images featured unusual people and places that were interesting as well as different—this was the particular appeal of these pictures. In the pages of the illustrated papers, pictures of Indians engaged in unusual, colorful, or bizarre "Indian" activities were a way to bring novel and eye-catching images to the American public.

Indian Rituals and Ceremonies

For white Americans, Indian dances, rituals, and ceremonies were an especially colorful and appealing activity. Except for certain residents of the West and Southwest, as Alan Trachtenberg has noted, most Americans in the last decades of the nineteenth century knew Indians as performers in Wild West shows and on display at world's fairs.[21] Following this theme, Indian dances and ceremonies were often depicted in the pictorial press as performances, strange and colorful activities that provided insights into Indian life, especially when these ceremonies were "primitive" and "deviant." Such rituals and ceremonies were ideal subjects for the pictorial press, which needed unusual and compelling pictures to lure readers to their pages—the more romantic or bizarre the better.[22] In 1864, for example, *Harper's Weekly* published an illustration of Indians dancing at a metropolitan fair in New York. The dancers, the paper explained, were part of "Bierstadt's Indian Wigwam," a popular program that gave visitors a chance "to study the habits and peculiarities of the aborigines."[23] The dance portrayed was the war dance, "as given on several occasions to the intense gratification of all spectators." The story concluded with a wistful nod to the presumed fate of the Indians, people who once "held undisputed possession of our continent," now reduced to dancing "for the pleasure of the pale-faced race, whose ancestors pushed them into obscurity and historical oblivion."[24] In this *Harper's* depiction, Indians were romanticized (and safe, even when performing a war dance) performers, colorful reminders of a once-great aboriginal American population that was no match for the march of Euro-American civilization and progress. The moral issues associated with this march were suggested here—"the pale-faced race, whose ancestors pushed them into obscurity and historical oblivion"—but only in passing. A brief report from a city fair was not the place to question Manifest Destiny and its tragic consequences for American Indians.

Leslie's published a vivid illustration of Indian dancing in early 1866, labeling it "Superstitions of the Indian Tribes—The Sioux Making Medicine"[25] (figure 2.2). The engraving, based on a sketch by an army bugler named C. Moellman, showed a number of Indians, many in silhouette, around a campfire in a moonlit Sioux village. Two figures dominated the illustration, one dancing with a tomahawk held high and the other stooped over a sacrificial animal, in this case a dog. The story explained more than the picture, noting that this ceremony was preparation for an attack, the savage way of "invoking the assistance of their gods before venturing their lives upon the field of battle."[26] The article focused on the strangeness of the ritual, including aspects that were not obvious. For example, the story noted that the medicine man and the chiefs involved in the dance were nearly nude, "retaining only that which decency requires." Equally strange was the method of animal sacrifice, which was hanging: "This method of killing their offering, is, we believe, peculiar to these prairie Indians." The dance proceeded with "the music of a wild chant, extemporized for the occasion," the story said, while one of the warriors chopped the carcass into small pieces for the medicine man and other warriors to eat. All this was too much for the *Leslie's* writer, who noted the "hideous" yelling of the dance and the consumption of "a plenteous supper of dog-meat." It was, the writer said, a "mummery"—that is, a ridiculous performance—that lasted until the "wee small hours of the night."[27]

This focus on the bizarre makes perfect sense given *Leslie's* penchant for the sensational and the working-class audience of the weekly. The illustration showed an apparently realistic and appealingly "primitive" tribal dance, drawing attention to the story, which revealed the shocking details of the Sioux ceremony—near nudity, discordant chanting, and a dog hung as a sacrifice before it was dismembered, roasted, and eaten. This was deviant but appealingly bizarre behavior, as *Leslie's* made clear in its story. In fact, the article opened with this justification: "The superstitious rites of savage nations will ever possess strange interest to enlightened minds, so closely do they resemble the religious observances of the classic Greek,

FIGURE 2.2. An army bugler named Moellman sketched this scene of a Sioux dance, an image that emphasized the strangeness of the dance and the ritual sacrifice—and consumption—of a dog.

the barbaric Goth, and the invincible Roman, of ancient days."[28] The superstitions of the Sioux, in other words, were akin to the rites and rituals of the ancient Europeans and, on that basis, could be appreciated by contemporary readers. This was also an argument for the popular ethnography of the day, an editorial position *Leslie's* embraced at the end of the article: "Though far from believing in the efficacy of these proceedings, we yet think as a religious observance this 'medicine-making' of the Sioux will not compare unfavorably with the superstitious rites of our own ancestors, before the light of Christianity had revealed to them the error of their ways." In this way, *Leslie's* explained the Sioux war dance in the context of earlier "primitive" peoples and their rituals, comparisons that *Leslie's* readers could use to understand the Sioux ceremony. For most readers, however, it seems likely that the dramatic image and the sensational elements of the story (roasting and eating dog meat!) overshadowed this more nuanced interpretation of the dance.

Scalping was another Indian practice that drew the attention of the pictorial press, even in ceremonial form. An 1874 Cary illustration captioned "Scalp Dance," for example, showed an unidentified tribe in their village celebrating a great victory, including a mock scalping.[29] The picture highlighted a group of dancing warriors, muscular and fierce, reenacting their battlefield successes. This illustration was,

Harper's declared, "a vivid picture of one of these wild scenes." The story explained the action:

> In the centre [*sic*] of the group are the squaws, ranged in a circle, and holding high above their heads the dripping scalps, fastened on the ends of long poles. Around this inner circle the warriors perform the wildest of all their dances, to the accompaniment of low measured grunts, interspersed with occasional outcries of the most hideous kind imaginable, while their painted faces are covered with the most horrible grimaces. Scalping knives are flourished, scalps shaken, and all manner of antics performed, to the great amusement of those who look on.[30]

This was powerful imagery, the kind of picture that added excitement to the pages of the illustrated press. Indeed, Cary's image and its explanatory story offered more excitement than factual information. The picture itself featured scowling warriors armed with knives in front of Indian women holding "dripping scalps" aloft. Under the headline "Sketches of Indian Warfare," the story began by recounting recent outbreaks of Indian violence in the West. "Helpless men and women and even little children have been subjected to bodily tortures that make one's blood run cold to think of," *Harper's* noted. The story, however, offered no details of a particular Indian attack or massacre. The story gave no information at all about these Indians, whom they had defeated, or anything else about their recent victory. In fact, generalized and terrifying Indian violence was the point of both the illustration and the story. *Harper's* did not present Cary's drawing as an ethnographic illustration, but an image of Indians in their natural state—dangerous, menacing, and hideous. These Indians, whoever they were, danced for glory in war and the defeat of their enemies, sure signs of Indian savagery.

One of the most dramatic Indian rituals, the Sioux sun dance, was depicted in a highly detailed two-page illustration in *Harper's* in early 1875. The illustration, signed by Jules Tavernier and Paul Frenzeny, was published above this caption: "Indian Sun Dance—Young Bucks Proving Their Endurance by Self-Torture."[31] The illustration depicted the third and final day of a tribal religious ceremony said to be "in honor of the sun." The illustration showed dozens of Sioux observing a test of masculine endurance in "a round inclosure" made of poles and buffalo skins and decorated with white and red flags. *Harper's* explained that scene was a rare look by "our enterprising artists" into a ceremony in which

> the young warriors of the tribe undergo various self-inflicted tortures for the purpose of proving their powers of endurance—such as piercing the skin and sticking into the wounds pieces of wood to which stout cords running from the central pole are attached. The whole weight of the body is suspended on these cords, producing the most excruciating pain, which is borne not only without flinching, but with every manifestation of delight.

All the young warriors, *Harper's* explained, "are naked, with the exception of a cloth about the loins, and their bodies are smeared with red, green, yellow, and blue paint."[32]

Given its dramatic and gruesome nature, this was a perfect Indian ritual for the pictorial press. This depiction of the sun dance, that is, included all the "Indian" elements needed to attract and amaze mainstream readers: a mysterious and exotic tribal ceremony, a solid dose of suffering and endurance, and a suggestion of masculine sexuality. No wonder Tavernier and Frenzeny sought to sketch this particular ceremony or that the editors in New York published it across two pages, their largest possible format. This sort of Indian illustration exploited the great strength of the illustrated papers: bringing pictures of exotic, faraway people and places into the lives of ordinary American readers.[33]

Indian rituals turned up in the pictorial press again in 1882, when ethnologist Frank Hamilton Cushing brought six Zuni men from the American Southwest to Washington, Boston, and other eastern cities. Cushing, described in *Leslie's* as an "enthusiastic member of the Ethological Bureau" of the Smithsonian Institution, was eager to show off his charges and—not coincidentally—promote his own role as the self-appointed spokesman, interpreter, and advocate for this apparently remarkable tribe.[34] *Leslie's* acknowledged this fact in the lead of its story, pointing out that organized Indian visits to the East were now routine. But with Cushing's help, the story continued, the Zuni visit to the East had been followed "with eager interest." The Zuni were a small but very old and interesting tribe, *Leslie's* explained, so fascinating that Cushing had resolved to join the tribe, "master their language, secure their confidence, and lay bare their mysteries."[35] Indeed, Zuni tribal ceremonies were depicted on *Leslie's* cover, which included one large and two small engravings of the Zuni chiefs performing their rites for a crowd of onlookers at Deer Island, Massachusetts (figure 2.3). The largest picture showed the men gathered on the beach, "filling their sacred vessels with water from the Atlantic."[36] A smaller picture on the top left of the page showed the men inducting Cushing into the "Order of the Bow," described as one of the tribe's highest and most influential secret orders.[37] The third illustration, published on the top right of the page, showed the Zuni chiefs rejoicing at the end of the ceremonies.

These pictures and the accompanying story were strong editorial material for *Leslie's.* As with the Sioux dance described earlier, the Zuni pictures were appealing and exotic. Dressed in elaborate traditional clothes and ornaments, the Zuni chiefs were presented as wondrous creatures from another time and place. Filling their vessels was, the caption said, an "ancient religious rite." In addition, this depiction of Zuni ritual came courtesy of a government official who lived with these people and understood their lives. Frank Cushing, according to *Leslie's,* was now a Zuni himself, having overcome early resistance to become an adopted member of the Parrot family and an elected tribal leader. All of this gave the *Leslie's* illustrations

FIGURE 2.3. *Leslie's* featured the exotic nature of Indian ceremonies in 1882 when a group of Zuni visited Deer Island in Massachusetts.

an extra air of authority, a gloss of scientific respectability that was unusual in other Indian illustrations. This authority also helped justify the exploitation of Zuni rites in the pages of the illustrated press, an intrusion into tribal customs that went unacknowledged at the time. Although it is unfair to hold these nineteenth-century figures to contemporary standards of cultural sensitivity, neither Cushing nor *Leslie's* had any apparent qualms about depicting Indian ceremonies or rituals, sacred or not. Cushing and *Leslie's* recognized that Zuni practices and customs were interesting and exotic, but they saw them as activities worth exploiting in the name of popular ethnography and pictorial journalism. On the face of it, the Zuni chiefs performed these ceremonies willingly, although it's difficult at this remove to know exactly what these men were thinking or how Cushing or others might have manipulated them during this trip.

Indian Ways of Death

The pictorial press was also interested in other sorts of Native American activities and rituals, including those surrounding death and dying. In March 1869, for example, *Harper's Weekly* published a full-page illustration of an Indian "burial" near Fort Laramie, Wyoming.[38] The scene showed three Indian mourners on horseback beneath a large tree with two wrapped bodies in its branches. The image, taken from a photograph by well-known photographer Alexander Gardner, was posed, although it documented the burial and mourners without apparent bias. The story, on the other hand, was generic. It provided no information about Gardner's photo or the circumstances under which it was taken and included no information at all about the Indians. Instead the story made note of various burial customs—including Egyptian embalming—and offered details from an earlier *Harper's Monthly* report on the items (arms, ammunition, food, and clothing) that usually accompanied the dead to the "Happy Hunting Ground."[39] The editors also pointed out differences between Christian and Indian burial customs, noting that Indians place the feet of their dead to the south, while Christians and most other groups bury their dead with the head pointing west "so that the face looked toward the rising sun." In this Indian portrayal, *Harper's* was less interested in the news about these burials—no newsworthy facts were provided—than in publishing an interesting scene from the Indian frontier by an established photographer. In other words, this illustration and its accompanying story were another example of popular ethnography, journalism that gave readers a look at some of the curious practices of Native Americans in their "natural" state.

Harper's published another image of an Indian burial in 1874, a half-page engraving of Indian women and children honoring a fallen warrior, his wrapped body held aloft by three long poles.[40] The most prominent of the mourners was a woman, perhaps the man's wife, looking to the body and offering a bowl of food or drink to the deceased. The scene, based on a Cary sketch, was respectfully rendered at a medium distance and betrayed no suggestion of condescension. The short article explaining the image, however, referred to the "affectionate superstition" surrounding Indian mourning.[41] *Harper's* presented this as a paradox. On one hand, Indians were "very attentive" to the dead, for which they could be praised. On the other hand, these gifts satisfied "the supposed wants of the dead," which was seemingly foolish and superstitious. As with many representations of Indian life in the illustrated press, Indians here were portrayed as curiosities, as cultural outsiders who were interesting but whose ways were odd and mysterious.

A similar theme appeared in *Harper's* in 1884 when it published a highly detailed, two-page illustration of an Indian funeral procession by artist Paul Frenzeny.[42] The picture showed a group of men and women mourners walking and riding alongside the wrapped body of a fallen warrior. Several of the mourners were singing; a woman on the right was beating a drum. Frenzeny's picture was a somber but respectful depiction that revealed (again) no trace of condescension. This was a significant image—the largest that *Harper's Weekly* could publish—yet the story that explained it was a two-sentence paragraph under the headline "Off for the Happy Hunting Grounds." The story, in full, reads as follows:

> When an Indian chief is carried to his place of burial, whether it be a grave or a rude platform of branches swung on the limbs of a tree, his body is preceded by a company of musicians, who chant his praises in rude strains. His famous exploits as a warrior and hunter form the burden of their song, and

with their sorrow for his death are mingled wishes for an even greater career in the happy hunting grounds to which his spirit has passed on.[43]

While the tone and language of this description were largely respectful, the funeral is presented (again) as a cultural curiosity. Frenzeny's illustration showed genuine mourning, but this was the mourning of Indians, whose funeral ceremonies were different from those of whites. This image was ethnographic, in fact, providing readers with an elaborate picture and a little information about Native American burial customs. What is notable, however, is what was missing in this account. The fallen warrior was unidentified by name or tribe. No place or time was reported, nor were readers given any information about the man's "famous exploits as a warrior and hunter." In all these ways, this portrayal was incomplete. It emphasized the odd spectacle of the funeral party (the drummer, the grieving singers) but offered none of the details surrounding the life being mourned.

A more controversial Indian practice—abandoning an elderly woman to die on the prairie—drew an unambiguous response in *Harper's*; it was uncivilized and un-Christian. The illustration, also by Cary, showed a grizzled, white-haired woman sitting alone amid scrub brush and grass[44] (figure 2.4). As her tribe exits the scene, wolves and vultures are already approaching, ready to pounce. "Left to Perish," the caption said, condemning this practice in decidedly Christian terms. "Only the Christian nations of the world provide hospitals and asylums for the sick and the infirm," the editors declared.[45] American Indians—except for the "partially civilized" tribes—leave the old and helpless to suffer and die, a legacy of their mistreatment of women. "They are degraded and despised; and are made to do nearly all the heaviest and meanest kinds of labor," the story explained. As for the illustration, it depicted an "old squaw whose days of usefulness are over." The editors could not resist dramatizing the woman's sad fate: "A few days will end all with her, and then the wolves and vultures, already instinctively forecasting her death, will feast upon her poor body, and leave her bones to bleach in the solitude of the wilderness." The article ended with a final appeal to Christian values: "Let us hope that the day may speedily come when the spirit of Christianity shall pervade the world, and make such crimes impossible."[46]

This portrayal of Indian practices leaves no doubt about the differences between the civilized and the savage world. Civilized Christians are humane and kind. They treat their women well. They also provide institutions for the care of the sick and elderly. Savages, on the other hand, mistreat women and the elderly, as documented so vividly in Cary's illustration. The old woman was "left to perish," *Harper's* declared, a characteristic of American Indians the paper extended to other barbaric peoples. "Uncivilized men almost every where leave those enfeebled by age to perish, and in some countries children kill their parents, and parents their children, when from any cause they become helpless and dependent." The paper's argument makes clear the presumed superiority of civilized, Christian nations (like the United

LEFT TO PERISH.—Drawn by W. M. Cary.—[See Page 447.]

FIGURE 2.4. The contrast between civilization and savagery was unmistakable in this illustration of an old woman abandoned by her tribe. Unlike the Indians, the editors wrote, Christian nations "provide hospitals and asylums for the sick and the infirm."

States) over the heathen peoples of the world. In so doing, it asserts an unexamined claim of moral superiority of "civilized" nations, ignoring the contradictions and failures in the civilized and Christian treatment of women and the elderly. The paper also makes a sweeping condemnation of all uncivilized Indians by assuming that all have the same inhumane practices.

This *Harper's* assessment was another telling example of Indian deficiency, presented in a way that made clear the differences between civilized and savage peoples. It was also compelling—but superficial—evidence of the barbarism and cruelty of Indian life, especially its lack of basic human decency. In both picture and story, *Harper's* revealed this Indian deficiency unambiguously. If there was a way to explain this scene in more sympathetic or culturally sensitive terms, neither Cary nor the editors in New York had the background, knowledge, or experience to do so. Moreover, *Harper's* had no interest or incentive to note the cruelties of Euro-American society; such comparisons would have to wait for a later date and a more detached perspective. In 1879, the savage nature of this incident was obvious and sensational—a fact that made it a better story for the illustrated press. This was effective visual journalism, an Indian picture story that was bound to register shock and disgust while also reaffirming Christian superiority and Indian inferiority.

Marriage and Male-Female Relations

Indian marital and sexual customs were a provocative way for illustrators to contrast the civilized with the savage. In fact, "Indians Swapping Wives" was the name of an 1870 Cary drawing for *Harper's Weekly*[47] (figure 2.5). Despite the title, the image itself was notably tame; it showed four unidentified Indians, a horse, and two dogs on the plains, with a low mountain rising in the background. *Harper's* claimed that the drawing was "an accurate sketch of the kind of trade that frequently takes place" among Indians.[48] Given Cary's travels on the northern plains, perhaps it was. In any case, the illustration showed two Indian men standing face to face in a Western landscape, negotiating a deal. One warrior, the story explained, was swapping an "old, homely wife" for "a young and pretty one, and a horse thrown in to boot." Importantly and more pointedly, the story added a moral dimension to this report. The headline set the tone: "Our Barbarian Brethren." The editors followed with this lead, rich in sarcasm:

> Our Indian fellow-citizens, it is well known, entertain very lax notions respecting the sanctity of the marriage tie—which, in fact, they consider any thing but a tie. The noble red man not only regards his wives as inferiors, but in the light of goods and chattels, and when tired of them trades them off in barter, or swaps them for another's.[49]

The text made clear what Cary's drawing suggested; namely, that Indian customs and mores were inferior to those of civilized people. Indians were uncivilized, after all, with no notion of proper—that is, Christian—marriage. Moreover, Indian men regularly denigrated women, something Cary signaled in the drawing by depicting the wives in a submissive stance, their heads bowed. All this was presented as typical of Western Indians; no tribe or location was published. Taken together, the illustration and story once again revealed Indian deficiency, documentary evidence for the moral superiority of Christianity and Euro-American life.

A more placid illustration of male-female relations appeared in *Harper's* in August 1876, when the paper published a drawing called "Indian Toilet"[50] (figure 2.6). This illustration featured a stereotypical Indian warrior—dour, dark-skinned, and large-nosed—wearing a decorated top hat, black and shiny. The man was sitting in front of his tepee checking his appearance in a makeshift mirror, preparing himself for some grand occasion. His wife was seated behind him, dutifully braiding his hair. A baby in a papoose was nearby. More ominously, the man's weapons, including an elaborate war club, were prominent in the foreground. The illustration was interesting in part because of the contrast between the domesticity of the scene—the tepee, the wife, and the baby—and the prospect of violence represented by the

INDIANS SWAPPING WIVES.

FIGURE 2.5. Indian wife swapping was a topic bound to attract readers—as well as moral condemnation. "Our Indian fellow-citizens . . . entertain very lax notions respecting the sanctity of the marriage tie," *Harper's* reported.

warrior's preparations and his weapons. The story provided additional insights into the scene, most of them critical of Indian life: "No dandy of civilization is more fastidious in regard to his 'make-up' than a young Indian warrior, or 'buck,' as he is called on the plains, whether in preparing for the war-path, a big feast, or an important council," the story began.[51] The illustration, the editors explained, was made by "our artist during a peaceful sojourn in an Indian village." Peaceful or not, the editors were unimpressed with Indian life: "The costume presents a curious mixture of the garments of civilized and savage life, and the effect is most ludicrous." The story went on to note that dressing this warrior for the occasion was woman's work. The "squaw," the article continued, "takes great pride in adorning the person of her own particular 'brave' in the highest style of the savage art." The story went on to describe how and when the colors of the paint could be applied, noting the fact that the colors changed by the season and that the paint was stored in curiously carved horns, hung in every tent or lodge. The story also claimed that Indian paint served as a way to avoid washing. "As a rule, Indians generally have an instinctive dislike to water, either as a beverage or for washing, and thus their faces are covered with alternative layers or crusts of dirt and paint."[52]

AN INDIAN TOILET.—[See Page 668.]

W. M. Cary

FIGURE 2.6. In the pictorial press, Indian men were often portrayed as arrogant and vain, dominating their women and dressing in ridiculous ways.

Cary's illustration was, on the surface, merely descriptive. It appeared to show what the artist saw in an Indian village and was, arguably, a straightforward representation of ordinary Indian life. Biographer Mildred Ladner saw it as a humorous dig at "the demeaning chores expected of Indian women."[53] But the story shifted that interpretation, emphasizing the deficiencies of Indians and their habits. The Indian man was presented as a dandy, far too concerned about his appearance than any civilized person should be. In addition, the warrior's top hat, an article of civilization, was presented as out of place and thus ridiculous, especially when combined with buckskin and the "savage" face of an Indian man. The scene was generic as well, stripped of place, time, and any tribal identification. By publishing "Indian Toilet," *Harper's* was highlighting the exoticism of the dandified (and unwashed) Indian warrior—a rather feminized male—in contrast to Euro-American males and, in the copy, making plain that Indian ways were inferior. Such domestic illustrations positioned Indians as social and cultural oddities, people with habits that were not simply different from "normal" Americans but also deficient and, in many cases, silly and pitiful.

Hunting and Camp Life

The daily activities of Indians were not especially newsworthy in the pictorial press. Yet the hunting and camp-life aspects of Indian life sometimes generated feature pictures and stories, especially if they were action-oriented. In 1874, for instance, *Harper's* published a Cary illustration of some unidentified Indians breaking a pony.[54] Set in a wooded Indian camp complete with tepees and a woman chopping wood in the background, the picture was action-packed—a contest between a wild horse, a barking dog, and several Indian boys. While two boys were trying to subdue the bucking animal with a rope, two others were desperately clinging to the horse's back and still another was hitting the ground. A brief story explained the scene. "The Indians have a rough but very effectual method of breaking colts," the story began. This business was "great fun" for the boys, *Harper's* reported, "but whether the colt enjoys the process is not so clear."[55]

This portrayal of Indian life was informative, to be sure. It provided a bit of excitement too, which helps explain why *Harper's* devoted a full page to the scene. Yet even here—in what could have been a somewhat neutral depiction of Indian life—the representation of Indians emphasized difference and deficiency. This method of taming a horse, after all, was "rough," even as it was "very effectual." In addition, the Indians in the scene were living in tents in a forest, dressed in buckskin, or, in the case of the most prominent Indian, bare-chested and muscular. Finally, this scene was presented—again—as a generic Indian camp, with no indication of a particular tribe, time, or place. In sum, this picture and story offered a view of Indian camp life that made plain a number of basic differences between Indians and whites. For the readers of *Harper's Weekly,* these were distinctly primitive people living a hard life very different from their own.

Another exciting part of Indian life was the hunt, especially the buffalo hunt on the open plains. *Harper's* published one such scene in 1858, a drawing by Felix O. C. Darley, one of its most accomplished illustrators. Set on the grass-rich prairie, "The Buffalo Hunt" showed a bare-chested warrior on his horse overtaking and attacking an imposing buffalo with his lance.[56] Another hunter pursues another animal in the background. Although the editors offered no specifics about this scene, they heaped praise on Darley's "striking and effective scene, [which] will no doubt fire the blood of our sportsman readers." This picture, one of several in this issue, "will do no injury to the high reputation which Mr. Darley has won by his former illustrations of Indian life," the editors proclaimed. Like Cary, Darley was a trusted artist and an old hand at illustrating Indian life, a fact that the editors used to promote his work. In addition, the editors made clear one purpose of this Indian illustration—to "fire the blood" of its adventurous male readers. In short, this illustration of Indian life was published because it was exciting, living up to the adventurous stereotype of Indian life on the plains. In the 1830s, Catlin had painted buffalo hunts in the West and helped make such scenes popular with the public. Twenty years later, Darley and his editors celebrated this quintessentially Indian activity.

Cary provided *Harper's* with a different sort of buffalo hunt in 1874 when he submitted a scene showing "Indians Killing Buffaloes in the Missouri River."[57] Two warriors with knives in their mouths were in the foreground of the scene, swimming alongside huge buffalo. In the background, other warriors pursued other animals in a canoe and small boat, while still other warriors on the right were dragging a carcass ashore for slaughter. Again, this was appealing material from the Indian frontier; the editors called it a "striking picture" and quoted from the artist himself in an accompanying story. Cary explained that the killing took place "toward evening of a sultry July day" near a fort on the Missouri. A dark cloud of dust began to rise, he wrote, followed by a low humming sound and then "a rumble like that of heavy thunder."[58] The Indians, Cary explained, were a friendly band, at the fort seeking protection from a hostile war party. While some of the warriors hunted with bows and arrows, these illustrated Indians "swam boldly into the midst of the herd and dispatched their victims with the knife." That night, the Indians made fires for a grand feast and "the garrison takes its share of the spoils within the walls of the fort," Cary reported.

The editors used the rest of the story decrying the fate of the buffalo at the hands of hunters, who had been killing the animals by the thousands for their hides alone. The editors offered several suggestions for saving the animals, including legislation, tariffs, and even the seizing of "green hides." The editors also invoked Indian-white relations in their preservation argument, noting that without the buffalo the Indians would be destitute, a grim situation that could threaten "scattered white settlements" in the West.[59] These were worthy arguments, of course, but they departed from Cary's illustration and his report on friendly Indians hunting and feasting at a fort on the upper Missouri. Nevertheless, the editors used Cary's information to have their say on two important matters: First, the buffalo must be saved from extinction and, second, the consequences of not saving the buffalo might unleash a new round of Indian violence against settlers. By the end of this story, *Harper's* had made it clear that some Indians at an unspecified place and time were a threat to whites—as most readers would have expected.

Indians Trading and Working

As noted earlier, Cary was one of the most prolific illustrators of ordinary Indian life. More than other Western artists, he took note of mundane domestic activities, including arrow making, which was the subject of a front-page engraving on the cover on *Harper's* in June 1870.[60] Cary depicted an Indian family—father, mother, two children, and a dog—seated outside a frontier fort. The woman was on the right, holding an infant in her arms, observing her husband at work. On the left a bare-chested young girl sat serenely at her father's feet next to the dog. The warrior dominated the center of the picture, holding an arrow in his right hand, a knife in his left. The accompanying story explained that the man was probably cutting "murderous grooves" in the shaft of the arrow so that it would be more lethal, "allow[ing] the blood to drain slowly but surely away." The story also explained how Indians used the bow in battle, praising their skill. On horseback, *Harper's* said, the Indian "instinctively takes to the bow, which he handles with marvelous dexterity." As for the arrows, they "are always made of ash or hickory, toughness being an essential quality." Beyond such description, the article criticized the arrow-making ability of Indian men, noting that this task was "generally intrusted [*sic*] by the warrior to his better half."[61]

As with most other representations of Indian lives in the pictorial press, this *Harper's Weekly* report provided almost no facts surrounding this scene. The Indians who appeared on the front page of the weekly were unidentified by name or tribe, nor was there any explanation of the circumstances that brought them to the fort, which was also unidentified. This lack of specifics suggests that this was not a news report at all; this was a form of popular ethnography, a broad examination of the ways of "the Western Indian," the very phrase that appeared in the second sentence of this article. Based on this evidence, eastern and midwestern readers had no need to know who these Indians were or how they might differ from other Western Indians. In this and many other cases, as we have seen, Indians in the illustrated press were simplified and made generic for ease of understanding.

One of the relatively few illustrations of Indians engaged in economic activity was the Paul Tavernier–Jules Frenzeny drawing "Indians Trading at a Frontier Town," published in *Harper's* in July 1875 (figure 2.7). This scene showed a number of

INDIANS TRADING AT A FRONTIER TOWN.

FIGURE 2.7. *Harper's* used this trading scene from Utah to belittle Indian men and contrast the ideal Indian man—a wooden statue—with actual Indian men, who were described as haughty and foolish.

Indian men and women at a storefront, having just arrived at a "border town" in Utah, probably Ogden.[62] This was an authentic picture, the editors boasted, having been "engraved from a sketch of an actual scene witnessed by our artists."[63] The two central figures in the illustration were an Indian woman carrying animal skins on her back and a dour-looking trader inspecting one of her pelts. Several blanket-clad Indians on the right side of the image were studying a wooden Indian outside a barbershop, while an Indian in the background admired a rifle, an item that he seemed likely to obtain with a successful trade.[64] The published engraving was detailed and apparently realistic, capturing a sense of business activity on the Indian frontier.

The short story that explained the illustration cast the scene in a different light. It offered a unflattering judgment on Indian gender roles, reporting that the "squaws, who do all the hard work, are loaded with skins," while the warriors "consider every kind of labor degrading to a man." The warriors "condescend only to do the bargaining," *Harper's* continued, though they were unlikely to succeed: "Indian cunning, supreme in border strategy, is never a match for the sharpened craftiness of the white trader in a bargain." The paper explained that the Indians rarely wanted money. "They want rifles, revolvers, knives, beads, sugar, cloth, and other articles which they can turn to immediate use," the story said. The story also pointed out the difference between these Indians, identified as Utes, and the romanticized Indian represented by the wooden statue. The statue was "the ideal Indian figure," *Harper's* said, "very unlike the real creature." Finally, *Harper's* assured its readers that this was a familiar scene, one that could be "witnessed in every frontier town where barbarism and civilization come in contact." In all these ways, both this image and its written explanation drew clear distinctions between Indians and whites. Indian men were lazy and abused their women. As traders, Indian men were no match for white traders. Even the barbershop's wooden Indian made plain the inferior nature of actual Indians, who were reduced to admiring the nobility of the statue. Tavernier and Frenzeny may very well have witnessed Indian trading in Utah, but the *Harper's* explanation of the scene was loaded with racial distinctions, all of which positioned the Utes as outsiders and, not surprisingly, deficient when compared to civilized people.

Another example of Indians at work was an 1877 drawing of some California Mission Indians making rope. Paul Frenzeny's documentary-style drawing showed several women and children at work under a covered outdoor workshop.[65] The Indians were shown twisting horsehair into rope using a large wheel-like device. A short article explained the scene. "The Mission Indians around Palo and San Diego, in Southern California, are dextrous workers in baskets and in ropes made of horse-hair," the article noted. The unidentified writer praised the artistry of the reed and grass baskets, noting their colors formed "a very pretty and even artistic combination." The baskets, the article continued, are so tightly woven that they are watertight. "They resemble the finest Japanese wicker-work, and are considered an indispensible article of kitchen furniture in the households of Southern California."[66]

The illustration and the overall message of the article were complimentary of the Mission Indians. They were shown at work and, more than that, making objects of beauty and utility. *Harper's* acknowledged the unusualness of this depiction: "It is seldom that American Indians are pictorially represented as otherwise engaged than in scalping, stealing, or hunting," the story began. "The above sketch forms an interesting exception to the rule."[67] With this language, however, the editors were sending a mixed message, noting the pervasiveness of illustrated Indian violence and contrasting it with this scene of Indian industry. To put it more bluntly, these Mission Indians were presented as "good" Indians; they demonstrated an admirable work ethic and high-quality craftsmanship. But the fact remained, as the editors noted, that other Indians were still "scalping, stealing, or hunting." For readers in New York, Boston, Philadelphia, Chicago, Cincinnati, and St. Louis—people unlikely to have any contact with the Mission Indians of Southern California—this was a decidedly "racialized" message, a bit of commentary that separated Indians

THE INDIAN AT WORK.—MAPLE-SUGAR-MAKING IN THE NORTHERN WOODS.—FROM A SKETCH BY W. M. CARY.—SEE PAGE 174.

FIGURE 2.8. Indians were rarely depicted as workers, but this *Leslie's* illustration of Indians making maple sugar was a notable exception.

from whites even as these "good" Indians were shown doing what the dominant society demanded that they do.

Another illustration of Indians working showed an unidentified group of Indians making maple sugar somewhere in the northern woods. This 1883 *Leslie's* illustration focused on a large fire and cauldron of maple sap hanging over it[68] (figure 2.8). An Indian on the right stirred the steaming syrup; a man on the left approached with another bucket of sap. Other Indians warmed themselves by the fire. On the far left, the artist showed a tapped maple tree draining its sweet sap into a bucket. In all these ways, the illustration showed industry and enterprise, two qualities rarely associated with American Indians in the popular press.

Despite this favorable depiction, the article explaining the illustration fell back on Indian stereotypes and generalizations. The story's headline and the lead sentence shifted the focus from this group of unidentified Indians to "The Indian." This switch from the particular to the general allowed *Leslie's* writers to make some sweeping comments about all Indians and their presumed relationship to work. The story opened with this pronouncement: "The Indian, when forced by circumstances, as he repeatedly has been, makes promises to the Government . . . to give up his depredations on the frontier and apply himself to regular pursuits."[69] The Indian says "that his heart is good," the article continued, and that he wishes to build schools and churches, to plant corn and wheat, and "to follow the white man's road." But, *Leslie's* added, these promises were usually made in the fall, "when the grass is scarce." In any case, the article went on, the Indian is now so thoroughly hemmed in by whites and their settlements that he has "no alternative but to work himself." Such work consists of trapping and collecting skins and making baskets and beadwork, as well as making sugar, *Leslie's* said. Sugaring was traditional work, *Leslie's* allowed, but now, thanks to cauldrons and other equipment obtained from whites, "they are enabled to make quite a business of it." This assessment of Indians and their relationship to labor was as sweeping as it was condescending, a broad editorial brush that grouped all Indians together as a single body and ignored many individual and tribal efforts to adapt to Euro-American society and assimilate. More significantly, the story overlooked many decades of white violence toward the tribes as well as government policies meant to destabilize and subdue Indians and hold on to the land. In short, the language and meaning of this story undermined the apparent industry shown in the maple-sugar illustration. This was, in effect, a catch-22 for this Indian representation, an approving illustration of Indians at work accompanied by an explanatory story that undercut the positive nature of the picture. In *Leslie's* in 1883, these industrious Indians could not be praised unconditionally in an illustration; their image had to be tempered by words that explained how and why they were working. Taken together, this was a patronizing representation of Indians at work.

Indians at Play

On rare occasions, Indians in the illustrated press could be shown at play, having fun. Cary portrayed one such scene in 1870 when he made a drawing of some Indians gambling for the possession of a female captive[70] (figure 2.9). As with other pictures, this dramatic scene was generalized, set somewhere on the prairie, just after Indians had overrun a wagon train. The violence of the scene was downplayed in both the drawing and the short explanatory article, both of which emphasized gambling. Cary's drawing centered on a group of kneeling warriors engaged in a game of chance. The article, "Indian Gambling," explained how the game was played:

> It is done by means of two sticks or stones. They take them in their hands and, holding them, behind their backs, separate them, or put them both together in one hand; then, bringing them forward, ask the opposite chief to guess which hand they are in. If there is one in each hand it counts nothing; if they are both together, and that hand is "guessed," he has chosen right. This process is repeated a certain number of times, until all have had their turn, when the

INDIANS GAMBLING FOR THE POSSESSION OF A CAPTIVE.—SKETCHED BY M. W. CARY.—[SEE PAGE 199.]

FIGURE 2.9. Despite the violence of this scene, this *Harper's Weekly* picture and the article that explained it emphasized Indians at play, gambling for the possession of a white woman.

one who has most often guessed right becomes possessor of the unfortunate captive. In this way the Indians often gamble away their horses, wives, and other possessions.[71]

Cary's drawing added drama to this scene, showing the forlorn and notably white-skinned young woman hanging her head as the Indians gambled beside her. Her unfortunate protector—husband or brother—was on the ground nearby, a warrior dragging his body toward the assembled Indians.

For Americans in 1870, this illustration was not about play but another example of Indian savagery on the plains. Attacks on wagon trains were the great fear of western emigrants, a fear that was often exaggerated and sensationalized in the press.[72] Indeed, this drawing was certainly fictionalized since it is unlikely that Cary witnessed this hostile scene firsthand. In other words, this was an imaginary scene, a Cary drawing based on secondhand reports from Western emigrants or friendly Indians. For *Harper's* and its white readers, however, this scene was symbolically—if not literally—true because it confirmed popular ideas about the dangers of emigration and the terrible consequences of an Indian attack. As with many such Indian drawings in the pictorial press, no victims were identified and *Harper's* gave no time or place for this incident. Nor was this "breaking" news; with its emphasis on gambling, it was not even an illustration of Indian violence. Like the emphasis on violence, however, Indian gambling—especially gambling over a helpless white woman—was a way of illustrating Indian cultural and racial inferiority, placing the savages on the margins of civilization.

Harper's published an example of Indians at play in 1874 with a half-page sketch of an Indian canoe race[73] (figure 2.10). The illustration showed two Indian men standing in their canoes, paddling furiously "on one of our broad Western rivers."[74] This was an action-oriented picture and these were strong, bare-chested men, their long hair streaming behind them. This picture was unusual because it showed Indian men enjoying themselves in friendly competition—very different from the "red devil" stereotype that appeared in illustrations of Indian-white violence. Even the explanatory story—only two sentences—avoided any suggestion of Indian violence. Instead, there was praise for Indian skill: "The Indians manage their slight birch-bark canoe with a marvelous dexterity to which few white men ever attain." When it came to racing canoes, at least, Indian men could be shown in the pictorial press as attractive, harmless, and highly skilled—even more skilled than white men. Notably, this occasion for praising Indian men was tied to a playful test of strength and endurance between warriors, not a contest comparing Indians and whites. This was an idealized and generic presentation as well, a sporting illustration between two unidentified warriors on an unidentified river at an unspecified time. Nevertheless, this image was refreshing because it showed Indian men in action in a nonthreatening leisure activity, a category of Indian life mostly overlooked in nineteenth-century popular culture.

Indian boys, presumably less threatening than Indian men, turned up in 1875 when *Leslie's* reported on tourists visiting an Indian village in Quebec. The half-page illustration by E. R. Morse showed a crowd observing several Indian boys who were demonstrating their marksmanship by "shooting at pennies."[75] The boys were from Lorette, *Leslie's* explained, an Indian settlement "principally engaged in the manufacture of snow-shoes and rude [primitive] toys."[76] The boys were part of the town's entertainment. "Visitors are importuned to offer small coins as targets, the coin being the prize of the successful marksman," *Leslie's* explained.

On its face, this was a neutral illustration depicting ordinary activities in the Indian village. Morse portrayed a peaceful—and playful—encounter between Indians and whites that appeared realistic and straightforward. On a deeper level, however, this illustration once again reinforced the idea of Indians as separate from—and opposed to—civilized life. Despite the village's efforts to make salable products, these boys were performing for tourists not with modern pistols or rifles, but with bows and arrows, the weapon of savages. In effect, these boys—although harmless in this scene—were

INDIAN CANOE RACE.

FIGURE 2.10. An Indian canoe race gave *Harper's* a chance to comment on Indian skill on the water, one of the few times the illustrated papers showed Indians in a friendly competition.

practicing savagery. In other words, this seemingly benign picture of Indian boys entertaining tourists was not a neutral depiction of Indians or Indian life. It was yet another visual reminder of the divide between civilized people and Indians, a divide that was taken for granted when Indian boys were shown "shooting at pennies."

Conclusion

Pictures of peaceful Indians engaged in ceremonial, domestic, and other daily activities were published irregularly in the last half of the nineteenth century. The number and variety of these pictures suggest a long-term popular interest in Indians and Indian life in the pictorial press, yet these pictures did not appear in the illustrated press randomly. Pictures of Indian life were produced when artists encountered peaceful Indians in the West or when Indians traveled to New York, Washington, and other eastern cities. Compared to pictures of Indian-white violence, such drawings were easy to create—and much less lethal. More importantly, artists made these pictures to fulfill a specific journalistic function; namely, to show white Americans what Indians looked like and how they lived their lives. Thus the focus for many Indian pictures was on significant and visible differences between whites and Indians—ceremonies, customs, social practices, and other "Indian" activities—all of which made clear that Indians were different from civilized Americans. These differences could be large or small, dramatic or subtle, but they were a journalistic requirement in peaceful Indian illustrations, the very element that made these pictures newsworthy and warranted their publication. In other words, most pictures of Indian life needed some compelling "Indian" quality to rise to the level of public interest; they needed to show something different, something appealing. These differences—real or perceived—were the whole point of such Indian images.

Beyond the focus on differences, another function of Indians in ceremonial and domestic illustrations was to "tame" the savages, to present Indians in ways that were understandable to white readers. If violent Indians represented a threat to social order and Euro-American civilization, Indians engaged in ordinary and nonviolent activities were made understandable and safer to the larger society. In contrast to pictures of Indians in action, which had excitement as a news value, some illustrations of Indian social and cultural life encompassed little or no dramatic action or impact. Instead, these images often focused on scenes of human or cultural interest, which appealed to readers because they seemed to explain Indians and Indian behavior. As suggested earlier, these sorts of Indian illustrations were a journalistic exercise in popular ethnography, an effort to tell visual stories about the ethnic other for a general audience of white readers.

Some of these illustrations were, in fact, documentary scenes, images that emphasized social and cultural differences in a detached, "objective" way. Yet the perceived neutrality of many of these images was undercut on occasion by the accompanying captions and stories, words that shifted the meaning of the illustration. This added meaning was a way of clarifying ambiguous images and producing specific interpretations or meanings that might not be apparent in the picture itself. Indeed, this sort of explanation was an important part of the meaning-making process in the pictorial press, a way editors could supply the social or cultural information necessary to explain (and often demean) the Indians in a particular picture.

The focus on differences also had larger political and cultural consequences. In the pictorial press, Indians were uncivilized, primitive people—the pictures offered powerful evidence of that. Indians were not merely different, however; they were often deficient. Thus Indian rituals and domestic life were depicted as inferior to the ways of white, civilized people, a characterization that routinely and automatically marginalized Indians and Indian culture to a broad swath of American readers. These ways of depicting Indian life, in turn, were part of the larger ideological and cultural process that made it difficult—impossible, actually—for Indians to be presented as ordinary citizens or legitimate political actors. This portrayal was not an accident, of course, but the product of popular and deeply held nineteenth-century ideas about Indians and their place in the political and social order.

CHAPTER 3

The Princess and the Squaw

*The Construction of Native American
Women in the Pictorial Press*

In June 1907, *Harper's Weekly* published a photograph of a newly
discovered portrait of "Princess Pocahontas."[1] The accompanying article explained
that the painting was one of only four known portraits of Pocahontas, a woman revealed as beautiful and dignified (figure 3.1). In fact, the article went to great lengths
to praise the young woman's character. She had been, *Harper's Weekly* proclaimed,
"a wild little heathen in the midst of a rude Indian tribe."[2] But her bravery—saving
Captain John Smith from execution by her kinsmen—had "won for herself enduring fame . . . to the sorely pressed colonists of Virginia." Moreover, Pocahontas had
been baptized. Transported to England, Pocahontas became "a bright example
for the Virginia Company to exhibit to the people of England of the first-fruits of
Christianity in the new colony, 'the little foreign princess, gentlest and sweetest of
savages, the first red Indian in whose heart had ever burned the love of Christianity.'"[3] The painting depicted an elegant young woman staring directly at the viewer,
her young son beside her. Pocahontas was beautiful and refined, her dark hair neatly
parted and combed, her neck graced with beads. Then there was her expression,
described in the article as "melancholy" and "said to have been habitual" with this
Indian princess. Both in words and in her portrait, Pocahontas was revealed in
Harper's Weekly as an ideal Indian woman, every bit as refined and womanly as an
English gentlewoman. She was "La Belle Sauvage," the article noted, "admired and
discussed in the highest circles of London." Captain Smith himself made this clear,
writing a letter to Queen Anne praising her "beauty, gentleness and courage."[4]

The facts about Pocahontas were rather different. She was not a princess in the
European sense, though she was the daughter of Powhatan (or Wahunsunacock),
a powerful Algonquian chief in tidewater Virginia, and she had married an English gentleman, John Rolfe.[5] She may—or may not—have saved the life of Captain
Smith, an incident that remains a subject of controversy among historians.[6] Even
the new Pocahontas portrait in *Harper's Weekly* was probably a different Indian
woman.[7] In spite of such discrepancies, the celebration of this portrait in *Harper's*

A NEWLY DISCOVERED PORTRAIT OF POCAHONTAS

By HELEN MARSHALL PRATT

This Portrait of the Indian Wife of John Rolfe, by an unknown Artist, is believed by competent Judges to have been Painted from Life

WHEN the Princess Pocahontas, having won for herself enduring fame by her signal services to the sorely pressed colonists of Virginia, set sail for England in the year 1616, her condition and appearance were so unlike those of the little Indian "maid of tenne" whom Captain Smith first saw with her chieftain father, that any new portrait of her that can be discovered cannot fail to be of interest.

Pocahontas, also known as Matoa, and Snowfeather (on account of her lightness of foot), and, after her baptism, Rebecca, had been a wild little heathen in the midst of a rude Indian tribe. But now she had been three years baptized and married, the honored wife of John (or Thomas, he is called by both names), who was "an honest and discreet English gentleman." The little son had been born to her; Captain Smith had sailed away to England, and she had been told that he was dead. Now, in the sunshine of a Virginia June, nearly four hundred years ago, she was setting out for the great world of England with Sir Thomas Dale, as a bright example for the Virginia Company to exhibit to the people of England of the first-fruits of Christianity in the new colony, "the little

foreign princess, gentlest and sweetest of savages, the first red Indian in whose heart had ever burned the love of Christianity."

On their arrival, Pocahontas was welcomed by Sir Thomas Stukeley, the Company's man, at the ship's side, and the gentleman bowed low to the princess. The Company provided for her and her son during their stay in London. Captain Smith wrote a letter to Queen Anne, the wife of James I., filled with praise of the beauty, gentleness, and courage of the Indian girl, commending her to the queen's friendly consideration, and asked that she be received as a princess whose husband's estate was "not able to make her fit to attend your Majesty."

The king and queen responded generously to this request, and graciously received her as one of royal blood, whose gentleness and native refinement could atone for her ignorance of courtly customs. Lord and Lady De la Warr acted as her social sponsors; "La Belle Sauvage" was admired and discussed in the highest circles of London, and at least one London tavern still retains the name by which she was popularly known. Gentlemen sent copies of her engraved portrait in their letters abroad, as the novelty of the hour. She attended those Masques which the queen so much affected, and in the queen's company. In his *Staple of News*, Ben Jonson introduces her, with other people of fashion, as "the blessed Pocahontas . . . the great king's daughter of Virginia." Dr. King, then Lord Bishop of London, made a great banquet in her honor, "in hopeful zeal by her to advance Christianity." And in all these appearances, "the lady did not only accustom herself to civility, but still carried herself as the daughter of a king, and was accordingly respected for her modest demeanor and interesting manner."

After ten months of apparently joyous living, a special ship was provided by the Company for her return to America, "sore against her will." Her health had suffered much from the change of climate, and she was very weak when taken to Gravesend to meet the ship. Here they were detained several weeks by adverse winds, and when at length she was taken on board the ship,

the princess's failing strength gave way and she died suddenly, March 29, 1617, and was buried in the church of St. George at Gravesend. A recently discovered letter of Mr. Rolfe addressed to Sir Edwin Sandys tells how deeply the wife's death was lamented by all, and that the son's life "greatly extinguisheth the sorrow of her loss, saying all must die, but 'tis enough that her child liveth." (*Virginia Hist. Mag.* 10: 136.)

Three portraits of Pocahontas are current. One a contemporary engraving by Simon de Pass, which appears in early editions of Smith's works, and has been copied and recopied until its original features are scarcely recognizable. The second portrait is owned by a descendant of the Rolfe family in Norfolk, and represents Pocahontas in court dress. It is undoubtedly contemporary, and that from which De Pass made his engraving. This painting was first reproduced by Wyndham Ribertson, Esq., in his interesting volume *Pocahontas and her Descendants*, in 1887. A third picture is known as the Sully portrait, and was made by the painter of that name from fragments of two or three early pictures, of the genuineness of which I have no information.

Recently, while living in England, my attention was directed to a fourth picture of Pocahontas, with her little son, owned by a descendant of the Rolfes at King's Lynn, Norfolk, which had never been copied, and its owner very courteously granted permission to have it photographed. This picture is reproduced with this article. The owner makes no claim whatever for the painting. It may be contemporary; it may be of later date. It was purchased by the family in London, about twenty years ago, and was said to have come from America. Certain features, however, point to an early origin. The peculiar shell earrings, set in silver, which the mother wears, are identical with those which are in the possession of the Rolfes of Heacham, handed down for three centuries as those of Pocahontas.

The face is distinctly that of a refined Indian girl; she was twenty-two at her death. The dress is a modification of her tribe costume. The melancholy expression which is said to have been habitual appears here. The child is a handsome boy of three or four. On the death of his mother, he was left in England to be educated, and later returned to Virginia, where he married and became a man of eminence, to whom many prominent families in Virginia, notably that of John Randolph, of Roanoke, trace their origin.

While Pocahontas resided in England, several prominent portrait-painters were in favor with the king and his court, of whom they painted numerous pictures. Among these were Nicholas Hilliard, Paul van Somer, Isaac Olivier, Mytens and Simon van der Pass, the Utrecht engraver, who also painted portraits. The last was only ten years in England, his visit there coinciding in date with that of Pocahontas. And undoubtedly at that time the current engraving of her was made, probably from the portrait named as second. Nicholas Hilliard had special license from James to paint portraits of the royal family. Paul van Somer was a Flemish artist of the court who excelled in accuracy of detail, and De Pass also was employed by him. Mytens, of The Hague, was a fine colorist: Isaac Olivier, a pupil of Hilliard, painted the family of James and the court.

FIGURE 3.1. Pocahontas—or a woman believed to be Pocahontas—was idealized in *Harper's Weekly* as an Indian princess, the embodiment of Native American beauty and feminine grace.

Weekly reveals a great deal about the idealization of Pocahontas in American popular culture. Indeed, Pocahontas was, and is, one of the most famous Native American women in history, an important and useful symbol for generations of Americans.[8] Since the beginning of the republic, historian Alan Trachtenberg has written, "the Indian princess Pocahontas has been widely adopted as an icon of the new nation."[9] Pocahontas's fame comes from her historical role as an intermediary between American Indians and Europeans. According to legend, she had selflessly thrown herself across Captain Smith's body, saving his life while defying her father and forsaking her own people. She had converted to Christianity, married John Rolfe, and taken a Christian name, Rebecca, a woman who, in Genesis, "was the literal mother of two nations."[10]

For all these reasons, Pocahontas was acclaimed as a powerful example of the triumph of civilization over savagery. Over time, Pocahontas became a convenient and flexible American symbol, setting the standard for the idealized Native American woman, a standard that—directly or indirectly—affected the way Native American women were viewed and understood. As documented in the following, Indian women were assessed not by their own values or customs, but by the romanticized idea of Princess Pocahontas—a woman of youthful beauty, motherly affection, ladylike gentleness, and dignity. Indian women who appeared to meet that standard could be praised in the pictorial press; those who did not could be denigrated or ridiculed.

Beginning with Pocahontas, this chapter describes and analyzes several popular ways that Native American women were constructed in news and feature illustrations across the lifespan of the two largest and most important illustrated newspapers, *Frank Leslie's Illustrated Newspaper* and *Harper's Weekly*.[11] The research examines how American Indian women—usually absent in other journalism studies[12]—were portrayed from the mid-1850s to the early 1900s, an era of western expansion, Indian warfare, and pacification, as well as rising expectations for (white) women. Following the ideas of Stuart Hall, the research locates signs of racial classification and difference in the representation of Indian women, including visual and verbal themes used to construct Indian women's public identities during this era.[13] On a cultural level, the study seeks to explain the representation of Indian women by linking them to popular Euro-American ideas about Indians generally and Indian women in particular, especially contrasting ideas about the Indian princess and the lowly squaw. The chapter also considers how these ideas and meanings might have resonated with the reading public during the final conquest and subjugation of Indian peoples in the American West. To address these issues, the chapter asks several questions. How were Indian women constructed in words and pictures? What verbal and visual differences separated Indian women from Indian men and from white women? What do these representations tell us about meaning of race and racial ideology in the pictorial press era? The research examines more than a dozen illustrations of American Indian women from *Frank Leslie's* and *Harper's*

Weekly, a sample large enough to include several significant themes and patterns.[14] By carefully examining these illustrations and associated captions and stories, the chapter explains how Indian women were represented—or *mis*represented—in the pictorial press and shows how these ideas and images operated as part of a long-standing national (and male) fantasy that constructed Indian women as symbolically useful outsiders, alternatively alluring or repulsive, but always contained by the dominant ideologies of Euro-American culture.

In the years following the Civil War, Indian-white violence was a rich source for illustrated journalism. Indian battles, ambushes, massacres, and the like often made exciting visual stories for *Leslie's* and *Harper's.* The Indians depicted in these pictures were almost exclusively men, routinely presented as threats to emigrants and frontier communities. Indian women, by comparison, were much less common in the pages of the illustrated press.[15] One reason for the absence of Indian women, of course, was their apparent lack of newsworthiness. Unless they were violent, especially colorful, or destitute, Indian women were easy to ignore. When Indian women were portrayed in the pictorial press, they were usually confined to specific roles at either end of a "respectability" spectrum, either as idealized Indian princesses or as downtrodden "squaws,"[16] themes that are examined in the following pages. On occasion, however, illustrators and editors represented Indian women in more neutral ways, departing from extreme stereotypes and allowing Indian women a more nuanced public presence. In addition, I argue that the pictorial press representations of Indian women were significant among the middle-class and elite readers of the illustrated press, most of whom were unlikely to encounter actual Indian women in their daily lives. For these readers, illustrations of Indian women were an important source of information about the appearance, character, and morality of these people.[17]

Indian Women as Territorial Symbols

Strange and exotic images of American Indians can be traced back hundreds of years in European history.[18] Given such fantasies and their long hold on the European imagination, the leap to exotic and sexualized American Indian women was not especially great. In the sixteenth century, various sorts of naked Indian women were used as symbols for the Americas.[19] An illustration published about 1575, *Vespucci Discovering America,* showed a regal Vespucci, clothed and standing, while America was symbolized by a prone, naked Indian woman.[20] During the colonial era, Philip Deloria discovered, Indian men and women were common symbols for the colonies in British political cartoons, eventually becoming a symbol of "enormous iconographic flexibility." The image of the Indian princess, Deloria adds, "allowed one to evoke female sexuality in picturing the fertile landscape or to show the colonies as available and vulnerable to the desires of English men."[21]

As noted previously, an idealized Pocahontas became part of the iconography of early America, a widely accepted representation of the transformation of America and its people from wilderness and savagery to settlement and civility. In time, Pocahontas also became a mark of "authentic" Americanness, a way for colonials and their descendants to prove their deep and mythical connection to the new continent. This was made clear in *Leslie's* in 1856 when the paper published an illustration of the "beautiful and intrepid Indian maiden" risking her body to save Captain Smith.[22] The story explained that "this remarkable incident" was proof of the power of love—she saved one Englishman and married another. Beyond that, her mixed-blood descendants were invoked to support the aristocratic credentials of the FFVs—first families of Virginia—who proclaimed "that the best blood of Pocahontas flowed in their veins."[23] Ten years later, *Leslie's* reprised this aristocratic theme, this time using a story and illustration about the grave of Pocahontas's father, the once-mighty Powhatan.[24] By 1866, the long-dead Powhatan could be safely recalled and celebrated as a "great chief . . . about whom so much of romance and history clings." Concerning Pocahontas, *Leslie's* again emphasized this idealized woman as the essential link to Virginia's aboriginal—and mythical—past. It is through her blood, *Leslie's* stated, that "the F.FV.'s boast that they inherit their aristocracy and fire."[25]

Another symbolic Indian woman turned up in *Harper's Weekly* in 1909 when the newspaper published a reproduction of a painting by Will G. Low.[26] *Prosperity under the Law* was one of four murals commissioned for the Lucerne County Courthouse in Wilkes-Barre, Pennsylvania. The theme of the painting, *Harper's* explained, was laudatory—it celebrated the Wyoming Valley's rich agricultural and mining heritage. The young Indian girl was the Wyoming Valley itself, home of "benign" justice and civilization. Notably, the Indian girl was an idealized, generic figure, clothed in a flowing, off-the-shoulder gown more European than Native American. In *Harper's,* her skin color was light, even lighter than the miner or the shirtless, highly muscled farmworker who appeared on each side of the painting. In all these ways, this imaginary Indian woman was transformed into an idealized figure and separated from the actual history of the Wyoming Valley, where living Indian women and their families had been displaced by white settlement. As with the Native American woman in the Vespucci illustration, this Indian girl—an Anglicized figure with no name and no tribe—represented nature and nature's bounty, pure and ripe for the taking.

Idealized Wives and Mothers

Like Pocahontas, many Indian women were portrayed in the pictorial press in their familial and domestic roles, roles also assigned to white women.[27] Such imagery is not surprising, given that these publications usually reproduced the ideologies of their (white) middle-class and elite readers, ideologies that were often traditional and conservative.[28] Often, this role revealed Indian women in a genteel, maternal position. In its first year of publication, for example, *Harper's Weekly* published a report on "Frontier Life in Washington Territory," drawn from a new book published (not coincidentally) by Harper and Brothers.[29] The report was illustrated by four drawings, one of which showed the interior of an Indian "hut" where several women sat around a fire. Although the image was too small to reveal specific details, several women were shown inside a dwelling with children (and a dog) in the scene. Notably, they were also depicted as passive, in contrast to the image of men on the same page, a fishing illustration notable for its activity. The story supports this interpretation, noting that these Northwestern Indians "live chiefly by chase and fishery"—male activities. In addition, the article emphasized the relative ease of their domestic work: "Their women," the correspondent concluded, "have an easier lot than generally falls to the Indian squaw."

An Indian mother also turned up in a group portrait published in *Leslie's* in 1857. The occasion was a visit to England by a group of Canadian Indians who were on exhibit at the Panopticon in London's Leicester Square (figure 3.2). The portrait showed the chief and warriors standing and kneeling above and behind four "squaws," one of whom held a baby, described as "an object of great curiosity and admiration to the [British] ladies."[30] The Indian women appeared dour and uncomfortable, their eyes averted. The article explained that the Indian mother's love was of particular interest: "It is singular to watch the mother while the baby is handed round to gratify the spectators. Her eyes never leave it for a moment." Much like a white mother, this Indian mother loved and protected her child, a point emphasized in *Leslie's*.

A more overtly idealized representation of Indian motherhood appeared in *Harper's* in 1872. A large illustration called "An Indian Mother" portrayed a tranquil family scene: father, mother, and sleeping child (figure 3.3). A short article explained the scene and emphasized the attractiveness of the Indian woman, a "princess" like Pocahontas. She was a Canadian, the article noted, of exceptional beauty:

> Years ago, when a mere child, her great beauty attracted the attention of the Prince of Wales at Niagara—she herself is a princess among her own people— and he admired her so much that he had her portrait painted for his private gallery.[31]

The image itself, sketched by "an artist tourist" identified as R. Emmet, showed the "princess" as notably lighter-skinned—and thus more civilized—than her husband (though not as white as her child). In contrast to her husband, the woman was further civilized by her neatly parted hair and "white" clothing. Her loving countenance and the tilt of her head suggested gentility, not savagery, an impression the text reinforced. The scene reveals, *Harper's* writes, "that the Indian character,

OJIBEWAY AND POTAWATAMIE INDIANS.

FIGURE 3.2. Indian women were front and center in this *Leslie's* portrait
of Canadian Indians in London in 1857. The baby, *Leslie's* noted, was
"an object of great curiosity and admiration to the [British] ladies."

when not debased by the worser [*sic*] influences of white civilization, is capable of
the same domestic traits that are found in our own households."

This illustration is, of course, a positive depiction of an unidentified Native
American woman. Both the image and the text include ideals of feminine beauty (like
Pocahontas) and domestic tranquility. But these positive attributes were offset by
the deeply ethnocentric and paternalistic nature of the representation. The Indian
mother was beautiful, but this was a "white" version of beauty. This was no ordi-

AN INDIAN MOTHER—[DRAWN BY SOL EYTINGE, JUN., FROM A SKETCH BY R. EMMET.]

FIGURE 3.3. The idealized Indian mother represented Indian women in safe and familiar terms. *Harper's* described this young mother as "a princess among her own people."

nary "squaw," after all. Indeed, she was an Indian "princess" capable of attracting European royalty. She was also an idealized Indian mother (again, like Pocahontas), more civilized than her husband and apparently unsullied by the corruption that accompanied the spread of civilization. *Harper's* concluded its explanation by assessing civilization's effects on Indian-white relations. The record shows, *Harper's* said, "that the race has been more sinned against than sinning." In this case at least, Indian motherhood was evidence for the idea that Indian women were like white women—people who deserved a better fate than the one they had been dealt in the conquest of the continent.

As these examples demonstrate, the Indian wife and mother was a common trope in the pictorial press. Like the portrait of Princess Pocahontas, images of Indian mothers revealed these women in culturally safe roles that readers could understand. This role could be easily romanticized as well, providing a positive way to represent Indian women and offering a counterweight to the much more barbaric images of Indian men. Like Pocahontas and white mothers, young Indian women could be praised for their gentleness and humanity, as when *Leslie's* emphasized the maternal concerns of the Indian woman in London.[32] Moreover, representing Indian women as loving wives and mothers was a way of reinforcing traditional family roles for American women in the face of rising challenges by suffragettes and other nineteenth-century women's rights advocates.

Working Wives and Old Squaws

When they were not idealized, Indian wives and mothers were frequently identified by the hardships and misery of their lives.[33] The pictorial press often labeled these women as "squaws." In contrast to Indian princesses or idealized Indian mothers, squaws suffered. They worked or begged. In 1875, for example, *Leslie's* published an illustration of Indian women at Fort Berthold on the Missouri River. The drawing showed a group of Mandan and other Indian women at work, carrying their rawhide boats to the river for a "berrying expedition."[34] Sixteen years later, *Leslie's* published a page of "character sketches" from Wounded Knee. Artist E. W. Kemble included two "squaws," one carrying a bundle of rations on her back, the other preparing jerked beef.[35] This contrasted with several portraits of men on the same page, including three "Fighting Men with War-Bonnets," none of whom was working. "Squaws," in other words, were not presented as genteel or refined, but as workers, often rough, rude, and grubby. Their labor rendered them dirty and inferior. Squaws, the illustrated papers made clear, lived a hard life, made harder by the roles they were assigned in tribal life—a society where the men were particularly lazy and arrogant.[36]

Much of this ideology can be seen in a half-page *Harper's* drawing published in March 1875 called "Indian Sledge Journey."[37] The scene, more apocryphal than real, showed an Indian family traveling in snow (figure 3.4). The woman was pulling the sled, loaded with a child, a puppy, and the family's belongings. Her husband, armed with a rifle, walked behind, a smaller presence in the engraving. The scene was dominated by the woman, who was clearly the focus of the illustration, as the explanation—with a hint of sarcasm—made plain: "Among the noble red men, in the division of labor[,] all the hard work falls upon the squaws; there is no question as to their mission in life."[38] That mission was to serve her husband and family through labor and sacrifice. The stoic sledge-puller was thus assigned a common role for "squaws" in the illustrated press—working on behalf of her family.

In 1873, *Harper's* published a larger criticism of Indian women, focusing most powerfully on their apparent place in Native American society. The occasion for this indictment was a large, heartrending, and seemingly harmless illustration of

INDIAN SLEDGE JOURNEY.—Drawn by William M. Cary.—[See Page 212.]

FIGURE 3.4. Indian women at work allowed the illustrated papers to condemn the apparent division of labor among the Indians. "All the hard work falls upon the squaws," *Harper's* explained.

an Indian woman with a baby on her back. "Squaw and Papoose" showed the unidentified woman at an angle from behind, so that her face was hidden while her baby's face was toward the viewer.[39] The woman stood before a log cabin, her hand outstretched toward the open door (figure 3.5). She was begging, presumably because she and her baby were hungry. The image took on greater emotional weight because the person in the cabin doorway was a child. The contrast could not be more direct: an Indian mother, unable to care for herself or her child, was forced to beg for food from a white girl.

This allegorical illustration, which lists no source, was explained in language that made no reference to the specific scene depicted. Instead, *Harper's* used the illustration to explain—and condemn—the hard lot of Indian women. The explanation began by noting, with evident irony, that the engraving "illustrates the way in which the noble Indian understands the duties and cares of maternity."[40] While the men hunt and fight tribal enemies, women were left to carry out "all the labors of life." This article listed all that these labors entailed:

SQUAW AND PAPOOSE.—[See Page 518.]

FIGURE 3.5. While some Indian women were idealized as princesses, others were "squaws," reduced to begging to support their families.

The Indian woman not only labors upon her buffalo robes, her moccasins, her straw baskets, and bead ornaments—that is, not only supports the family, as is the province of men to do—but she performs all, or nearly all, the domestic labor about the camp. She is the hewer of wood and the drawer of water; she dresses, sews, turns, and adorns the skins which are to serve as the apparel of her family; she makes the tents, puts them up, drives in the stakes, and fastens the ropes, and then . . . takes the tents down again and bears them away upon her back.

And what of Indian men? They "swagger along unburdened and indifferent, or dart about on their steeds. They no more think of helping their squaws than of flying."

In words and in this engraving, Indian women were portrayed as hardworking but abused individuals. They might have some redeeming qualities, but they were bound to the gender roles of Indian society and unable to exercise their own will. This assessment was wrong and far too broad to encompass all Indian cultures,[41] but it probably made perfect sense to the editors of *Harper's*. From the perspective of nineteenth-century whites, the social and cultural roles of Indian women with tribal society were little known and regularly misunderstood. Indeed, this article equated very different tribes from Maine to Mexico in one overarching statement. Moreover, as noted earlier, the article offered no other information about the origin or circumstances of the illustration. What *Harper's* readers were left with was a stark comparison between Indian and white cultures. Indian men used squaws as laborers, while whites honored their women and men shared in the hard work. In *Harper's,* such comparisons lived up to the paper's self-proclaimed mission as "A Journal of Civilization."

The image of the Indian woman as crone turned up in *Harper's* again three years later (figure 3.6). This illustration showed an "old squaw" bent over at a frontier station "begging for food."[42] The blanket-clad woman faced the reader, supported by her cane, in front of two frontiersmen. The men, sitting on a boardwalk in front of a log building, appeared skeptical. The man closest to the woman was leaning back in his chair. Though he made eye contact with the beggar, he appeared unwilling to give her food—or anything else. The second man leaned forward, but he too seemed unmoved by the woman's plight. The story explaining the illustration identified the woman as Sioux and assured its readers that the scene was accurate— "a portrait from life," as they put it.[43] Her condition, *Harper's* explained, was the tribe's fault: "Her people have probably gone off on some marauding expedition, leaving her to die or subsist by the charity of the white people."

This image of Indian women—as beggars—was not entirely inaccurate. In the conquest of the West, the Sioux and many other tribes were forced to give up their traditional ways. Bison herds were being decimated as continuing Western development, ill-advised government policies, and widespread corruption reduced the plains tribes to dependence and poverty. Nevertheless, this illustration reinforced the popular view that Indians were cruel and uncivilized people. The tribe was out "marauding," after all, leaving the old woman to fend for herself. As a visual symbol, this downtrodden Indian woman could be seen as a stand-in for the plight of all Indians—people on the wrong side of history and progress, people from primitive and static cultures with little hope for the future. Like this "old squaw," *Harper's* implied, many Indians needed white charity to ward off hunger and eventual extinction.

Perhaps the most effective illustration of downtrodden Indian women in the pictorial press was artist Henry Farny's "Toilers of the Plains," a full-page *Harper's* drawing published in 1884.[44] As its title suggests, this drawing showed unidenti-

AN OLD SQUAW BEGGING FOR FOOD—SCENE AT A FRONTIER STATION.—[SEE PAGE 234.]

FIGURE 3.6. Older Indian women were often described as "squaws." In this case, *Harper's* blamed the tribe, writing that "her people have probably gone off on some marauding expedition."

fied, blanketed Indian women gathering firewood on the prairie (figure 3.7). The principal figure was holding a knife and an ax, with a bundle of sticks across her back. Two other women, also carrying firewood bundles, followed her. The scene, which included no place or time, presented a bleakly romantic scene of rolling grasslands and distant mountains, decorated with a bison skull on the far right. The accompanying story offered only pity for the women and contempt for the men from an unnamed plains tribe. "The noble red man never debases himself . . . to the performance of any drudgery," the article began. "War and the chase absorb all his energies," the article continued, so that the fieldwork was "relegated to the squaw."[45] In Farny's picture, the editors wrote, "we are shown several of these poor creatures, who have been searching the almost treeless plains for fire-wood with which to cook food for their lazy masters." This interpretation emphasized the deficiencies of Indian life, positioning the women as "toilers" and "poor creatures" while indicting Indian men as falsely "noble" and far too proud to work. Such language once again reinforced the presumed subservient role of Indian women and their lowly status in the Indian social hierarchy. In words and images, this trope made

FIGURE 3.7. In 1884, artist Henry Farny dramatized the unhappy fate of Indian women, seemingly destined to work and suffer.

clear the differences between Indians and whites, an ethnocentric comparison that put Indians in a decidedly inferior light.

Indian Women as Objects of Ridicule

When not idealizing Indian princesses or emphasizing the sorry state of squaws, the illustrated papers sometimes offered a view of Indian women as merely silly or immature. One of the most prominent examples of this quality was a front-page illustration in *Leslie's* in April 1870 (figure 3.8). The image, "The Sick Indian Girl—An Incident of the Plains," was based on a photograph by A. J. Russell.[46] It showed the girl crouched in front of a small tepee, watched over by a medicine man standing serenely behind her. The image was unusual in that it depicted ordinary Indian life. Moreover, it was a static scene with no trace of hostility or violence. The illustration, then, was more of a cultural curiosity than a newsworthy event. Yet neither photographer Russell nor *Leslie's* was content to let the image speak for itself. Inside the issue, the editors ran a short explanation of Russell's encounter. The photographer told *Leslie's* that he "proposed to restore her to perfect health by taking her photograph!" The article continued:

FRANK LESLIE'S
ILLUSTRATED
NEWSPAPER

Entered according to the Act of Congress in the year 1870, by FRANK LESLIE, in the Clerk's Office of the District Court for the Southern District of New York.

No. 761—VOL. XXX.] NEW YORK APRIL 30, 1870. [PRICE 10 CENTS. $4 00 YEARLY. 13 WEEKS, $1 00.

THE SICK INDIAN GIRL—AN INCIDENT OF THE PLAINS.—FROM A PHOTOGRAPH BY A. J. RUSSELL.—SEE PAGE 99.

FIGURE 3.8. The sick Indian girl was presented sympathetically in this *Leslie's* illustration, though the accompanying story poked fun at her illness.

The dusky aborigine assented. Raising herself partly up, the picture was taken as we have reproduced it. When handed to the patient to look at, she became so delighted with her "counterfeit presentiment" that she forgot all about her indisposition. She was restored, almost instantly, to perfect health![47]

As word of her cure spread quickly among the tribe, the photographer said he might, had he desired, "have had the pleasure of photographing every 'sick Indian' living under the shadows of the Rocky Mountains." The story dramatically changed the meaning of the illustration. It turned what could be seen as an unbiased, documentary image into a commentary on Indian gullibility. The story made clear that the Indian girl and her tribe were superstitious and thus ridiculous since, as all of *Leslie's* readers would know, cameras do not cure illness.

Leslie's published a similar illustration of Indian women a few weeks later. Again, the picture itself appeared relatively innocuous. Over the caption "Indian Women and Children at Their Toilets," the front-page engraving showed a group of Indians standing and sitting, cleaning and dressing themselves and their children.[48] Like the sick Indian girl, this was a relatively dull scene (figure 3.9). The caption explained the illustration and revealed much about the editors' attitude toward Indians, especially their personal habits and character. The article began with a general commentary. Readers who had formed their opinions of Indians based on James Fenimore Cooper's novels, the article explained, "will be doomed to disappointment on seeing the gentle savage of the Plains and the Rocky Mountains."[49] The actual Indian, the article continued, "is not a charming creature in morals, manners or habits, and the combined efforts of soldiers and missionaries have not resulted in making an angel of him." The article listed several Indian deficiencies, including serious faults (stealing) and several petty issues (not eating meals at regular hours).

The article then turned to the washing in the cover illustration. The children got most of the water, *Leslie's* stated, because Indian women "wash themselves only at rare intervals." Worst of all, there was little decorum among them:

> No fastidiousness or simulated modesty is exhibited at these toilets, and each aboriginal matron strips her darlings without regard to visitors or weather. Soap is not in favor with the Indians, and combs have not attained a high degree of popularity.

In addition, Indians were often vain: Give a Plains Indian "a well-shaped hand-mirror," the newspaper reported, and you will have "a friend forever."

This *Leslie's* article revealed much about the news value of this front-page scene. While not especially newsworthy, the illustration documented little-known details about Indian people and their lives. But the article went beyond factual information, offering an unflattering evaluation of Indian grooming habits. Cleanliness seemed to matter a great deal in *Leslie's,* an emphasis that put Indians in an unflattering light. As in many other cases, *Leslie's* ethnocentric comparisons of whites and In-

ON THE PLAINS.—INDIAN WOMEN AND CHILDREN AT THEIR TOILETS.—FROM A PICTURE BY OUR SPECIAL PHOTOGRAPHER.—SEE PAGE 21.

FIGURE 3.9. Illustrators sometimes focused on Indian hygiene and grooming, giving editors a chance to criticize the habits of Indians in their natural state.

dians automatically impeached the ways of Indian women, casting them as cultural outsiders who could be ridiculed as insufficiently proper, clean, or civilized.

Indian Women as Craft Workers and Exotics

Over time and with the increased contact between Indians and illustrators, other ways of representing Indian women emerged in the pictorial press. One significant theme for representing Indian women in the last years of the nineteenth century was through their craftwork. This theme was especially useful in the American Southwest, where the quality of the crafts was high and the people—Pueblo, Navajo, Hopi, and others—were suitably colorful and ripe for journalistic exploitation. Yet the pictorial press showed an interest in Indian craftwork much earlier in the century. Veteran *Harper's Weekly* artist Theodore Davis, for instance, published an engraving of two Navajo women weaving a blanket in September 1866.[50] The scene showed the women working at their loom, their half-finished blanket stretched above them (figure 3.10). This was a refreshingly placid illustration, with no hint of prejudice or ill will. The image was accompanied by a brief report from Davis. He located the scene at the southwestern ranch of "Maxwell, an old frontiersman." Maxwell's ranch, Davis wrote, was protected by 600 Utes ("his chosen defenders"), with Navajo people as servants. The blanket itself was a special one, being prepared for presentation to the secretary of the interior. Davis explained the value of Navajo weaving:

> The Navajo blanket is an article more sought after than one would suppose. It sells readily, if a good one, for from a hundred to a hundred fifty dollars, according to pattern or quality. They are woven so closely that water can be carried in them; and as a protection against the chill winds of the plains they are equal to the best fur robes.[51]

Taken together, the drawing and the story showed an appreciation for Indian craftwork, a theme that became increasingly romanticized in the closing years of the nineteenth century.[52] This theme also demonstrated a way that Native American women could appear in the press in a new light, shedding some of their "savagery" and appearing colorful and more "authentic." This positive representation applied more to women than men, however; Indian men still presented a physical threat to white settlers.[53] Yet even as a positive representation, this illustration and story focused on Navajo skill but denied the women an individual identity. Davis identified high-quality Indian craftwork with tribal traditions, but separated—and devalued—the work of the individual Navajo women, none of whom were named. Such a view overlooked the labor involved in producing such goods, as if the blankets had, in effect, woven themselves.

In 1889, *Harper's* published a heavily illustrated, four-page article on Southwestern Indians called "The Heart of New Mexico." This article included two illustrations of blanket-clad Pueblo women carrying pots called *tinajas,* or water pots, on their heads, as well as five drawings of individual pots.[54] Pueblo pottery, usually produced by women, soon became symbols of "authentic" Indian craftwork, prized by collectors and tourists.[55] In fact, one of these scenes—a smiling and finely dressed Pueblo woman—quickly became an important visual symbol—and eventually a cliché—of Southwestern Indian life.[56] This image, in fact, is an example of the "touristic gaze," a socially approved way of celebrating Indian culture, presenting Indian women as interesting, colorful, and culturally "other." This picture also had the effect of view of removing these women from the day-to-day struggles of Indian life—a topic alluded to in the article—and in this way reducing their lives to visual

INDIAN SQUAWS WEAVING A BLANKET.—[Sketched by Theodore R. Davis.]

FIGURE 3.10. Illustrator Theodore Davis documented the weaving skills of Indian women in this scene from New Mexico in 1866.

"postcards"—images that appeared authentic, but that were superficial and highly circumscribed.

In these illustrations, Pueblo women were identified with the craftwork. The article explained that Pueblo "squaws" were busy women. Since most Indian men were "averse" to labor, the article claimed, Pueblo women "attend to all the house-work, make most of the pottery and basket-ware, grind the corn or grain for bread and *tortillas,* and find time, besides, to do such fancy-work as their lords and masters may require for their various trappings."[57] Like Navajo blankets, Pueblo pottery was considered a part of the Indian-white economy. "Pitchers, cups of numerous shapes and quaint outlines, images of animals . . . and an almost endless variety of nondescript articles, are produced for the delectation of innocent travelers and for commercial transaction known in the Indian lingo as 'heap swap,'" *Harper's* noted.[58] In this article, the emphasis on craftwork and the tourist trade highlighted the pottery, not the women. Four individual pots were illustrated on one page, for example, with this caption: "Pueblo Tinajas, ornamented in red and black." The women who made these pots or displayed them on their heads remained unnamed and, except for their labor, unexamined. Their lives, their artistic traditions, and the conditions of their pottery production were not illustrated or explained.

The traditional dances of Southwestern Indians provided another way to depict Indian women, a focus on ritual that was a marker of exotic difference.[59] In 1890, *Harper's* published a full-page illustration of the "Tablet Dance" of the Santa Domingo Pueblo in New Mexico.[60] The drawing, based on a photograph, documented a scene from the dance, which was explained in the accompanying article. The illustration showed both male and female dancers lined up across the page. A line of Indian and white onlookers watched from the background. The story discussed the community's preparations for the dance as well as the actions of the dancers and the clothing of the male and female dancers. In all its elements, this representation positioned the Indian women as interesting tribal people. Notably, this representation was free of overt gender bias or racial stereotyping, though it did emphasize the "otherness" of the Santo Domingo dancers. "The women are dressed in a dark blue single garment, consisting of a double blanket reaching to the knee," the article explained. As for the women themselves, they were highly decorated: "Their cheeks are painted vermillion, and they carry a bunch of green cedar in the left hand. Upon their heads is the wooden head-dress or *tabla* of thin board, fifteen inches high."[61] This representation avoided the stereotypes of most earlier representations, portraying the women as colorful exotics, people worthy of interest because of their beautiful but strange native ceremonies.

A similar illustration in 1893 reinforced the exotic nature of the Southwestern Indians. This illustration, by painter Joseph Henry Sharp, depicted the Harvest Dance of the Pueblo Indians.[62] Again, this drawing showed men and women dancers and explained their ceremony in ethnographic terms. As might be expected, Sharp emphasized the spectacle of the dance, including its most colorful aspects. He wrote:

> Rows of gaily dressed Apaches, Navajos, and Pueblos on horseback encircle in quiet dignity the enthusiastic actors, while a little farther off the whole scene is framed in by the gleaming walls of the white and yellow houses, whose roofs are crowded with men, women, and children clad in their richest holiday garments, in strong relief, and the distant mountains and deep blue sky.[63]

This depiction again placed Indian women in a ritualized setting, emphasizing the "otherness" of Indian ceremonial life. This emphasis on the exotic ignored the more ordinary aspects of daily life in the pueblo, although it did depict these people as human beings in a culture worthy of serious attention. Such illustrations offered a highly romanticized image of these Southwestern Indians, an identity that abandoned the old "squaw" stereotypes by creating and reinforcing a newer, more colorful Indian stereotype.

Idealized Indian Beauty

As noted earlier, the Princess Pocahontas trope began in the early colonial period. This theme endured across the decades and remained a popular way to represent Indian women, even in the late nineteenth and early twentieth centuries. As a result, Indian women who transformed themselves and became "civilized" could be represented as would-be princesses. This was clearly the case in *Leslie's* in 1880 when the newspaper published an illustration of a living Indian "princess." The engraving showed a demure woman known as Bright Eyes—even her name was appealing. Bright Eyes was an Omaha woman who became newsworthy as a supporter of the Ponca tribe in its long-running dispute with the federal government. Her image, taken from a photograph, was notable in several respects. First, Bright Eyes was shown in her modern clothing, not her traditional Omaha attire. Her dress appeared modest, with a high ruffled collar and ruffled cuffs at her wrists. Bright Eyes held a purse at her side. The portrait showed a civilized and proper young woman, a person very different from a poor "squaw."[64]

The favorable presentation of Bright Eyes was appropriate given her public role. The caption itself highlighted that role, calling her "The Ponca Indian Maiden Advocate."[65] As an advocate (and as a maiden), Bright Eyes presented herself as more civilized and less savage than other Indian women, an identity that comes through in the illustration. In fact, Bright Eyes *was* more civilized than many Indian women. Her father was a prominent mixed-blood Omaha and French trader and her given name was Susette La Flesche. She attended school in the East and spoke proper English.[66] For all these reasons, *Leslie's* found it easy to portray Bright Eyes favorably. Moreover, she was on a mission of mercy, seeking help for her tribal friends, the beleaguered Poncas.

The accompanying story supports this interpretation. In it, Bright Eyes was described as eloquent and attractive. Indeed, the unidentified (male) writer was smitten: "She was attired in a blood-red wrapper, which draped itself in willowy curves over her lissome form."[67] He continued, "Her face is a delicate oval, her complexion olive, her hair the color of a raven's wing." Taken together, the story and the illustration presented Bright Eyes with none of the negative stereotyping associated with Indian "squaws." But this depiction was an exception to the rule. Few Indian women of this era were as newsworthy as Bright Eyes was and fewer still possessed her apparent poise, charm, and beauty. Like Pocahontas, Bright Eyes was exempt from the harshest rules that governed the imagery of Indian women. As with Pocahontas, Bright Eyes could be idealized as one of those rare Indian women who transcended negative racial boundaries and became a figure of popular adulation.

Idealized Indian princesses were useful cultural symbols in the pictorial press. These women could be honored for overcoming the limitations of their race and represented in the pictorial press as beautiful, loving, exotic, and innocently sexual, imagery that separated them from the drudge role assigned to other Indian women. It seems clear, too, that the idea of the idealized Indian woman operated as part of a long-standing male fantasy focused on the exotic outsider, the "cultural other."[68] Reporters, illustrators, and editors—almost all men—perpetuated this image in the illustrated press because it resonated with larger cultural themes about women generally and about selected American Indian women in particular. Like Pocahontas, young, beautiful, and "civilized" Indian women could become symbols of idealized "feminine" qualities such as fertility, natural abundance, and the virtues of civilization.

Conclusion

This chapter identifies and analyzes several important ways that Native American women were represented in the illustrated press. Although the categories described here are not exhaustive, the research found that many Indian women in the pictorial press were placed in one of two culturally constructed categories: princesses or squaws. Either way, Indian women were marked as different from whites, a safe and controlled "cultural other." Young, beautiful Indian women and mothers could be cast as "princesses," while old, poor, and "uncivilized" Indian women were depicted as "squaws." As we have seen, both *Leslie's* and *Harper's* employed these categories routinely, though there were differences between these papers. *Harper's* emphasized the poverty and hardship of Indian women, often suffering at the hands of Indian men, while *Leslie's* sometimes ridiculed Indian women for their silliness or grooming habits. In keeping with its "civilizing" theme and its more elite readership, *Harper's* depicted Indian women as craft workers and exotics, a category not prominent in *Leslie's*. This gave the *Harper's* a way to represent Indian women in more touristic and anthropological terms, avoiding old stereotypes by creating newer, more "advanced" ones. Neither weekly produced significant illustrations of ordinary or "normal" Indian women, a depiction that would render them unremarkable and thus "invisible" in the pictorial press.

Indian women during this era were subject to a powerful representational process that set them apart from white women while also supporting traditional Euro-American gender roles. Indian women in the pictorial press were different but they were also safe for public consumption—constructed by white, male illustrators for white readers who had preconceived ideas about their inferiority. In addition, artists and editors had an economic incentive to create interesting and engaging

Indian women, representations that would command attention on the printed page. Little wonder, then, that illustrations of Indian women were narrowly conceived and categorized, limited to a few familiar stereotypes. Little wonder that young and beautiful Indian women could be represented as "civilized" Indian princesses. Little wonder that "squaws" were shown as drudges and beggars. These were biased representations of Indian women, of course, but they demonstrate how the pictorial press constructed ideologically useful Indian women during this period. In fact, unbiased or "objective" representations of Indian women were nearly impossible in nineteenth-century journalism, which had no modern sense of journalistic fair play and no meaningful concept of cultural pluralism.

The business of representing Indian women in the illustrated press also involved implied comparisons to white women. These comparisons were necessarily ethnocentric, based on the presumed superiority of Euro-American culture and rooted in the nineteenth-century social Darwinism of Herbert Spencer and John Fiske.[69] This evolutionary philosophy, distinct from Darwin's biological ideas, placed Indians on a low evolutionary rung, well below the elevated position occupied by Europeans and Euro-Americans. This view purported to explain why Indians were "savages" and why, from the "civilized" point of view, Indians lacked the social and material progress of Euro-Americans. Such ideas, deeply embedded in American culture, turned up repeatedly in representations of Indian women in the illustrated press. Artists, illustrators, and journalists relied on long-standing concepts of race and difference to form their images of Indians in the press. Nevertheless, as we have seen, Indian women were treated more sympathetically than Indian men. Popular ideology shaped the representation of some Indian women as princesses and mothers, some as exotics, and some as unlovely creatures ruled by their men, forced to work or fend for themselves while the men hunted, fought, or simply loafed. In *Leslie's* and *Harper's,* Indian men were regularly portrayed as the worst of the race—lazy, warlike, and unreliable. By that low standard, Indian women received relatively benign coverage in the illustrated papers.

CHAPTER 4

Making Images on the Indian Frontier

The Adventures of Special Artist Theodore Davis

On the bright Manhattan morning of April 2, 1867, illustrator Theo-dore Davis happened to meet his *Harper's Weekly* boss, Fletcher Harper, taking his "constitutional walk down Broadway." According to Davis, Harper—whom Davis called "the Commander-in-Chief"—was surprised to see his illustrator. "Why are you not with General Hancock's Indian Expedition?" Harper asked. Davis did not need to be asked twice. By his own report, he took less than thirty minutes to pack a sketchbook, his "pet" Ballard rifle, and "a few minor necessaries" before boarding a train. "The third morning after," Davis wrote, "I was at Junction City, Kansas, nearly two thousand miles from New York."[1]

This incident captures two important aspects of Indian war reporting in the post–Civil War era. First, it indicates a level of popular interest in the Indian frontier, an interest Fletcher Harper was eager to editorially exploit—and to bankroll. Second, the story illustrates the significance of the on-the-scene pictorial journalist. In the age before photojournalism, an experienced Civil War illustrator like Davis was a valuable staffer, a visual journalist who could make the taming of the American West vivid for thousands of *Harper's* readers. Thanks to Fletcher Harper's deep pockets and Theodore Davis's intrepid spirit, armchair adventurers all across the East and Midwest could see—and almost hear—the pounding of Cheyenne and Arapaho ponies on the western plains.

As one of the first illustrators to go west after the Civil War, Davis was a significant source of imagery from the Indian frontier. Davis first traveled west in late 1865, taking a Butterfield stage ride across the Kansas plains to Denver and recording several Indian attacks, fights he described and illustrated for *Harper's Weekly* and *Harper's New Monthly Magazine*. Davis also covered the Kansas campaign of Gen-eral Winfield Scott Hancock, where he accompanied the colorful George Armstrong Custer and produced several influential illustrations of Indian fighting.

THEODORE R. DAVIS.

FIGURE 4.1. After years covering the Civil War for *Harper's Weekly,* artist Theodore Davis traveled west in 1867 to cover the Indian wars, rifle in hand, two pistols in his belt.

Davis was well suited to battlefield reporting. Besides years of experience illustrating the Civil War, Davis had both the nerve and the will to succeed in the rough-and-tumble business of Indian campaigning. A drawing made at Fort Harker in Kansas in 1867 (figure 4.1) shows Davis with fringed buckskin clothes, a broad hat, and two pistols stuck in his belt. He is holding a rifle and has what appears to be a knife strapped to his lower leg. Historian Robert Taft has argued that Davis's personality and energy served him well on the frontier. "Possessed of a buoyant and sunny disposition," Taft wrote, "he made friends wherever he went. No journey was too fatiguing to allay his interest in new sights and new experiences, and any danger lent added zest to all his numerous enterprises."[2]

This chapter describes and analyzes the frontier illustrations and writings of Theodore R. Davis in the early postbellum period. The chapter argues, first, that Davis was an influential source of popular imagery about the Indian frontier. More specifically, the chapter identifies two Davis illustrations in particular—an 1866 drawing of an Indian attack on a stage and an 1867 depiction of the arrow-strewn remains of several cavalrymen—as important images that helped shape popular ideas about Indians and Indian fighting in the last half of the nineteenth century. I also argue that Davis's depictions of Custer's victory over Black Kettle at the Washita River—drawings Davis made in New York—advanced significantly Custer's reputation as an Indian fighter, a reputation that became famously controversial at the Little Bighorn River in 1876. In all these ways, the chapter makes the case that the Indian war journalism of "special artist" Theodore Davis offers important insights into the popular understanding of Indians and Indian warfare in postbellum America.

Theodore Davis and the Rise of the Illustrated Press

Theodore Russell Davis was born in Boston in 1840. Little is known of his early years, but he was in Brooklyn in the mid-1850s, where he studied with Henry

W. Herrick, a wood engraver and designer.[3] Davis probably received informal instruction from James Walker, a Mexican War veteran who created a well-known painting of American troops storming Chapultepec.[4] The extent of Davis's training is unclear, but he is known to have exhibited a crayon drawing at the American Institute in 1856.

Whatever his artistic beginnings, Davis was skilled enough at age twenty-one to begin working as an illustrator, traveling south shortly before the outbreak of the Civil War with William H. Russell, a correspondent for the *London Times.* He was in New Orleans in 1861, but his drawings from the city were confiscated in Memphis by Confederate vigilantes.[5] At *Harper's Weekly,* Davis became one of the paper's most important artist-correspondents, providing drawings and stories from a variety of locations in the war.[6] In July and August 1862, for example, Davis provided stories and drawings of Union naval activities on the lower Mississippi River around Vicksburg. Later in the war, he accompanied General William T. Sherman on his destructive sweep through the South.[7] According to his *Harper's Weekly* obituary, Davis was wounded twice during the war, so severely at one point that he almost had a leg amputated. Davis, *Harper's* said, served on the staff of General Logan and was appointed military engineer at the siege of Vicksburg. The paper also reported that he turned down a colonel's commission in order to remain a special artist with *Harper's.*[8]

Davis went west for *Harper's* soon after the Civil War, motivated to some degree by the need for the excitement of war. Davis's daughter, Caroline Pennypacker, told historian Robert Taft as much in 1939:

> Returning to New York after the close of [Civil War] hostilities, he seemed restless and dissatisfied, as all correspondents and soldiers are after a sudden let-down. Noticing this, Harper's, his publishers, inquired what he would like to do. And to their considerable inquiry his prompt reply was: "Send me out to the western plains where Custer is seeing action." This request was immediately granted and Mr. Davis was given an assignment on the then dangerous plains of our far West.[9]

Davis's travels through Indian country generated significant frontier writing and imagery. His trip in 1865 and 1866 documented several Indian raids on the overland stage line; his 1867 trip produced important images of Indian fighting associated with Custer. Although Davis soon returned to New York, he continued to supply Western illustrations for *Harper's* for several more years.[10] Davis retired to Asbury Park, New Jersey, sometime in the 1880s, where he continued to do freelance work, even designing a dinner service for the White House of Rutherford B. Hayes. He died in 1894, apparently suffering from old wounds and the hardships of army life.[11]

Popularizing an Indian Motif

One of the most well-documented stagecoach attacks in the history of the American West occurred in late 1865 in western Kansas. A Butterfield stage carrying Davis, Butterfield vice president General W. R. Brewster, and several others was approaching the Smoky Hill Springs station when a band of Cheyenne and Arapaho warriors suddenly appeared. Davis sounded the alarm and began firing. The battle was on.

Davis wrote about this incident four times and illustrated it twice. His first report was datelined, "HEADQUARTERS IN A 'DOBE,' (*Indians on every side*,) SMOKY HILL SPRINGS, Nov. 25, '65," a report published in the *Rocky Mountain News*.[12] The article outlined his journey from Atchison to Denver. The trip started peacefully enough, but before long Davis and his companions began hearing reports of Indian troubles. Near the Ruthton station, the travelers met a stage party that had been attacked. This group included L. K. Perrin, a correspondent for the *New York Times*. Perrin told Davis about his group's fights with Indians, including fighting from a buffalo wallow, a scene Davis later illustrated for *Harper's Monthly*. Davis also heard and reported on several instances of Indian cruelty, including Perrin's graphic report of a stock tender at the Downer station that the Indians had roasted over a slow fire. "He cried so piteously that they cut his tongue out," Davis reported.[13]

As for the raid at Smoky Hill Springs, Davis offered only a brief account. His entire report consisted of the following paragraph:

> We had just reached this station when we were attacked by a large group of Indians, who did not fight, but run [*sic*] as soon as we opened on them from the coach windows. Gen. Brewster fired twice at a white man. The ambulance was captured, but the Doctor [Whipple] and his men escaped. We are corralled, and the Indians are trying to burn us out.[14]

The next paragraph, dated the following day, quickly resolved the standoff: "We are out of the Indian country, and safe. Ho! for Denver—where we hope to find our friends." Notably, Davis does not mention a single death or injury as a result of the Smoky Hill Springs raid.

Davis's second report also appeared in the *Rocky Mountain News*. It provided additional details of the attack and, significantly, this time the Indians appeared more menacing. Writing in the third person, Davis picked up the action:

> Mr. D., the moment that he gave the alarm, picked up his rifle and sent its contents at the most gaudily gotten up Indian, who not liking the dose ran off. On the other side of the coach, Gen. Brewster was peppering away at a white man, who seemed to be the leader of the party.[15]

The Indians retreated, Davis wrote, only to appear again in pursuit of the station's livestock. Davis reported on his own role in protecting the cowboys and their animals: "The Indian was within a few paces of the stock herder when Mr. Davis sent the interior arrangements of his Ballard rifle into Mr. Indian's back, causing a series of very curious gyrations on the part of the Indian who was tied to his horse, so [he] saved his scalp."[16]

Davis also provided new details about the attack on Dr. Whipple and his ambulance. At first, he noted, it seemed as though the doctor and his men could withstand the enemy fire. But more Indians appeared. Recalling the image of the roasted stock herder, Davis wrote, "Then we had visions of roast Surgeon, fragments of amputated Surgeon, 'a devil of bones' Surgeon *a la mode*."[17] No such roasting occurred, however, and, with the support of Davis and his group, the doctor and his men made it to the station safely, though they were forced to abandon the ambulance and its medical supplies.

The fighters regrouped at the station where they plotted their defense and evaluated the enemy's intentions. "The picking up of a few unconsidered trifles in the way of scalps, horses and mules was being done as a sort of side remark," Davis noted. He offered a grim assessment of the situation: "This we look upon as a neat bit of strategy to be met in one way, and that 'Chivingtonian.'"[18] This was a reference to John Chivington, the leader of the 1864 attack on Black Kettle's camp in western Colorado, a bloody, one-sided affair that soon became known as the Sand Creek massacre. Clearly, Davis and his companions had seen enough of Indian violence.

Davis's third report on the stage attack appeared in *Harper's Weekly* in early 1866.[19] This account described the stage route and other logistical details concerning the trip. The Indian raid was told through an excerpt from Perrin's *New York Times* story. The details were largely the same, though in this report, unlike the previous two, there was no mention of a white man among the Indians. Perrin also supplied some numbers; according to his count, fifteen Indians had made the original charge on the stage, and another fifteen or twenty Indian had menaced the ambulance.[20]

The fourth and most complete Davis account of the stage attack was published in *Harper's New Monthly Magazine* in July 1867. This long, leisurely story provided personal details about the travelers, including the fact that Davis served as the party's cook, while one of his companions became the primary "chip-gatherer," picking up dry buffalo chips as fuel for the fire. Davis also laced his narrative with a strong dose of anti-Indian rhetoric. Regarding the idea of meeting "friendly" Indians on the plains, Davis was skeptical. "An Indian, like a rattlesnake, may be trusted only when his fangs are removed," he wrote, "otherwise it is well to give him a wide berth, or be prepared to kill him on sight."[21]

Davis's magazine narrative repeated the story of his group's meeting with Perrin's party and quoted the *Times* report at length, including new details of the stock herder's torture:

One poor fellow they staked to the ground, cut out his tongue, substituting another portion of his body in its place. They built a fire on his body. The agonized screams of the man were almost unendurable; about him were the Indians dancing and yelling like demons.[22]

This horrible scene evidently impressed Davis, because he drew it for the magazine, even though he did not witness it himself. The *Monthly*'s caption on the image dripped with sarcasm: "LO, THE POOR INDIAN," it read.[23]

Davis's story of the Smoky Hill Springs raid was similar to earlier stories, but in this version the Indians did not simply run off. Indeed, they shot many arrows at the stage, though Davis reported no casualties. The number of Indians attacking the stage increased, however, from Perrin's count of fifteen to Davis's new estimate of "nearly a hundred mounted Indians."[24] Finally, the white man, earlier thought to be a leader of the attacking warriors, was not mentioned in this report.

Despite these factual differences, they were exciting tales, and Davis provided a number of equally exciting illustrations. The most important of these was Davis's April 1866 *Harper's Weekly* drawing—republished as part of the *Harper's Monthly* story—of the stage racing around a bluff toward Smoky Hill Springs pursued by Indians (figure 4.2). Davis showed the frantic driver, whip in hand, urging his mules ahead. A passenger next to the driver fired his pistol at the approaching Indians. Although Davis had experienced the attack, the drawing's point of view was not what he had seen; like his *Rocky Mountain News* article, it was a third-person rendering, drawn from the perspective of a bystander.

Nevertheless, it was an action-filled image, full of drama and the thrill of the chase. The image of Indians attacking white travelers in the West was so popular, in fact, that it was repeated in various guises over the years and became a visual cliché, one of the most obvious ways to represent the Indian threat in the West. Davis did not begin this trend. Art historian Ron Tyler believes that the first such image was an 1854 illustration by John Russell Bartlett called *Apache Indians Attacking the Train and Party of a Boundary Survey*.[25] A similar image of a wagon train under attack was created in 1856 by painter Carl Wimar, a German immigrant who traveled up the Missouri River in search of material. Tyler notes that Wimar never witnessed any such attack, but was inspired by a fictional account in the work of French novelist Gabriel Ferry. Wimar's painting, *Attack on an Emigrant Train,* was completed while Wimar was studying in Dusseldorf, and Tyler has pointed out that Wimar's wagons were more European than American and that his Indians were dressed in bright colors, not buckskin.[26] Nevertheless, an engraved version of Wimar's painting was published in *Ballou's Pictorial,* an early illustrated journal, in 1857, where it became popular and spawned many similar images.[27]

Davis contributed to this motif in important ways. He was, after all, the only one of these artists to experience an Indian attack firsthand, a point noted in his four written versions of the incident. Few other stage attacks, in fact, were as well publicized as the one between the Davis party and the Cheyenne and Arapaho at Smoky Hill Springs. Moreover, the evolution of the four stories over time demon-

ON THE PLAINS—INDIANS ATTACKING BUTTERFIELD'S OVERLAND DISPATCH COACH.—SKETCHED BY THEODORE R. DAVIS.—[SEE PAGE 269.]

FIGURE 4.2. The Indian stagecoach attack became a part of the mythic West, turning up in illustrated papers, dime novels, fine-art paintings, and Buffalo Bill's Wild West show.

strates that Davis recognized and exploited the dramatic nature of the attack. This exploitation explains the disappearance of the white man mentioned in the first two reports, a detail that would certainly complicate the meaning of the fight. It also explains the rising number of Indians who attacked the stage and the evolution of the attack from a single paragraph in the *Rocky Mountain News* in 1865 to a long, sometimes sensational narrative in *Harper's Monthly* in 1867. Over time, Davis's Indian adventure expanded to meet the needs of both his editors and his readers—a desperate chase, whizzing arrows, and Indian barbarity. Davis's drawings reinforced this image, showing brave travelers at the far reaches of civilization. The significance of Davis's work was greater because his illustrations were widely circulated, appearing *Harper's Weekly* and *Harper's Monthly,* publications that reached thousands of readers around the nation. All this was the stuff of Western mythology and, in time, Western artists as prominent as Frederic Remington and Charles M. Russell painted versions of the Indian stage attack. Buffalo Bill's Wild West show also regularly reenacted a similar incident, an Indian "attack on the Deadwood Stage Coach."[28] In the twentieth century, the incident became part of many Western movies and television shows.[29] Davis did not originate this image, but his work as a writer and illustrator in the 1860s certainly promoted this image in the popular press at a time when the nation's attention was turning west.

The transformation of the stagecoach attack from an obscure incident on the plains to a legendary part of Western lore can also be explained by the mythic simplicity of the event.[30] In its most basic terms, this image illustrated the clash between civilization and savagery. The stage was a symbol of American progress, and the Indians were useful enemies, symbols of the untamed (but not untamable) West. The attack also provided a useful opportunity to demonstrate the virtues of the civilized life, a chance for brave frontiersmen and soldiers to show their mettle. On this level, the Indian attack on the Smoky Hill Springs station could be seen as an attack on civilized America and the noble task of Manifest Destiny. Davis himself—armed with his Ballard, two pistols, pencils, and a sketchpad, was a near-perfect example of a civilizing agent in the west, an easterner-turned-frontiersman who was brave, good-hearted, and able to survive on the frontier.

Davis, Savagery, and the Rise of Custer

Thanks to Fletcher Harper, Davis traveled west a second time in 1867 to document the Indian campaign of General Winfield Scott Hancock. The expedition turned out to be a failure because Hancock had ambiguous orders to fight the Indians or not, depending on their temperament.[31] In any case, Hancock never engaged in any significant fighting. Despite this lack of action, Davis produced several important illustrations, images that added to the idea of Indian savagery and boosted the reputation of George Armstrong Custer as an Indian fighter.[32] As journalism historian Elmo Scott Watson has written, Davis provided "the best contemporary accounts we have of the beginning of Custer's career in the West."[33]

Davis's most significant drawing from the Hancock campaign was also his most sensational. The illustration (figure 4.3) showed the skeletons of several cavalrymen—the remains of Lieutenant L. S. Kidder and his men—lying on the prairie, all of them pierced with arrows. Several soldiers from the search party—including a figure thought to be Custer himself[34]—contemplate the horrors of death on the plains. It is a shocking image, all the more so because of the profusion of arrows in each body. *Harper's Weekly* ran the illustration on the bottom of its front page, a placement guaranteed to attract attention and inflame anti-Indian feelings.

The accompanying story reported the apparent circumstances of Kidder's demise. "It appears from our correspondent's report of this melancholy affair, that Lieut. Kidder, who had lately reported for duty with his Company, stationed at Fort Sedgwick, was ordered to take ten men as an escort, follow the trail of General Custer, and deliver to him some important dispatches from General Sherman," *Harper's* reported.[35] Unfortunately, Kidder never caught up to Custer and was overwhelmed by hostiles. "From appearances there is no doubt that the party was attacked by a

FIGURE 4.3. The grisly fate of Lieutenant L. S. Kidder and his men was bound to attract attention in *Harper's Weekly*, powerful evidence of Indian savagery.

party of three or four hundred Indians, who drove them into a ravine, where they were speedily killed. The remains were too horribly mutilated to enable the officers to recognize any of the party. They were buried on the spot where they fell."[36]

Unlike the torture of the stock herder Davis heard about and illustrated on his first trip west, Davis was a witness to the aftermath of Lieutenant Kidder's ill-fated mission. His illustration was straightforward and gripping; there was no need to exaggerate this tragedy. In fact, it is likely that Davis or the *Harper's* engravers softened this illustration considerably, depicting skeletal remains rather than more shocking images of mutilated bodies.[37] Yet the shocking nature of the image could not help but stir anti-Indian emotions among the readers of *Harper's Weekly*, a self-proclaimed "Journal of Civilization." Such illustrations were powerful evidence for the need to extend that civilization across the continent, to put an end to Indian atrocities even if it meant the extermination of some tribes. As we have seen, Davis knew the savagery of Indian fighting firsthand and he was not the least bit romantic about the cruel ways of the warriors. His image of cavalrymen's bones on the prairie added one more atrocity to the long list of murders, raids, scalpings, and the like that white Americans held against the Indians of the plains. As with the stage attack, the Indian atrocity story was a familiar trope in the last half of the nineteenth century. By illustrating the death of Lieutenant Kidder, Davis and *Harper's Weekly* made this atrocity more vivid and gave it attention it might not otherwise have received. Davis's drawing also reinforced the idea of Indian mutilation, a fact of frontier warfare that was easy to sensationalize. Indeed, the Kidder image is similar to an illustration published in *Harper's Weekly* only three weeks earlier, an image of the slashed and punctured body of Sergeant Frederick Wyllyams. He was killed by Indians near Fort Wallace, Kansas, where his body was photographed. The photograph was brutally graphic, but *Harper's* used it as the basis for a somewhat more tasteful drawing published July 27, 1867.[38] Like Lieutenant Kidder and his soldiers, Wyllyams's body was shot full of arrows. As suggested previously, such visual representations of mutilation and death at the hands of Indians fostered an important element of Indian warfare in the postbellum era; that is, images of Indian atrocities became another cliché, a favored way to represent the Indian wars. Through his illustration of Lieutenant Kidder—not to mention his repetition of the roasted stock herder story in 1866—Davis did his part to reinforce this image of warring Indians.

Davis also helped pump up the reputation of George Armstrong Custer, the officer he had followed during the Hancock campaign in 1867. Although neither Hancock nor Custer could claim a battlefield victory in that campaign, Davis's familiarity with Custer and his Indian fighting turned out to be useful the following year when Custer attacked Black Kettle's camp on the Washita River in what is now western Oklahoma. While working in New York in December 1868, Davis produced several seemingly realistic drawings of the so-called Battle of the Washita, Custer's first major Indian victory.

The attack on the Washita was part of General Sheridan's new Indian campaign, a plan designed to succeed where Hancock had failed. The idea was to surprise the southern plains tribes at their winter camps, where they would be vulnerable.[39] The plan worked and the attack on the Washita killed Black Kettle, a well-known Cheyenne peace chief and survivor of the Sand Creek massacre, as well as many other Cheyenne men, women, and children. Custer's men, the Seventh Cavalry, captured fifty-three women and children as well as 875 horses, ponies, and mules, animals they later slaughtered to keep the Indians from using them again. The army burned the village and all its provisions. The Seventh Cavalry lost twenty-one men; eleven more were wounded. The attack appeared to be a great victory, and was generally hailed as such by the press and public. But for the Cheyenne as well as Custer's critics, it was less a glorious battle than a cold-blooded massacre, and it has remained controversial among native people to this day.[40]

In *Harper's Weekly*, however, the Washita attack was a huge success, and Davis did his part to reinforce that notion. Although the stories emphasized the planning of Generals Sherman and Sheridan, Custer was singled out for his efforts. "General CUSTER on this occasion won fresh laurels," *Harper's* reported.[41] The paper also published Sheridan's official report on its front page, a report that praised Custer

THE SEVENTH U. S. CAVALRY CHARGING INTO BLACK KETTLE'S VILLAGE AT DAYLIGHT, November 27, 1868.—[See Page 811.]

FIGURE 4.4. George Custer's career as an Indian fighter was boosted by his surprise attack on Black Kettle's village in 1868. The illustration was imaginary, as neither Davis nor any other artist witnessed the fight.

and blamed Black Kettle and his band for committing "depredations on the Saline and Solomon rivers, in Kansas."[42] Deeper in the issue, Davis provided several drawings of the fight and its aftermath. Notably, the captions on each image identified the fight with Custer. One illustration, "General Custer's Command Marching to Attack the Cheyenne Village," showed the troops walking and riding across the snow-covered prairies of present-day Oklahoma.[43] Another image (figure 4.4) showed the attack itself, charging soldiers entering the village of tightly packed tepees.[44] With soldiers entering from the right and Indians defending from the left, it was a gripping image of Custer's victory. The third Davis illustration (figure 4.5) was published a week later. It showed the aftermath of the fight: "The Indian Campaign—Prisoners Captured by General Custer."[45] In this drawing, Davis showed a group of weary, windblown prisoners trudging through the snow with a horse and travois. Several soldiers with sabers drawn look on from the rear. The scene is bleak; the Indian situation so desperate that it might very well elicit sympathy for the captured Indians.

Despite the apparent realism of these images, *Harper's* never claimed its special artist was on the scene. Nevertheless, these images were important to Custer's reputation as an Indian fighter. They made his victory over Black Kettle highly visible and thus "real" to thousands of readers in New York, Washington, and around the nation. In addition, these stories and the illustrations added to Custer's reputation

THE INDIAN CAMPAIGN—PRISONERS CAPTURED BY GENERAL CUSTER.—SKETCHED BY THEODORE R. DAVIS.—[SEE PAGE 830.]

FIGURE 4.5. Theodore Davis dramatized the march of Cheyenne and Arapaho prisoners captured by Custer's Seventh Cavalry following the attack on Black Kettle's winter camp in Indian Territory.

as the bravest and best of the Indian fighters, a cavalry officer willing to march his men all night to achieve victory. Such publicity reinforced Custer's reputation as a flamboyant and heroic public figure, a status he took into his final battle on the hills above the Little Bighorn River.

Of course, the *Harper's* drawings were all fictional. Davis created them in New York, far from the Washita River. True, he had been to the plains and he knew Custer as well as the details of Indian fighting. Davis's experience in the field added credibility to the *Harper's* illustrations. But whatever their credibility, the images were probably effective in creating authenticity, the illusion of observed reality. The illustrations were effective visual journalism, based on fact and drawn from experience. Both in the pages of *Harper's* and in fact, Custer's men traveled long and hard through driving snow in order to surprise the Cheyenne village. The Seventh Cavalry did achieve an apparent victory and it did take prisoners, themes that were reinforced in Davis's drawings. Symbolically, then, it probably did not matter to the public that Davis was in New York during the Washita campaign. For readers of *Harper's Weekly*, the overall truth of the victory was what mattered. At a time of western expansion, the country needed army victories over Indians—the

Hancock campaign had failed to produce even one—and it needed heroes. With a little help from *Harper's Weekly* and Theodore Davis, Custer's victory over Black Kettle could fill the bill.

Conclusion

Theodore Davis's success in creating frontier imagery can be traced in part to his personality and experience. By all accounts, Davis was a friendly, engaging character. An 1865 report in the Central City (Colorado) *Miners' Register,* for example, referred to "his charming manners." As Davis was leaving town, the *Register* bid him fond farewell: "He goes, and with him a full share of public esteem. Farewell Davis."[46] Such "public esteem" surely helped Davis through the hardships of western travel. Davis also brought years of battlefield experience to the Indian frontier, a fact that helped him focus on the most interesting and vivid aspects of Indian warfare. Davis was also valuable as both a journalist and illustrator, providing *Harper's* with exciting stories and even more exciting illustrations. As a result, Theodore Davis made the most of his two trips west for *Harper's Weekly,* creating a small but powerful number of frontier illustrations that shaped popular opinion about Indians and the Indian wars for many decades.

This chapter makes the case that Theodore Davis was one of the most important and popular sources of imagery from the Indian frontier in the postbellum era. Because he went west so soon after the Civil War and because he created several illustrations that captured key elements of Indian fighting in the West, Davis deserves serious attention. After all, his writings and illustrations of the attack at Smoky Hill Springs made it the most famous stage attack in American history—despite the fact that no members of Davis's party were killed or injured. Yet this attack, and others like it, had both popular appeal and cultural resonance. As noted earlier, the stage attack came to represent something more than a few moments of terror on the plains of western Kansas; it became a vivid and useful symbol of the taming of the West. That helps explain its long life in nineteenth-century dime novels and Buffalo Bill's Wild West show as well as its appearance in twentieth-century movies and novels, from John Ford's *Stagecoach* to Thomas Berger's *Little Big Man.*

Similarly, Davis's illustrations of arrow-pierced skeletons on the plains became immediately infamous and provided powerful evidence that the Indians deserved to be punished. Like the stage attack, this and other graphic images of Indian violence worked on a deeper level. They were, of course, naturally and automatically sensational, which gave them great emotional weight with a wide swath of American readers. They also reinforced the divide between the "blameless" white victim and the bloodthirsty savage. Who, after all, could not feel compassion for the victim, his body pierced and broken? In addition, such images made plain the terrible barbarity of the Indian enemy, people so uncivilized and unfeeling that they tortured the living and mutilated the dead. Such images produced a combination of high emotion and moral clarity that was almost mythic in nature. The arrow-pierced bodies of white soldiers made the enemy horribly real while also justifying the destruction of the evil Indians, a destruction that was morally necessary for the building of the West and the continuation of American progress. The Davis illustration of Lieutenant Kidder's bones helped drive home this point.

Finally, as we have seen, Davis did his part to boost the reputation of George Armstrong Custer as the great Indian fighter. This is Davis's most dubious achievement, for unlike his earlier drawings, it was based not on fact but on his vivid imagination. Nevertheless, Davis knew the territory and he used his knowledge to create illustrations that could have been real—and were accepted as such. As with his earlier work, Davis's images served a larger cause, bringing Custer's victory over Black Kettle to a national audience of readers far from the Oklahoma plains. Davis's drawings of the attack on the Washita made it a *public* victory over the Cheyenne, a victory the public wanted and the army—and Custer himself, of course—was eager to claim.

Perhaps what gives Davis and his illustrations their significance is what we might call the "vividness principle." By traveling across the plains and making the experience of Indian fighting and death both personal and concrete, Davis communicated the frontier experience to thousands of readers in a powerful way. Real or imaginary, fair or unfair—and they were usually unfair—these Western and Indian images were powerful because they captured and fed the public imagination. They were immediate and emotional, vivid in ways that written journalism was not. In the aftermath of the Civil War, Davis's illustrations were part of a popular and highly effective visual process that created and sustained a host of culturally useful but biased and highly inflammatory ideas about Indians and Indian life, ideas that remain in the public discourse about American Indians to this day.

CHAPTER 5

Illustrating the Indian Wars

Fact, Fantasy, and Ideology

One of the most gripping images of the nineteenth-century Indian wars appeared on the cover of the *Illustrated Police News* on July 13, 1876.[1] The illustration captured the precise moment when an unidentified Indian warrior fired his rifle at point-blank range into the chest of General George Armstrong Custer. Another unidentified warrior—dark, muscular, and wild-eyed—was advancing on Custer at that same instant, tomahawk at hand, ready to strike. Custer's body recoiled from the bullet, yet his right arm remained outstretched, his sword pointed toward the Indians as his face turned upward, bathed in light.

This illustration, the first published rendering of the Battle of the Little Bighorn, was a complete fabrication, of course, since no artist or photographer was at the scene to document the details of Custer's death.[2] Moreover, the unexpected Sioux and Cheyenne victory, Custer's fame as a Civil War leader and as an Indian fighter, and the lack of firsthand reports from the battlefield left a huge information gap that the newspapers—and the illustrated press—rushed to fill. The *Police News* illustrator knew his role: to create a hero, a great soldier cut down by the savages. By showing the deadly work of vicious warriors—and by fixing the dying general's eyes on heaven—the *News* illustrator assured readers that Custer had indeed died a heroic death, a martyr to civilization. Six days later, veteran illustrator William de la Montagne Cary published his own heroic vision of Custer's Last Stand in the *New York Daily Graphic*[3] (figure 5.1). Like the image in the *Police News,* it showed a glorious Custer, saber in hand, the last white man standing in a heap of dead and dying warriors, soldiers, and horses. The *Daily Graphic* admitted that no eyewitness was present to record the Last Stand, but said that Cary's illustration "was made from careful descriptions of the country and the dispositions of the forces sent to us by our correspondent who visited the scene of the battle."[4] Despite this claim, Cary's image was highly speculative, the second of many hundreds of imaginary Last Stand images produced by artists and illustrators across the decades of the nineteenth and twentieth centuries.[5] It is no exaggeration to say that Custer's Last Stand became *the* visual emblem of the nineteenth-century Indian wars, an iconic

FIGURE 5.1. Artist W. M. Cary was nowhere near the Little Bighorn in 1876, but that did not stop him from producing an early (and imaginary) illustration of Custer's Last Stand, a soon-to-be iconic image that celebrated the doomed heroism of Custer and his men.

scene that, for white Americans, symbolized the violent but necessary triumph of civilization over savagery in the American West.

Fictionalized Last Stand illustrations were hardly the first pictures of Indian-white violence in American visual culture. In fact, colonial artists and printers had been illustrating Indian-white conflicts since the days of Mary Rowlandson, the Massachusetts woman whose 1682 captivity narrative inspired an entire genre of dramatic stories and violent images.[6] By 1804, painter John Vanderlyn imagined the death of a white American patriot at the hands of two British-inspired Mohawks in his work *Murder of Jane McCrea*.[7] In the middle of the nineteenth century, improvements in printing technology and an increased demand for newsworthy images meant that more Americans than ever could see realistic-seeming pictures of Indians as well as violence and war. The Civil War, in fact, proved to be a circulation boon for the pictorial press, which employed scores of "special artists" to follow the troops and draw pictures of battlefield action and other aspects of the war.[8] The papers also employed a number of military officers to sketch the action, pictures that were redrawn in New York and turned into wood engravings. These images were published as news, but they worked on an ideological level as well. As Robert Craig has noted, such illustrations were interpretations of experience that transcended the immediacy of the news event itself. In Craig's words, "They stood for honor, glory, camaraderie, compassion, [and] hard work."[9] The popular interest in war pictures persisted throughout the Civil War and became a compelling editorial and economic incentive for Indian war coverage in the illustrated press. Only months after Lee's surrender at Appomattox, Alfred Waud and Theodore Davis, two veteran *Harper's Weekly* illustrators, headed west to sketch Indians and Indian-white violence.[10] Thus many Indian battles, skirmishes, and other violent Indian encounters were prime material for the post–Civil War pictorial press, adding excitement and a dose of heroism to the often-staid imagery that filled the pages of the illustrated papers.[11]

This chapter describes and analyzes some of the most significant illustrations of Indian-white violence in the post–Civil War era. The research builds upon an observation by Walter Lippmann, who noted in 1922 that most journalism "is not a first hand report of the raw material. It is a report of that material after it has been stylized."[12] Illustrated Indian-white violence was often secondhand and highly stylized, as the Last Stand images demonstrate. The chapter examines a small but representative sample of illustrated Indian-white conflicts that appeared in the pictorial press, especially the two leading illustrated newspapers, *Frank Leslie's Illustrated Newspaper* and *Harper's Weekly*. These examples, drawn from the 1860s and 1870s, document several major and minor incidents of the Indian wars and shed light on popular attitudes about Indians and Indian-white violence. The chapter asks several questions: What kinds of Indian-white violence did the pictorial press depict and how was it represented? Which ideas and themes were emphasized and which were downplayed? What explains the mixture of fact, fantasy, and ideology in these illustrations? By addressing these questions, the research seeks to develop a deeper understanding of violent Indian-white imagery and to explain the larger meanings associated with these images. As the following pages show, the meanings attached to violent Indian-white images were often complicated and sometimes contradictory, shaped by myriad cultural and ideological forces in play at each historical moment.

Imagining Indian-White Violence

This analysis divides images of Indian-white violence into two broad categories: (1) realistic—or what purported to be realistic—news illustrations of actual Indian-white battles and conflicts, and (2) imaginative, allegorical illustrations of Indian-white violence, generic images unconnected to a particular time and place. Typically, both types of illustrations were published with explanatory captions and stories, texts that worked to "fix" the dominant meaning of the image and often—but not always—reinforced the meanings of the image. As explained in the following pages, both types of illustrations focused on dramatic moments of violent action, but neither type of illustration was likely to be particularly accurate or factual. That is, illustrated Indian-white violence was almost always a mixture of fact and fantasy, a combination of limited real-world observations, interviews with participants or reports from witnesses, and some measure of invented or imagined details. Realistic battlefield illustrations were always less "real" and more imaginary than the pictorial papers claimed. When *Leslie's* or *Harper's* had artists on the battlefield—a rare circumstance—these artists were limited to particular views of the fighting, a lack of time to make detailed drawings, and the obvious and immediate danger of being killed or wounded.[13] It was much easier—and safer—to produce Indian war scenes before or after the actual combat; that is, within the confines of an army camp. In fact, camp pictures make up a substantial portion of Indian war illustrations in the pictorial press.[14] Other scenes related to Indian violence, such as the hanging of thirty-eight Sioux warriors linked to attacks on white settlers in Minnesota in 1862, were relatively easy to illustrate because they were planned events that allowed artists time to make on-the-spot sketches.[15] Camp and other static scenes from the field did not show action, but they did help establish the authority of the pictures through their proximity to the violence.[16] On-the-spot battlefield artists added credibility to their pictures through interviews with the soldiers involved, sources that were firsthand but also subject to their own limitations and biases. In most cases, artists were nowhere near the fighting, which meant that these illustrations were constructed entirely from interviews with participants or written accounts from the scene, often second- or thirdhand sources with their own biases and constraints. For all these reasons, news illustrations of Indian-white combat were highly imaginative constructions made up of bits and pieces of fact, observation, speculation, hearsay, and wishful thinking. This combination of the actual and the imaginative was a principal feature of Indian-white warfare as illustrated in the pictorial press. Although the illustrated papers promoted the idea that its Indian-white pictures were faithful renderings of real-world events,[17] the pictorial press more often provided—and its readers accepted—illustrations that were plausible but speculative re-creations of Indian-white combat. Not surprisingly, most of these images served a larger ideological purpose, portraying Indians as vicious barbarians and glorifying whites as defenders of civilization.

The second category of illustrated Indian-white violence was also plausible although—unlike the combat scenes—quite imaginary and unconnected to real-life events. These images were not reports of actual events, but allegorical pictures of Indian attacks and threats, illustrations that appeared real but were actually representative images of Indian-white violence. These images served as vivid symbols of ongoing Indian-white conflict in the West. *Harper's Weekly* acknowledged the symbolic nature of such pictures in 1870 when it published a full-page picture of a family of settlers defending their cabin from an Indian attack. "Though not designed to illustrate an actual event, our picture . . . this week is something more than a mere fancy sketch," the editors explained. "Scenes like the one so graphically imagined and portrayed by our artist are unhappily of too frequent occurrence on our far

Western frontier," *Harper's* continued, "where the whites and the red men seem fated to wage a warfare that can cease only with the extermination of the aboriginal inhabitants."[18] These illustrations, therefore, were not news reports of real violence from the frontier; they were representations of the sorts of Indian violence that had happened to some settlers at some places and times, and, as in this case, they were published as warnings about the Indian frontier and as reminders of the larger struggle between civilization and savagery. These imaginary pictures were acceptable to readers because they met readers' expectations, even as the illustrated papers themselves helped create and repeat these expectations. As with the illustrations of real-world battles, these images served a larger allegorical function, attempting to visually document and justify the ongoing conflicts between Indians and whites in the West.

On occasion, however, the pictorial press offered more ambiguous messages about Indians in the West, publishing pictures of imaginary violence alongside commentary about the mistreatment of Indians. Such stories reflected the long-standing Euro-American ideal of the Noble Savage and the post–Civil War rise of Indian rights activists in Boston, New York, and other eastern cities, a movement that reminded Americans of the price of conquest and the moral consequences of Manifest Destiny. Significantly, these ambiguous representations of Indian violence were tied to imaginary incidents where no actual soldiers or settlers died, violence that was much easier to forgive than real-world violence. Although these mixed-message representations were relatively rare, the very fact of their appearance in the pictorial press is evidence of a shift in the anti-Indian ideology in the last half of the nineteenth century—at least when the violence was imaginary.

Fact and Fiction in Indian War Illustrations

The violence of war has long been a recognized feature of news and news making, of course, and nineteenth-century Indian-white violence was no exception. In the case of the pictorial press, the decades-long war between whites and Indians in the West provided an opportunity to publish exciting pictures of danger and heroism, action-oriented illustrations likely to capture the imagination of readers in eastern and midwestern cities and towns far from the scene. Pictures of battles and skirmishes between Indians and the army were among the most dramatic and significant Indian illustrations of the pictorial press era. These illustrations were dramatic in part because they were inherently newsworthy, as violence usually is. In 1863—and with plenty of Civil War stories and pictures filling its pages—*Harper's* published a full-page illustration of a cavalry charge against a hostile Sioux village in "The Battle of White Stone Hill" in present-day North Dakota.[19] Based on an officer's sketch, the image showed saber-wielding soldiers on horseback overrunning a band of dark-skinned warriors, an action-packed picture of military triumph guaranteed to attract readers. Violent scenes were also ripe for heart-tugging language and imagery. In late 1879, for example, the Ute war gave *Leslie's* the opportunity to run a dramatic full-page illustration of the burned-out ruins of the White River Agency in Colorado.[20] The illustration, based on a sketch by Lieutenant C. A. H. McCauley, showed destroyed wagons and fences as well as piles of ashes. The illustrations also depicted two groups of soldiers, each contemplating the graves of the Indian agent, Nathan Meeker, and the agency clerk and postmaster, W. H. Post. The accompanying story was equally dramatic. "Everywhere murder, riot and arson had held high carnival," McCauley reported. "Many of the savages . . . were drunk at the time of the outbreak, having obtained arms, ammunition and whisky from white men trading secretly on the reservation," he continued.[21] In vivid language and imagery, *Leslie's* made clear that these Indians were threats to civic order and all that was good. "Instead of the harvest of peace," McCauley concluded, "the harvest of death has come, and cruel barbarism has swept all civilization away."

As noted previously, Indian-white violence could be used to tell stories of Indian treachery and military valor even during the Civil War. In its coverage of the continuing violence in Dakota Territory in 1863, for example, *Harper's Weekly* published a half-page engraving on its cover showing the "Murder of Lieutenant Beever by the Sioux Indians"[22] (figure 5.2). A wealthy Englishman, Beever was an aide to General Henry Sibley, the officer in charge of the Sioux campaign.[23] The illustration showed Beever surrounded by warriors in a forest, victim of an ambush. Beever's horse has fallen and lies on the ground, apparently dying, while Beever fires his pistol at an advancing warrior. His actions are in vain, however, as five other Sioux are closing in, including a prominent warrior on the left whose arrow is ready and another on the right who has a tomahawk poised overhead. This illustration is striking because of its focus on Beever's heroic but doomed situation. He is still standing, fighting gamely to the end. But the Sioux are all around him and his death is imminent.

This was dramatic stuff, a climatic moment of violence that *Harper's* used to attract attention and add news value to the paper's images. It was a true story too, as *Harper's* reported inside the issue. But the illustration was clearly a fictionalized drawing, the creation of an artist who did not witness the ambush. *Harper's* noted this fact, but maintained that the sketch was "a truthful one, so far as could be gathered from the examination of those who visited the scene immediately afterward."[24] In this image and in many similar illustrations, the gap between reality and the editorial imagination allowed for a certain artistic license—extra drama and invented details—that *Harper's* supplied in the interest of an exciting picture. It is also telling that *Harper's* labeled Beever's death a murder—implying Indian criminality—when the incident was part of a military campaign. The paper's depiction of Beever's bravery also reinforced popular ideas about treacherous Indians—people who would, if they had the chance, ambush and slaughter every white soldier (and civilian) in the West. In short, this depiction of an Indian attack is typical of the violent Indian trope in the pictorial press, visual journalism that corroborated the nineteenth-century need to fight and subdue the "Demonic Indian."[25] Moreover,

MURDER OF LIEUTENANT BEEVER BY THE SIOUX INDIANS.—[See Page 687.]

FIGURE 5.2. The deadly Indian ambush was a familiar theme in the pictorial press, exciting illustrations that brought Indian violence into the homes of middle-class readers.

this 1863 illustration prefigures the visual elements of the Fetterman and Custer massacres that were to come. Like those images, this illustration emphasized Indian aggression and celebrated a courageous soldier standing tall amid the swarming enemy, firing one final shot and killing one last warrior before he falls. This violent incident was a tragedy for Lieutenant Beever, to be sure, but his death was magnified and made meaningful as part of the ongoing struggle between civilization and savagery, a heroic struggle that *Harper's Weekly* was happy to imagine, dramatize, and publish on its cover.

A more muted illustration of army valor can be found in images of the Fetterman massacre, which took place near Fort Phil Kearny in Wyoming.[26] In December 1866, a Civil War veteran named William J. Fetterman disobeyed orders from the fort's commanding officer and led some eighty men into a trap set by Lakota, Cheyenne, and other warriors, fighters that included High Backbone and Crazy Horse. Lieutenant Colonel Fetterman and all of his men were killed and their bodies mutilated, facts that sparked outrage in the press. The *Chicago Tribune's* headline was typical: "Horrible Indian Massacre."[27] *Leslie's* published a full-page illustration of the battle

THE MASSACRE OF UNITED STATES TROOPS BY THE SIOUX AND CHEYENNE INDIANS, NEAR FORT PHILIP KEARNEY, DAKOTAH TERRITORY, DECEMBER 22nd 1866.

FIGURE 5.3. When Sioux and Cheyenne warriors overran Lieutenant Colonel William Fetterman's troops in 1866, *Leslie's* emphasized scalping, vivid evidence of Indian brutality.

and a brief story, which blamed the disaster on the fort's commander, Colonel Henry Carrington, and included this dramatic line: "Not a man escaped to tell the tale."[28] Although no whites survived the attack and none of the soldiers at nearby Fort Kearny knew exactly what happened, *Leslie's* produced a fictional yet bloodcurdling picture of the battle based on telegraphic reports from the West[29] (figure 5.3). The artist imagined a sprawling mass of vicious Indians and dying soldiers. In the center right of the drawing, the artist showed a triumphant warrior with two arms aloft, one hand holding a scalping knife, the other a bloody scalp. Another Indian on the far right was similarly jubilant. In fact, most of the prominent Indians in the scene had tomahawks and knives at the ready. The soldiers, in contrast, were on the ground, dead, dying, or begging for mercy. Lost in the background, deep in the chaos, one brave soldier—perhaps Lieutenant Colonel Fetterman himself—was astride his horse, his saber held high for a final blow against the swarming warriors.

Harper's Weekly also produced a full-page illustration of the Fetterman battle, although it was published more than two months after *Leslie's* picture.[30] Like *Leslie's*, *Harper's* imagined a crowded field of fearsome warriors and victimized soldiers amid horses and clouds of dust. The *Harper's* artist put a final few of Fetterman's men at the center of the picture, taking their last shots as the warriors closed in.

Harper's did not offer a vision of a heroic Fetterman, perhaps because he was the officer who led his men into a trap even after he had been forbidden to do so.[31] If Fetterman was one of the soldiers shown fighting in the *Harper's* picture, he was unidentified, surrounded, and helpless.

Dire though the Fetterman illustrations were, they were also the stuff of successful pictorial journalism. Both pictures were visually arresting and the *Leslie's* illustration was notably violent, although the gore of scalping and death was understated by the limitations of black-and-white wood engraving. These illustrations were also highly fictional representations created in New York from telegraph and official army reports that were themselves speculative and incomplete. Despite this dubious provenance, it was true that Fetterman and his men had been overrun and killed in a bloody battle in Wyoming, as the illustration made clear. If some of the drawing's details were wrong—if, for example, the men had been scattered across a wider battlefield—that did not change the terrible facts of the battle. In other words, neither the *Leslie's* nor the *Harper's* artists who produced these drawings knew exactly what happened to Fetterman and his men, nor could they show with any accuracy how the battle ended as the warriors swept across the field. Nevertheless, both illustrations provided readers with a broad sense of the fight and how it might have looked, realistic-appearing images that revealed the horrors of Indian violence and the desperation of the doomed soldiers. From this journalistic perspective, the particular details of the battle were less important than a more general sense of Indian bloodlust and white victimization. Within these bounds, then, both *Leslie's* and *Harper's* delivered realistic and "true" pictures of the Fetterman fight, even though the scene was imagined and many of the details were invented. Moreover, the pictorial press did not present these illustrations as literal or eyewitness accounts, even if some readers chose to interpret them that way. These illustrations, that is, were works of visual fiction that were emotionally and ideologically true. As such, these scenes filled a journalistic space between reality and imagination, which was the best (and only) way for the pictorial press to tell the story of the Fetterman fight in pictures and fulfill their visual mission. Indeed, this was the conceit of the pictorial press, the journalistic negotiation that both the editors and readers tacitly agreed to in nineteenth-century visual journalism. The pictorial press supplied the pictures—images that varied widely in veracity—and the public accepted them for what they appeared to provide; namely, illustrations of actual people, places, and events that *could* be accurate and that reinforced the powerful and deeply seated idea of evil Indians and valiant soldiers.

By the time George Armstrong Custer and his cavalry attacked the Sioux and Cheyenne village along the Little Bighorn River in the summer of 1876, the general outline of the doomed Indian fighter was well established. That was evident in the Last Stand as imagined by W. M. Cary for New York's *Daily Graphic* (see figure 5.1). As with the Fetterman illustrator a decade earlier, Cary was far from the scene and created his illustration based on secondhand reports, several standard features of plains Indian fighting (tomahawks, lances, horses), and a liberal dose of trium-phalism. Like the Fetterman battlefield, too, the Last Stand battlefield was imagined as a mass of men and horses, living and dead. As with the surrounded Lieutenant Beever and Fetterman's unfortunate command, Cary focused on the last moment of Custer's life, the split second before his final, fatal wound. This moment allowed Custer one last moment of glory, one final blow against the savages.

In both cases, this climatic moment also provided a visual answer to the ques-tion that haunted both the Custer and Fetterman massacres. What happened to these doomed soldiers? How did they die? These questions, of course, provided a creative opening for scores of illustrators and artists in subsequent decades, all of whom used their artistic skills to imagine the horrors of an Indian massacre and create plausible pictures of the battle that readers would accept and appreciate. For his part, Cary did that so successfully that his illustration established the tableau and set the tone for the outpouring of Last Stand depictions that were soon to come.[32]

The principal difference between the imaginary Fetterman battlefield as rendered in *Leslie's* and Cary's Last Stand illustration for the *Graphic* was the heroic portrayal of its commanding officer. If Lieutenant Colonel Fetterman was portrayed in the *Leslie's* image, he was not identifiable and not heroic. Cary's Last Stand drawing, by contrast, put Custer in the center of the action, bathed in light. Custer was unmistakably glorified, the last man standing. The differences between the Fetter-man and Custer depictions are easy to explain. While Fetterman was an obscure officer until his death, Custer was a public figure well before the Little Bighorn. In fact, Custer had been a Civil War hero, portrayed on the cover of both *Leslie's* and *Harper's Weekly,* fearlessly charging the Confederate lines.[33] By the end of 1866, he had proven himself as an Indian fighter based on his successful attack on the winter camp of Cheyenne chief Black Kettle along the Washita River. In 1876, he was a part of a major military campaign against the hostile Sioux and Cheyenne of the northern plains. These factors account for the almost-instant mythology that materialized after Custer's death. These factors also explain Custer's heroic depic-tions in the illustrated press. As noted earlier, Custer was at the center of Cary's picture. This and many other subsequent images presented Custer as the doomed but valiant hero who, following the ideology of the era, could be seen as a symbol of Manifest Destiny and the ongoing struggle between civilization and savagery. In fact, the shock of Custer's defeat at the hands of the Indians ensured that this "doomed hero" image would become popular and be reproduced for years to come, as indeed it was. Cary's illustration became a model for hundreds of popular depictions of Custer's Last Stand, an influence that over time ranged from pulp novels and comic books to the fine art of Frederic Remington and other Western painters.[34]

Perhaps because the *Police News* and the *Daily Graphic* had already pictured the valor of the Last Stand, *Leslie's* illustrated the Little Bighorn story not with battlefield drama but with a reverential portrait of the late general, his right hand tucked neatly into his uniform.[35] Although a static image, this portrait conferred status to its subject, reinforcing the idea that Custer was a great soldier and martyr to American civilization.[36] The following week *Leslie's* published a map of Custer's and Crook's movements across the plains and mountains and, more dramatically, a sketch of unidentified troops riding through a Montana valley, a lone warrior watching from above.[37] This was an altogether fictional drawing. It showed the army from the enemy perspective, after all, and featured an armed Indian in the foreground, so close he could readily kill the artist. The story published with the sketch explained little of the scene. It started not with a report on the fighting, but with a description of the Montana scenery. "He is indeed a singular being who fails to be influenced by the grand chain of lava peaks which tower up in the east as far as the eye can reach[,] . . . their cold gray summits bald and frosted here and there with streaks and patches of snow," the article said.[38] The story buried the battle news—that General Crook had fought the Sioux on the Rosebud River and "claimed a great victory" and that Custer and his men had been massacred on June 25.[39]

For its part, *Harper's Weekly* ignored battlefield news and emphasized imaginary sentiment. The paper devoted a full page to artist C. S. Reinhart's side-by-side pictures of a West Point solider before and after the battle[40] (figure 5.4). The "before" scene, "Romance on the Hudson," showed an idealized young couple courting on a bench at West Point. The couple, unidentified but certainly suggestive of Custer (a West Point graduate) and his beloved Libby, was holding hands, apparently deep in love. This drawing appeared alongside a more gruesome picture labeled "Reality on the Plains." As the caption suggests, this "after" drawing depicted the discovery of soldiers' bodies on the battlefield, the dead stripped of their shirts, pierced with arrows. The most prominent figure in the drawing, a wounded trooper, stood solemnly over the body of the former West Point cadet. The dead soldier's left arm was outstretched, his fingers near a portrait of his true love.

This illustration was pure fantasy, of course, intended to elicit sympathy for soldiers lost on the plains, especially the brave Custer. For this purpose, no names were needed; every *Harper's* reader could connect the late General George Armstrong Custer to these images. To complete this idea, *Harper's* published a sentimental poem on the following page. "Never was [a] month like the month of June," the poem began, "Her wreath of roses and lovers' moon."[41] A few lines deeper in the poem, these immortal lines:

> Wait till the fearful war-drum rolls:
> In the bitter hour that tries men's souls
> He will win the honors that she shall wear,
> Till her woman's heart grows proud to bear
> A name that a nation loves to boast,
> And write with those that she honors most.[42]

ROMANCE ON THE HUDSON—

REALITY ON THE PLAINS.—[See Poem, Page 618.]

FIGURE 5.4. Responding to the death of Custer, *Harper's* artist C. S. Reinhart produced contrasting panels—the romance of a West Point cadet and the fatal reality of Indian fighting in the West.

There was more such verse, some of it describing an Indian ambush in romantic terms:

> Crack of rifle and savage yells!
> Poisoned arrow and hissing shot
> Pour from the ambush thick and hot.
> Red blood, flowing from manly veins,
> Dyes with crimson the burning plains.[43]

These words, and the illustrations they explained, were a highly fictionalized way of dealing with the loss of a military hero and the national grief that followed the news from the Little Bighorn. The Indian victory over Custer had impressed itself on the nation in a powerfully emotional way, so much so that *Harper's Weekly* was moved to respond not with a realistic-seeming news illustrations of the Last Stand, but sentimentally and symbolically, with words and images that expressed the national mood. Reinhart's contrasting images enlarged private love to the level of a national tragedy, simultaneously damning the savages and praising the fallen hero and his lost love. No Indians were shown in these illustrations and none was needed. It was enough for *Harper's Weekly* to show an arrow piercing the officer's body, a vivid reminder of the price Custer—and by extension, all American soldiers—were paying as they attempted to subdue the savages and bring civilization to the northern plains.[44]

Invented Indian Violence

Unlike newsworthy war illustrations featuring Beever, Fetterman, and Custer, the pictorial press also featured other pictures of Indian-white violence that were wholly imaginary, unconnected to specific events. These illustrations were allegorical and ideological, constructed pictures of generic Indian-white conflict intended to tell larger stories of the American West. Freed from the facts, artists and illustrators could use their skills to imagine particularly dramatic moments that epitomized the national project of taming the West. One example of this sort of symbolism appeared as a full-page illustration in *Harper's* in early 1866[45] (figure 5.5). This image showed two white riders, described as a "mounted messengers," fleeing from a band of mounted, attacking Indians. As with Lieutenant Beever's death scene, this was a vivid and dramatic image—even the horses appear excited. The attacking Indians have already surrounded and killed one messenger; the other rider is firing back at his attackers with a pistol. The closest Indian, in fact, has been hit and is reeling on his mount. But the messenger is outnumbered; his situation appears desperate.

This illustration, based on a sketch by S. B. Enderton, was published without a story, a sign that it did not depict a specific Indian attack. As a symbolic fantasy, it included all the elements of an iconic scene of Indian-white violence, unambiguous visual components that would in time become a Western cliché. The white messengers (the good guys) were under attack from marauding Indians (the bad guys), who were unmistakable enemies of civilization. This was an apparent ambush, too, a tactic favored by the hostile tribes of the plains. For readers in eastern and midwestern cities and towns, this scene must have been emotionally true and ideologically significant, visual confirmation of the savagery of the Indians and the danger of the Western frontier. Indeed, this sort of dramatic and dangerous illustration was just the sort of image that the pictorial press could furnish to its readers as needed, adding excitement to the issue and capitalizing on its visual advantage over the daily press, which lacked the ability to bring large and highly detailed pictures into its readers' lives. In the post–Civil War era, this illustration was also the kind of Indian-white violence that must have seemed largely true, even when the specific details were invented. In contrast to the fictionalized depiction of Lieutenant Beever's actual death, this image showed a generic Indian attack on unidentified messengers. This was fictional violence, not news, but it would have appeared "real" to most readers, who would assume—correctly, in many cases—that something like this must have happened to some messengers at some place and time.

MOUNTED MESSENGERS ATTACKED BY INDIANS ON THE PLAINS.—[SKETCHED BY S. D. EDMSTON.]

FIGURE 5.5. Travelers on the plains lived in fear of Indians, a fear stoked by pictures of such attacks, even when no artist witnessed the violence.

Invented realism and the civilizing project on the plains were also at the heart of a *Harper's Weekly* illustration published in 1868. This full-page image, drawn by Little Bighorn artist W. M. Cary, showed a band of Sioux warriors sneaking up on a prairie homestead as the farmer plowed his field behind a team of oxen[46] (figure 5.6). What is notable here is that the illustration was drawn from the point of view of the Sioux attackers, as if Cary were a part of the war party. *Harper's* viewers, like the Sioux themselves, were placed behind a split-rail fence, watching and waiting for just the right moment to strike. "Sioux Indians of Nebraska appear to be the most troublesome," the paper explained. Although a peace treaty had recently been signed, the story said, Indian "depredations and outrages" continued.[47] Not coincidentally, the editors did not claim this illustration was made in the field. Again, this was a generic scene: "Our illustration . . . shows the mode of warfare practiced by these predatory bands upon the unsuspecting and defenseless settlers."[48] In other words, *Harper's* was tacitly acknowledging that this was an imaginary picture of hostile Indians on the plains. Neither Cary nor any other artist witnessed this scene, but for *Harper's* readers this was probably beside the point. This illustration, in other words, represented something larger than one act of violence; it was a symbol of many such Indian attacks and, in that sense, it

SIOUX INDIANS IN AMBUSH PREPARING TO ATTACK SETTLERS.—Drawn by W. M. Cary.—[See Page 262.]

FIGURE 5.6. W. M. Cary created this surprise attack on a Western homestead from the perspective of the Sioux, a dramatic point of view imagined by the artist.

represented the perceived—and ongoing—Indian threat to settlers living on the Great Plains. Readers knew which side to root for.

Another fictional Indian attack strengthens this point. In September 1867, *Harper's Weekly* published a version of a Currier and Ives print called, dramatically enough, "The Last Shot"[49] (figure 5.7). This image showed a dismounted, buckskin-clad mountain man fending off an Indian attacker. The mountain man appears alone and vulnerable, sitting in the grass as a tomahawk-wielding warrior jumps from his horse, ready to kill. Fortunately for the white man, his pistol—pointed directly at the warrior—holds a final shell. As in the Indian news illustrations, the lithographers captured the incident at a climatic moment, smoke bursting from the pistol's barrel as the Indian clutches his chest and begins to fall. This scene is highly dramatic, of course, but it is also an imaginary incident with a reassuring message for the paper's armchair adventurers. In contrast to the Fetterman massacre a few months earlier, this white man survives, his final bullet a symbolic blow against savagery on the plains. The editors provided no story to explain this scene, though they did provide the commercial source of the image: "From a Picture Published by Currier and Ives." In fact, this was a page of visual storytelling from a popular lithography firm that sold pictures of idealized American life. "The Last Shot" was, that is, presented

THE LAST SHOT.—[From a Picture published by Currier and Ives, 152 Nassau Street, New York.]

FIGURE 5.7. Dramatic scenes of Indian-white violence—exciting but quite imaginary—enlivened the coverage of the West in the pictorial press, as in this Currier and Ives picture from 1867.

more as nationalist entertainment than news, a reification of a scene from Western life that Americans in the post–Civil War era found exciting and "true," at least in an emotional and symbolic sense. That would explain its publication in the pages of an illustrated paper, where it added zest to the weekly's pages and confirmed—or reconfirmed—the inevitable triumph of civilization over savagery. The picture also reinforced the idea of Indians as dangerous villains, eager to dispatch any and all travelers on the long trek west. As noted earlier, this sort of Indian attack was routinely presented as news in the illustrated press. In this case, however, the "Demonic Indian" was presented as the stuff of legend, safely contained (and dispatched) on the printed page and marketed to middle-class readers as a thrilling feature of the American West.

Ambiguous Representations

In September 1876, *Harper's* published a large and particularly powerful image of imaginary Indian-white violence in the West. The picture took up most of two pages, but the image offered more myth than news. In fact, the engraving was pure allegory,

ATTACKED BY THE INDIANS.

FIGURE 5.8. The heroic American pioneer dominated this illustration of Western expansion in 1876, but this theme was undermined by the accompanying story, which criticized federal Indian policy and expressed sympathy for the Indians.

an American tale of triumph on the frontier that must have happened somewhere at some time—or many times. In any case, *Harper's* provided no time or place for an actual attack like the one presented. The illustration showed a group of white emigrants defending their wagon train from an Indian assault[50] (figure 5.8). One bold pioneer dominated the scene, a knife in his belt, his rifle at the ready. The man faced the viewer directly, standing tall, resolute and ready to defend his family. Behind him, a wounded horse struggled for life. On the left side of the illustration, a woman tended to a wounded traveler, while two frightened children peered out from the covered wagon and an older man reloaded a rifle. On the right, a group of mounted Indians charged into the picture, bearing down on the pioneers, one of whom was firing back at the attackers. The *Harper's* caption stated the obvious: "Attacked by the Indians."[51] Like the climatic military scenes described previously, this life-or-death drama on the prairies was bound to catch the attention of eastern and midwestern readers.

The story with it amplified and explained the scene in sweeping and nationalistic terms. It began with the Pilgrims, recounting their early encounters with the Indians and—surprisingly, given the violence of the engraving—defended the Indians and went on to provide a logic for their actions. "They were the owners of the soil, and the white settlers were the invaders and intruders," *Harper's* reported. The Indians were friendly, the story continued, and wished to live in peace with the whites. "Had the settlers recognized the rights of the Indians and treated them fairly, [and] kept faith with them . . . there would have been no desolating Indian wars," the story noted. It continued in this vein:

> It is undeniable that all of our Indian wars have been provoked by the whites. Every treaty made with the Indians has been violated as soon as it was for the interest of whites to break it. Despoiled of their lands, demoralized by whiskey, taught treachery and fraud by the "superior" race, it is but natural that they should fight for the possession of their lands or that they should be cruel and vindictive in their methods of warfare.[52]

There was more along these lines: Canada had treated its Indians fairly, avoiding much of the violence found in the United States. Even here, when tribes had been dealt with honorably, they had made great strides toward civilization, as Bishop Henry Whipple, a leader in the nascent Indian rights movement, had argued. Thus the dramatic *Harper's* scene:

> Such incidents as the one depicted in our double-page engraving are the natural result of our Indian policy. We have taught the Indian to regard the whites as enemies. We have cheated, despoiled, and demoralized them, and now affect to be surprised when they turn upon us, and defend the integrity of their lands with all the brutality and cruelty of savage warfare.[53]

The article concluded with a reference to the popular nineteenth-century idea of the vanishing Indian, noting, however, that it was no credit to either Christianity or civilization that the settlement and development of the West "should be accompanied only by the extermination of these races."

In its language and tone, the article was at odds with the dominant theme of the illustration it purported to explain. The illustration told a simple, easily understood story of brave pioneers defending themselves against violent Indians. The article, however, told a less compelling tale, recounting the causes of Indian-white conflicts in American history and providing reasons for Indian resistance. Careful readers would have noted the contrast between the words and the image. Yet given the size and power of the picture—and the fact that the white Indian fighter was the visual center of the illustration and its most heroic figure—casual readers could easily miss this contradiction. For these readers, the message of the illustration was as clear as the caption itself: "Attacked by the Indians." In other words, the visual power of the *Harper's* illustration trumped the more sympathetic, nuanced historical explanation of Indian warfare. Indeed, the dominant theme of the image—heroic white resistance to savagery—was clear, especially since it was published less than three months after the Little Bighorn.

An 1871 *Leslie's* cover also illustrates the ambiguous presentation of Indian-white violence in the post–Civil War era. The illustration—one imagined by an unidentified artist—showed an armed and animated warrior leading his horse down a stream. The caption highlighted the meaning of the image: "On the War-Path 'Water Leaves No Trail'"[54] (figure 5.9). The warrior, identified inside the issue as Sitting Bull, was presented not as a portrait of the man himself, but as a symbol of all dangerous Indians. The drawing showed an agitated, dark-skinned warrior, armed with a tomahawk as well as a bow and arrows, leading his excited horse downstream. This Indian, who bore no resemblance to the real Sitting Bull, was not a Noble Savage. This was a fictional Sitting Bull depicted as a dangerous man, all the more so because he was on the run, as *Leslie's* explained:

> "Dead men tell no tales," says the white transgressor; and the crafty Indian, driven mile by mile from the hunting-grounds of his fathers, and inflamed with the white man's fire-water, murmurs as he is the object of murderous pursuit, or, from an intention to contest the right of being evicted, applies his war-paint and girds himself for wily movement, "Well, water leaves no trail."[55]

This Sitting Bull was "crafty" and "wily." He was "inflamed" by alcohol too, making him more treacherous than he had been. Yet this evil Indian theme was softened considerably by an explanation deeper in the story. Like *Harper's* in its wagon train story, *Leslie's* provided an explanation for Indian violence. "At the East," *Leslie's* noted, "we wonder why the Indian troubles are not suppressed." But, the article continued: "Little thought is given to the encroachments on the Indian reservations, and to the tricky dealings of agents and adventurers, or to the necessities of the aborigines." *Leslie's* continued this theme, noting the fact—rarely acknowledged in the press—that "all [the Indian] depredations are occasioned by whites themselves." The construction of the railroad, for example, had pushed Sitting Bull and other Indians to the brink. The cover illustration, *Leslie's* said, revealed "the straits to which these natives are reduced."

With these words, the article contradicted the Indian treachery emphasized in the cover illustration. The story explained that Sitting Bull and his tribe had been pushed to the limit and were not so much fighting whites—contrary to the "war-path" of the caption—as trying to save themselves. In this illustration, Sitting Bull was not the hunter, but the hunted. In fact, the article ended by emphasizing this theme, noting the "anxiety" of the horse and his master, who feared "the sudden appearance of a Gatling battery, or some other instrument of extermination." In short, *Leslie's* text changed and complicated the meaning of the cover illustration, pulling back from the violent Indian stereotype presented so boldly on the cover. Given the vividness of the illustration (and the fact that it was the cover image), it seems safe to say that the picture, not the text, carried the dominant meaning in this case.

Following the humanitarian push by eastern reformers and "friends of the Indians," these illustrations of imaginary Indian-white conflict gave the pictorial

FRANK LESLIE'S ILLUSTRATED NEWSPAPER

Entered according to the Act of Congress, in the year 1871, by FRANK LESLIE, in the office of the Librarian of Congress, at Washington.

No. 837—Vol. XXXIII.]   NEW YORK, OCTOBER 14, 1871.   [PRICE, 10 CENTS. $4 00 YEARLY. 13 WEEKS, $1 00.

ON THE WAR-PATH—"WATER LEAVES NO TRAIL."—SEE PAGE 72.

FIGURE 5.9. This Indian "on the war-path" was identified as Sitting Bull, a "wily" Indian inflamed by alcohol. Despite this portrayal, *Leslie's* story blamed whites for Indian violence and expressed sympathy for the plight of Indians.

press an opening for more moderate views of Indians and their place in American society. Unlike newsworthy depictions of real-world Indian violence, which were automatically condemned in the illustrated press, generic and fictionalized violence could be presented in more moderate terms. This ambivalent approach was a way that both *Harper's* and *Leslie's* bridged the increasingly wide gap between the treacherous Indian of popular lore and a more sympathetic—and in many cases, accurate—depiction of Indians who were fighting for their very survival. The *Leslie's* illustration reinforced the idea of the "Demonic Indian"—thus meeting the expectations of many of its readers—while the story explained the Indians' dilemma and expressed sympathy for the general plight of Indians, an editorial position that was humane and morally defensible to other readers. In this way, *Leslie's* and *Harper's Weekly* could offer ambivalent Indian representations in their pages, continuing to highlight Indian savagery in their pictures but offering explanations and sympathy in their stories.

Conclusion

On December 26, 1868, *Frank Leslie's Illustrated Newspaper* published a fictionalized Indian war illustration called "The Battle of Washita"[56] (figure 5.10). The drawing showed cavalry and foot soldiers charging into Black Kettle's winter camp, sabers drawn, rifles firing. Some Cheyenne were dead or dying; others were attempting to flee. One Cheyenne woman was resisting in vain, her tomahawk helpless over her head as a soldier stiff-armed her neck. The artist imagined a heroic General Custer too, mounted on a black horse, serenely observing the attack. This illustration, created from official reports and press accounts, differs markedly from the images of Indian-white violence described previously because it featured white aggression toward Indians, including women and children. Indeed, the Washita attack was so one-sided that it has come to be known as the Washita massacre.[57] In this instance—rare in the postwar period—the illustrated press depicted white violence toward Indians. The facts of the campaign help explain this portrayal; it was a successful army attack led by a highly newsworthy officer. Not surprisingly, the accompanying story—Custer's official report to his superior, General Phil Sheridan—justified the army's aggression. "The Indians were caught napping for once, and the warriors rushed from their lodges and posted themselves behind trees and in deep ravines, from which they began a most determined defense," Custer wrote.[58] The soldiers managed to rescue two white children, but another child was not so lucky. "A white boy held captive, about ten years old, when about to be secured, was brutally murdered by a squaw, who ripped out his entrails with a knife," Custer reported.[59] For *Leslie's* readers, such language helped justify the army's aggression. These Indians were savages. They had kidnapped white children. They brought the violence upon themselves.

THE BATTLE OF WASHITA—THE ATTACK ON BLACK KETTLE'S CHEYENNE CAMP, WASHITA RIVER, INDIAN TERRITORY, BY THE SEVENTH REGIMENT CAVALRY UNDER MAJOR-GENERAL GEORGE A. CUSTAR, Nov. 27th.—See Page 225.

FIGURE 5.10. The illustrated papers often showed Indians attacking whites, but in this case *Leslie's* imagined Custer's attack on the Cheyenne and Arapaho—men, women, and children—at the Washita in 1868.

Despite this example of white aggression, most illustrations of Indian-white violence during this period depicted Indians as the source of the violence. This followed the expansionist ideology of the era, a time when Indians were easily imagined as savages, natural enemies of civilization. For their part, the pictorial press represented Indian-white violence in a highly imaginative way, using a combination of fact and fantasy in the service of a larger national story. As noted earlier, some Indian war illustrations were based on field sketches or reports from Indian-white battles, a news-making practice that gave the pictorial press a claim to accuracy and verisimilitude. Other violent images were wholly imaginary, based not on specific incidents but capturing a general, emotional truth about violence on the Indian frontier. Significantly, both types of illustrations included fictional details, elements of fantasy that served an ideological function. Beyond adding excitement and drama to the pages of the illustrated press, both categories of Indian-white imagery helped create heroes, honor victims, and demonize villains. Thus Indian war illustrations glorified Lieutenant Beever and General Custer, agents of civilization who lost their lives fighting the savages. These and similar images became, in effect, iconic public memorials to the fallen, a journalistic way of honoring the victims of Indian violence and reinforcing the rightness of Manifest Destiny. The imaginary pictures created heroes as well, depicting generic messengers and settlers as stand-ins for average Americans in the West. These images, too, marked Indians as villains.

As noted previously, the illustrated papers sometimes presented ambivalent portrayals of Indian violence. These depictions were purely allegorical images; they presented the Indian threat broadly, leaving room for more nuanced commentary and interpretation. The editors of the illustrated press deployed symbolic pictures of Indian-white violence as a way of explaining the long-standing "Indian problem." While these pictures were visually exciting and stereotypical, the accompanying text provided context and explanation that the illustrations could not. The pictorial press was open to such stories for both ideological and geographic reasons. The ideological reason was the enduring idea of the Noble Savage, an idealized, natural being that had a long hold on the American imagination, even during the Indian-white violence following the Civil War. In terms of geography, *Leslie's* and *Harper's* were New York–based publications focused largely on urban stories and pictures, including soft news topics like fashion and leisure from eastern cities and Europe. Indian raids on the dusty plains were newsworthy, but this violence was not a serious threat to the cities or the nation. In the urbanized East, in fact, it was possible to hear and understand the Indian side of the story. White crusaders and activists who called themselves "friends of the Indians" lived and worked in eastern cities, where, on occasion, they could influence the editors of the illustrated papers. These activists helped open a space for more detailed and informed reports of Indian-white violence, stories accompanied by pictures that still offered the thrill of frontier danger.

Another explanation for such mixed messages may lie in the continuing confusion over the place of Native Americans in the popular imagination. As many historians and observers have noted, American Indians were both loved and hated from the colonial era on.[60] Noble Savages were celebrated for their natural virtues and dignity at the same time that their more hostile compatriots were demonized for their bloodlust. Indians could be featured on maps and official documents as symbols of the continent and its bounty, but also shown as barbarians and agents of Satan. This dichotomy in the American mind was unresolved in the nineteenth century, playing itself out in visual culture and the press. Artist George Catlin, for example, painted respectful portraits of the Indian people he lived with and came to know in the 1830s on the upper Missouri.[61] But painter Charles Deas offered a much darker vision of Indians in America in his 1845 painting called *The Death Struggle,* a terrifying image of an Indian and a trapper fighting over a beaver pelt, both men out of control and plunging over a cliff to their deaths together.[62] This was a none-too-subtle metaphor for the United States itself at an earlier time—Indians and whites locked in a struggle that could have annihilated the Indian race and injured if not destroyed Euro-American society.

In sum, Indians were represented in fictionalized and divergent ways during the post–Civil War era because white Americans could not settle on a single idea of who Indians were or what they meant to American society. As art critic Robert Hughes put it, "Whites had been praising, deriding, or trying to be objective about the first Americans ever since they crossed the Atlantic."[63] Thus Indian violence toward whites, which was regularly and easily highlighted in the illustrated papers, was sometimes softened by explanatory stories that portrayed that violence in more sympathetic terms. This was a sign of white guilt, perhaps, but it was also a small editorial acknowledgment of the serious and very real mistreatment of Indians across the decades of American history.

CHAPTER 6

Making Sense of Savagery

*Native American Cartoons
in the* Daily Graphic

Five weeks after Lakota and Cheyenne warriors overran and killed every soldier accompanying George Armstrong Custer at the Battle of the Little Bighorn, New York's *Daily Graphic* published a front-page cartoon of two Indian men (figure 6.1). The Indian on the right was shown sitting on a log in the woods, staring serenely into the middle distance. He was clearly a warrior, but a peaceful, nonthreatening one, despite his bare chest, buckskin leggings, bear-claw necklace, and a bow and many arrows. The Indian on the left, however, was an altogether different Indian. He was clearly dangerous—darker, meaner, well armed, alert, and ready. He was shown astride his well-muscled pony before the wild majesty of the Rocky Mountains, a pistol in one hand, rifle in the other. The caption below these figures was simple and ironic—"The Noble Red Man"—but the subcaptions made the meaning of the two Indians more obvious and more poignant: The "good" Indian was tagged "Cooper's Romance," while the "bad" Indian was labeled "Custer's Reality."[1]

The visual contrast between these two Indians was both stark and significant. In the wake of Custer's ignominious defeat in eastern Montana, these contrasting warriors captured the extremes of Indian imagery in nineteenth-century pictorial journalism. Indeed, both figures made sense in the cultural milieu that followed Custer's defeat. The reading public, especially in the East, had become accustomed to Indians as imagined by James Fenimore Cooper in his popular *Leatherstocking Tales.* These were the romanticized Noble Savages, natural aristocrats of the eastern forests, seemingly well mannered and easily controlled. Significantly, too, most Americans in the last half of the nineteenth century believed that Indians were an inferior and doomed race, destined to disappear quietly into the past as civilization advanced inevitably across the continent. But Custer's defeat had challenged the idealized Indian figure, making clear Western Indians were still a threat to American progress and underscoring the continuing dangers of the frontier. In fact, the Custer Indian's firearms on the cover of the *Daily Graphic* could be seen as evidence of

FIGURE 6.1. The dual nature of the Indian character had been long debated in the press, a debate illustrated by this side-by-side comparison of Indians in the wild.

corruption among Indian agents and traders, another challenge to the taming of the wilderness and the pacification of the Indians. In the summer of 1876, the *Graphic*'s readers would be much more concerned about the reality of Indian violence than Fenimore Cooper's literary Indians. In this and other Indian cartoons, the editors of the *Graphic* were signaling a popular shift in the public perception of American Indians, from benign to savage Indians. This cover also implied that something had to be done to pacify these Custer Indians, to force them into harmless and neutralized Cooper Indians—a move the *Graphic* was happy to support.

This chapter considers Indian cartoons and illustrations in the *Daily Graphic* at two historical moments: before and after the Battle of the Little Bighorn. Not surprisingly, the Seventh Cavalry's defeat at the Little Bighorn was a watershed event in Indian representations in the *Daily Graphic*, a paper that generally ignored Indians until it reviled Custer's killers in a number of vicious cartoons. In short, the *Graphic*'s Indian cartoons before and after the Little Bighorn can be read as a public sign of the shifting political and cultural meanings that surrounded Indians and their role in late nineteenth-century American life. As historian Thomas Milton Kemnitz has argued, editorial cartoons can be seen as a "primary visual means of communicating opinions and attitudes or of 'summing up' situations."[2] Significantly, cartoons are a highly dramatic editorial form as well, capturing key themes and ideas succinctly in popular and understandable images. The *Daily Graphic,* a new illustrated journal, depicted Indians in two distinct visual forms: in political cartoons and in news illustrations.[3] As we shall see, the *Graphic* deployed cartoons to support its editorial positions and emphasize anti-Indian ideology, especially after the Little Bighorn. The paper's news illustrations, however, were generally more straightforward, lacking the overt racism and bias of the cartoons. In this way, the *Graphic*'s imagery revealed the paper's ambiguity about Indians and Indian policy. This research focuses on the *Daily Graphic,* a New York City newspaper that became the world's first illustrated *daily* newspaper.[4] The *Graphic* played an important role in the history of American visual journalism, a role that deserves greater scholarly attention. The *Graphic*'s Indian images also merit greater scrutiny, especially since the paper thrived at a time when the Indian wars were bloody and frequent. Despite this fact, scholars have largely ignored the *Graphic* and its Indian coverage. In his book on political cartoons, for instance, Roger Fischer devoted a chapter to the Indian cartoons in *Harper's, Judge, Puck,* and other journals, but not the *Daily Graphic.*[5]

The Rise of the *Daily Graphic*

The Daily Graphic Company was incorporated in October 1872, capitalized by Canadian investors at $500,000. The money was raised, a former *Graphic* illustrator wrote, "on the belief that certain Canadians had discovered a photo-lithographic process that would revolutionize the illustrating and printing business."[6] Those Canadians, William A. Leggo and Joseph Desbarats, became the paper's publishers, and, in fact, they had developed a method for the Canadian *Graphic* that "allowed original drawings, photographs, or engravings from other publications to be transferred photographically to lithographic stone, eliminating the need for hand-carved wooden blocks."[7] The *New York Daily Graphic* began publishing in March 1873, and was immediately successful. After only two months, the paper boasted a circulation of 100,000, making it the largest evening paper in the world.[8] More significantly, the *Daily Graphic* pioneered a new form of visual journalism, one that was faster and, arguably, more accurate. In announcing their enterprise, Leggo and Desbarats claimed that the paper's "illustration of events will be as accurate and pleasing and elegant as any word-painting in the text."[9] More pictures made the *Graphic* more educational, the editors argued, because the paper could publish images of life in far-off places, including illustrations from European newspapers and magazines.[10] Images also opened the *Graphic* to nonreaders, including immigrants who had not mastered the English language. Even Mark Twain weighed in on that point, writing to the editors of the *Daily Graphic* that it was a "marvelous paper." His tongue firmly in cheek, Twain declared, "I don't care much about reading (unless it is some traquillizing [*sic*] tract or another) but I do like to look at pictures."[11]

The paper aspired to national significance, a claim the editors promoted on the paper's second anniversary in March 1875. "The paper is sold on the stands of newsdealers in nearly every city in the United States," they wrote. "It undoubtedly has a regular circulation outside the city exceeding the combined country circulation of all the other evening papers, and larger than the country circulation of most morning papers."[12] The time was ripe for an illustrated daily journal, they argued, and "this paper meets a want no other [newspaper] satisfied." The *Graphic* was also suitable for all readers, the editors bragged, "all classes and conditions of men and women, and how well it satisfies the wants of the family circle, the bourse, the club, the boudoir, and the study."[13] On its third anniversary, the editors of the *Daily Graphic* again congratulated themselves on their success and praised their brand of visual journalism. "Three years ago to-day the first number of The Daily Graphic was issued," the editors noted. "Everybody pronounced the project wild and predicted its failure."[14] Yet the *Graphic* lived, the editors responded, as "a paper of exceptionally high character." Not only that, its pictures were better than ever: "The illustrations have strikingly improved both in spirit and in finish, and have found an ever-widening audience." In 1874, the American managers of the *Graphic* broke with the Canadians and their technology, a move that resulted in expensive litigation and contributed to the paper's eventual failure. The *Graphic* was also damaged by the growth of illustrations in other New York dailies, including Joseph Pulitzer's *New York World*. With the rise of the *Graphic*, Pulitzer biographer George Juergens wrote, "Pulitzer and his staff came to see in illustrations a great, unexploited medium of communication, and elevated it from an occasional novelty to an important tool in reporting the news."[15] Despite its slow start, the *World* began to run more illustrations and cartoons, Juergens found, eventually competing with and overtaking the *Graphic*. "The correlation between the *World*'s expanding use of pictures for entertainment and the *Graphic*'s demise in 1889 is too direct to be coincidental," Juergens concluded.[16]

Despite its relatively short life, the *Graphic* was an impressive pictorial paper, recognized for its timely and extensive use of illustrations and cartoons. Former *Graphic* illustrator S. H. Horgan called the paper "a marvel of its time."[17] Among its more prominent illustrators and cartoonists were A. B. Frost, Fernando Miranda, E. W. Kemble, W. A. Rogers, and Livingston Hopkins, a cartoonist who went on to greater fame in Australia, where he worked for the *Sydney Bulletin* during the nation's Federation period.[18] Like *Frank Leslie's Illustrated Newspaper* and *Harper's Weekly*, the *Daily Graphic* used allegorical cartoons to represent news makers and news events. New York City, for example, was represented as "Father Knickerbockers."[19] In a cartoon advocating improved river navigation, the paper pictured an ailing old man labeled "Father Mississippi."[20]

Among students of the nineteenth-century Indian wars, the *Daily Graphic* is best remembered for publishing the first illustration of Custer's Last Stand, an image published thirteen days after the news reached New York. The *Graphic*'s speedy response to Custer's demise was a major scoop for the paper, which beat *Harper's Weekly* by ten days.[21] The picture was entirely imaginary, though the *Graphic* claimed that the picture was created "from sketches and descriptions by our special correspondent."[22] In fact, the illustration was the work of William de la Montagne Cary, an experienced illustrator who had traveled in the West and had considerable knowledge of Indians and Indian fighting, but who was nowhere near the Little Bighorn in June 1876.[23] Nevertheless, Cary's illustration was immediately popular, glorifying the gallant Custer and setting a standard for dozens of notable Last Stand images, almost all of which featured the courageous Custer standing tall over a heap of wounded men and horses, surrounded by scowling warriors. Cary's *Daily Graphic* illustration was widely reprinted, eventually turning up in *Harper's Weekly*, *Leslie's*, and *St. Nicholas*, as well as in a popular Currier and Ives print.[24] Significantly, Cary's image got a number of details wrong, including the sabers Custer and other cavalrymen were shown wielding.[25] But accuracy was not necessary or even desirable in Little Bighorn depictions. After Custer's spectacular death at the hands of the Indians, the public did not want accuracy as much as it wanted a mythic hero—something Cary and the *Graphic* supplied.

Before the Battle

Indian images were uncommon in the *Daily Graphic* in 1874, except as spirits. During the fall of that year, the *Graphic* published a series of letters reporting on the spiritualist movement then in vogue in parts of the United States. The letters were the work of Colonel Henry S. Olcott, employed by the *Graphic* to investigate reports of strange phenomena at the Eddy homestead in Chittenden, Vermont. Olcott described numerous encounters with ghostly figures, some of whom were Indians. On November 10, 1874, for instance, Olcott's letter was called "The Smoking Squaw."[26] The featured squaw, Honto, was illustrated as an indistinct female figure wearing a long dress and—being Indian—smoking a pipe (figure 6.2). Three other Indian women also appeared to the spiritualists that night, including one that Olcott described in conventional terms:

> She was a very short woman, not above five feet high, and of a very much darker complexion than Honto. She wore a dress of dark blue or black . . . trimmed with bands of large beads that clattered as she walked. Her moccasins and leggings were also trimmed with them, and her hair was very long and thick, and hung free down her back.

Other Olcott letters identified more Indian spirits, both men and women, identified as Black Swan's Mother, Bright Star, Daybreak, White Feather, and Santum.[27]

"THE SMOKING SQUAW."

FIGURE 6.2. The *Graphic* imagined an Indian spirit, a woman named Honto, when it reported on the spiritualist movement in Vermont in 1874.

Yet Honto was the most prominent of these ghosts, turning up in a number of other stories and drawings. On November 17, 1874, the *Daily Graphic*'s illustrators showed the spiritualists' efforts to weigh and measure Honto. She was about five foot three, which should have put her weight at about 135 pounds. But Honto's weight proved confounding to Olcott, measuring as high as eighty-eight pounds and as low as fifty-eight.[28] More significantly, Olcott described Honto performing exotic activities—dancing, ringing a bell, and playing the organ.

The meaning of Honto and the other Indian spirits is not explained in Colonel Olcott's letters. In some ways, the Indians were similar to other exotics who appeared to the spiritualists at the Eddy farm, a group that included black Africans, Russians, Kurds, and Asians.[29] Long-dead Vermonters also appeared at the Eddy farm. Like these white spirits, the Indian spirits may have represented a link to the American past, a way for these seekers to deepen their connection to the land and its original inhabitants. In the nineteenth century, after all, Indians were widely believed to be a disappearing race, destined to fade into history in the face of advancing Anglo-American civilization. For the New England spiritualists, as for ordinary *Graphic* readers, the possibility of harmless Indian ghosts—ghosts who danced and played the organ—must have been a fascinating "what if" encounter with the spiritual world of ancient America.

Whatever the case, the editors of the *Graphic* did not appear fully convinced by Colonel Olcott's reports. Although the paper published his letters, the stories were inside material, published as entertainment, not serious news. In fact, Olcott's letters probably inspired the *Graphic*'s December 7, 1874, cartoon endorsing science—depicted as a Lady Liberty–style figure—shown banishing superstition.[30] The *Daily Graphic* criticized spiritualism again in a series of front-page cartoons in early December 1874. These drawings, by Livingston Hopkins, were labeled "Our Comic Artist Among the Spirits." In the center of the page, the cartoonist depicted his own image, which was surrounded by drawings of his adventures in spiritualism. After consulting a medium (who asks the cartoonist for a fee of five dollars), an Indian character named "Bringybotlywiski (Big Smoke)" materializes and has several encounters with a cartoon version of Hopkins. Besides the silly (and demeaning) name, Hopkins imagined Big Smoke in stereotypical terms with high, prominent cheeks, a small forehead, and a wide mouth (figure 6.3). The character's hair was wild and unkempt, a sign of his lack of proper grooming. Big Smoke was adorned with a huge presidential medal, typical of many actual Indians who had negotiated with whites, as well as a pipe.

This cartoon Indian, like Colonel Olcott's ghostly Indians, was not a threatening figure. After the cartoonist pricks Big Smoke with a pin "to test his genuineness," the Indian feigned violence—inspecting the cartoonist's scalp—but accepted the cartoonist's apology, and (naturally) finished off a bottle of whiskey. "And Big Smoke expresses himself perfectly satisfied," the caption explained. The last cartoon shows Big Smoke growing hazy in front of a cigar store, still holding his empty whiskey bottle.

This sort of cartoon Indian was both playful and stereotypical. Cartoonist Hopkins reinforced the all-too-real problem of the drunken Indian, but in imaginary and comedic terms. Big Smoke, after all, was a spirit, his appearance and behavior exaggerated for comedic effect. He was a wild Western Indian, not a romantic Eastern one, but he was also silly and harmless, an Indian the *Graphic*'s readers could chuckle over and appreciate. This Indian image, in other words, represented a kind of "soft" prejudice against Indians, a way of subtly emphasizing the inferiority toward Indians that was taken for granted in the last half of the nineteenth century. The *Graphic*'s readers would have no difficulty identifying with the cartoonist against Big Smoke, seeing the Indian as an object of derision and ridicule. Yet the prejudice in the cartoon was not openly hostile or mean-spirited. Refreshingly, too, the cartoon was free of violence. The suggested violence of the scalp inspection, Hopkins and his editors could claim, was merely a joke, without overt bias or racism. Nevertheless, Big Smoke, a wild and alcoholic cartoon Indian, was clearly positioned on the wrong side of progress and civilization.

In contrast to such cartoons, Indians appeared in more neutral terms in March 1876, when the *Graphic* published nine pictures from Fort Sill in present-day Oklahoma.[31] These illustrations included views of fort buildings as well as a thatched-roof

Materialized spirit of Bringybotlywiski (Big Smoke).

FIGURE 6.3. Cartoonist Livingston Hopkins
took a comic tour of the spiritualist movement
for the *Graphic* in 1874, imagining his encounters with a cartoon spirit Indian, a drunk called
"Bringybotlywiski."

structure labeled the "Summer Hut of Caddo Indians." A more popular Indian dwelling, a tepee, was also shown, listed as the "Home of a Comanche Chief." The only Indian individuals illustrated in the series were two Indians leading a horse with a travois into the Indian agency. These Indians were small figures, unidentified by name or tribe. The *Graphic* explained that these scenes were based on photographs and argued that they were "a group of very accurate sketches representing scenes and characters at Fort Sill." The link between photography and accuracy is notable here, an appeal to the camera's documentary eye as a way of establishing visual fidelity to the place itself. It is notable, too, that the photographs were all medium-distance shots, a distance that kept specific individuals and detailed cultural information out of the pictures. Of the three Indian-themed illustrations published in the *Graphic,* two tribes were named in connection with their traditional housing, but no individual Indians were identified and no specifics of the housing were published. In this instance, then, the photographic source of Indian illustrations ensured the accuracy of the scenes but omitted close-up illustrations of individual Indians or their cultures.

In a front-page cartoon published a year before the Fort Sill illustrations, the *Graphic* commented on the Indian-white conflict raging in the Black Hills. The cartoon showed a fierce, armed, well-muscled Indian standing guard over the disputed lands. A sign posted behind the warrior made clear the nature of the Indian's anger: "The United States by Solemn Treaty Pledges That the Lands Shall Be for the Exclusive Use of the Indians."[32] The top right corner of the cartoon included an inset, a circle with two warriors attacking a white mother and her child. Below, also on the right, the cartoon showed an approaching miner armed with a rifle, his wagon loaded with "Mining Stores."

THE DAILY GRAPHIC

AN ILLUSTRATED EVENING NEWSPAPER

39 & 41 PARK PLACE.

VOL. I—NO. 45.　　　　NEW YORK, THURSDAY, APRIL 24, 1873.　　　　FIVE CENTS.

OUR NEW INDIAN POLICY—WHICH IS THE SAVAGE?

FIGURE 6.4. The *Graphic* turned the power of its cartoons against the army during the Modoc war of 1873, criticizing soldiers for scalping Indians.

At first glance, the cartoon appears to be anti-Indian, but the commentary inside quickly dispels that interpretation. In fact, the *Graphic* editorial condemned the recent formation of the Sioux City and Black Hills Transportation Company in strident terms: "When white men break their most binding engagements in this way," the paper said, "it is no wonder that Indians should employ the 'means which God and nature have placed in their hands' to defend themselves."[33] In this instance, the *Graphic* recognized the duplicity of federal dealings with the Sioux and the paper used the miners' Black Hills invasion to scold the U.S. government. While this position stopped short of deep-seated Indian sympathy—the cartoon did depict two warriors killing a mother and child, after all—it was much more evenhanded than much of the Western press, and even some Eastern papers. Early in its editorial life, in fact, the *Graphic* was sympathetic enough to publish a front-page cartoon critical of Army violence against Indians, in this case the Modocs in northern California (figure 6.4). The cartoon showed a soldier with his feet on a dead Modoc warrior, proudly holding the man's bloody scalp. The caption drove home the anti-violence message: "Our New Indian Policy—Which is the Savage?"[34]

After the Battle

The number of Indian cartoons in the *Graphic* increased in the weeks following Custer's defeat, as did their hostility.[35] One of the most inflammatory anti-Indian cartoons, published on the newspaper's front page, depicted a half-Indian, half-buck creature who—having just killed and scalped a U.S. soldier—has just been shot by another soldier[36] (figure 6.5). The *Graphic*'s caption left no doubt about the specific target of this cartoon. It read, "The Right Way to Dispose of Sitting Bull and His Braves." The half-buck, half-Indian figure was not Sitting Bull, however, but an animated, extremely hostile symbol of Sitting Bull and his kind, Indian "bucks" who were wild men with no regard for human life. Violence from savages of this sort, the cartoon made clear, must be fought with greater violence. This was not a subtle message, nor was it meant to be. For the *Graphic* and its readers, the death of Custer and his men called for vengeance, even if that meant more bloodshed on the plains.

This and similar *Graphic* cartoons were among the most virulent of the anti-Indian images published in the weeks after Custer's death; neither *Harper's Weekly* nor *Frank Leslie's Illustrated Newspaper* was as openly hostile in their illustrations. What explains this difference? It's not clear, but it may be that the *Graphic* took an extreme anti-Indian position in order to gain attention and attract readers in the highly competitive New York newspaper market. As a daily illustrated paper, the *Daily Graphic* lived up to its name and beat its illustrated competitors. In sum, economic forces are a likely explanation for the speed and tone of the *Graphic*'s anti-Indian illustrations. Taking a strong anti-Indian position, after all, was likely to be popular among most of New York's commercial class, some of whom stood to gain from the subjugation of the plains Indians and the opening of the West.

FIGURE 6.5. In response to the Sioux and Cheyenne victory over Custer, the *Daily Graphic* unleashed a hideous Indian killer, half-man, half-beast, his bloody hands clawing the air.

On July 8, 1876, more than a week before the Indian-buck cartoon, the *Graphic* published an angry anti-Indian cartoon by Livingston Hopkins, a cartoon that advocated Indian extermination.[37] The cartoon showed a large Uncle Sam, complete with top hat and striped pants, chasing a group of retreating Indians (figure 6.6). Uncle Sam is holding a scythe labeled with one word: "Extermination." The caption added to the effect of the drawing: "The True Solution of the Indian Problem." Notably, the *Graphic* did not raise any moral concerns on its editorial pages regarding extermination. In fact, the call to exterminate the Sioux and other hostile tribes was common in many quarters of the press in mid-1876, though few newspapers displayed this idea as boldly as the *Daily Graphic*.

THE TRUE SOLUTION OF THE INDIAN PROBLEM.

FIGURE 6.6. Custer's defeat at the Little Bighorn brought out the worst instincts of the
Graphic, including this extermination cartoon by Livingston Hopkins.

A month after the Little Bighorn, the *Graphic* published a cartoon highlighting the problematic bond between Western Indians and Eastern humanitarians
(figure 6.7). The image depicted an armed, stern-faced but unidentified warrior
next to a forlorn image of the Reverend Wendell Phillips, a well-known Indian
sympathizer.[38] The image showed the men physically connected by a band between
their bodies, a link labeled "Our Common Humanity." This idea was meant to be
ironic since the visual cues in the cartoon did not suggest commonality. Phillips, in
fact, was turned away from his Indian brother, seemingly unhappy to be connected.
The warrior was unhappy too and, even worse, holding a large, bloody knife in his
left hand. The caption reinforced the irony of the cartoon: "Blest Be the Tie That
Binds." Below the caption, the *Graphic* printed a fake Phillips quotation:

> This, my friends, is the gallant Sioux whom Du Guesclin, Chevalier Bayard,
> and Sir Philip Sidney would receive as a brother. We are bound together by a
> common humanity, and oh! Let us assist each other to the best of our powers.
> Let us furnish the heads, and this dear brother shall scalp them.[39]

If all of this was not ironic enough, the *Graphic* offered a pointed clarification
inside the paper. The drawing, the editors noted, showed Phillips and "his *pro-
tégé,* the noble Sioux." The story explained the front-page quotation: "It will be
remembered that in a recent letter Mr. Phillips was futile enough to liken the Sioux
braves to Chevalier Bayard, Sir Philip Sidney, and Du Guesclin." The paper would

FIGURE 6.7. The Little Bighorn offered the *Graphic* an opportunity to question the ties between Indians and the Eastern humanitarians, such as the Reverend Wendell Phillips, a noted supporter of Indians.

have none of this: "The Sioux are simply bloodthirsty devils and Mr. Phillips is a deluded man."[40] The *Graphic*'s words and images were unmistakable: The Sioux were murdering demons and no amount of humanitarian praise would change that.

In an allegorical cartoon published on the *Graphic*'s front page in late July 1876, the paper identified the economic forces behind the Custer debacle.[41] C. S. Reinhart's drawing showed an encounter between three generic figures—an Indian, a civilian trader, and a soldier—at a trading post (figure 6.8). The scene was imaginary but not unusual; the trader was selling a rifle to an Indian. Money was changing hands and the Indian was admiring his new weapon. The soldier was not amused, however. Ramrod straight and resolute, he was cuffing the trader, who frowned at the soldier with a fearful look. If the dynamics of the scene were not sufficiently clear, a sign in the background made the nature of the transaction more explicit: "A Sleek Post Trader. Guns, Ammunition & Supplies Always on Hand." Finally, the cartoon's caption made plain the policy implications of the cartoon: "The True Way to Prevent Massacres by Indians." Below the caption, the editors published this admonition from the soldier to the trader: "You Rascal! How Am I to Keep Order on the Frontiers with You Selling Rum and Rifles to the Indians! If I Can Get Rid of You, the Sioux Will Be Quiet Enough."

FIGURE 6.8. Within weeks of the Little Bighorn, the *Graphic* softened its criticism of Indians. This cartoon faulted corrupt Indian traders who sold guns to the Indians to line their own pockets.

This cartoon illustrated the widespread belief that corrupt traders were the primary source of Indian arms, a belief that had a basis in fact. Indeed, the cartoon trader was obviously despicable, with "bloody" cash in hand and a guilty look on his face. More surprising, perhaps, was the calm demeanor of the cartoon Indian, depicted without rancor. He was smiling—a rare image in the illustrated press—a warrior admiring his new rifle. In this illustration, the so-called Indian problem was not the Indian's fault, or at least not entirely. The real culprit was the "sleek post trader," a completely unprincipled character driven by money. As for the army, its representative was a paragon of virtue, protecting the nation's frontier by reining in the excesses of alcohol and armaments in the West. Given the *Graphic*'s calls for extermination and its visual denunciation of Indian violence, this cartoon represented a break in the wave of anti-Indian visual propaganda in the *Daily Graphic*.

By October 1876, the *Graphic* was able to depict the war in the West in more or less neutral terms. In a series of five realistic sketches—not cartoons—the *Graphic* presented "Scenes of General Crook's Campaign Against the Sioux" without reference to hostile Indians.[42] Instead, the sketches showed the Western landscape ("Sheridan's Butte on the Yellowstone"), soldiers hunting buffalo, and Crook's headquarters in the field. The only Indians shown in these five images were the Shoshone, allies of the army, who were shown "Making Medicine" around a campfire. Notably, the accompanying explanation of the Shoshone ceremony was serious and respectful, a sign that these Indians—unlike the Sioux—were "good" Indians. The one reference to "bad" Indians here was under a drawing of the steamer *Yellowstone* being "Fired on by Indians." Yet no Indians appeared in the sketch and without the caption, readers would not have known that the *Yellowstone* was under attack. Taken together, these images illustrate a more routine representation of Indian campaigning, one marked more by drudgery and boredom than by adventure and heroism. This is significant because both the artist in the field and the *Graphic*—a publication only recently seething with anti-Indian hostility—passed up an opportunity to vent their rage at Sitting Bull, the Sioux, and Indians generally. In this instance, neither the artist nor the editors in New York felt compelled to publish violent or hateful illustrations.

A few days later, the *Graphic* published another realistic illustration of an Indian potlatch in British Columbia under its "Incidents of the Week Illustrated" label.[43] This drawing, which showed a mass of Indians in front of two tepees, offered more cultural information than anti-Indian hostility. As the story made clear, the event was a "scramble" for $15,000 worth of goods such as blankets and guns, items being thrown from the top of the tepees. Together, the illustration and the story mark these Indians as different from "civilized" whites, but—and this is significant—not violent or hostile. In fact, by publishing this drawing as one of its "Incidents of the Week," the *Graphic* was normalizing this Indian cultural activity, bringing it into daily journalism and explaining it in ways that ordinary readers could understand and, with a little imagination, appreciate.

Similarly, in late October 1876, as the Centennial Exhibition in Philadelphia was ending, the *Graphic* published a realistic appreciation of Indian material culture.[44] A three-column drawing from the exhibit hall showed visitors admiring a tepee—or "tent," as the caption put it—flanked by several totem poles. A well-dressed (white) family examined the tepee from the left side of the illustration, watching a woman and girl in the doorway of the structure. No Indians were shown, and, significantly, the illustration betrayed no animosity toward Indians nor any hint of Custer's recent defeat. In a news illustration in the exhibit hall, it seems, Indian culture could be separated from Indian violence and presented without anti-Indian bias. In the *Graphic,* this was yet another way of making Indians "safe" for public presentation, securing a benign place for Indians in late nineteenth-century visual culture.

Notably, all of these "neutral" illustrations of Indians were news drawings, not cartoons. This fact appears to underscore the rhetorical nature of the inflammatory postbattle Indian cartoons cited above. To put it another way, the *Graphic*'s cartoons were the paper's form for its editorial invective and racial allegory; its news sketches and illustrations were a place for realism and factual details. These illustrations, after all, were based on actual events and, as such, represented the paper's more traditional Indian reporting and visual journalism.

Conclusion

As documented previously, the *Daily Graphic*'s neutral and even positive news stories and illustrations in the weeks after the Little Bighorn helped balance the wave of incendiary anti-Indian cartoons and editorials that followed the battle. Although anti-Indian cartoons dominated the pages of the *Graphic* following the Custer battle, editorials and some illustrations soon suggested a break in the paper's anti-Indian campaign. Thus, the *Graphic* presented a "Cooper Indian" as a counterpoint to the savage "Custer Indian" only five weeks after the battle. The *Graphic* noted that the romantic Cooper Indian no longer existed, yet the paper's editorial located—and praised—just such Indians, people who were on the path toward civilization. Some Indians, the *Graphic* noted, were redeemable people, savages who were actually capable of civilization. Sitting Bull and the Sioux who defeated Custer's Seventh Cavalry, however, remained on the wrong side of this divide, depicted as evil Indians who had to be punished and controlled—or even exterminated. In short, the *Daily Graphic* made clear distinctions between peaceful and savage Indians, a distinction not always common in other U.S. newspapers. In an editorial in August 1876, for example, the *Graphic*'s writers laid out the specific differences between good and bad Indians. Good Indians, the paper said, were "independent sovereigns," while bad Indians were "wards of the nation."[45] Good or bad, the editorial continued, Indians "cannot be exterminated like so many wolves." The paper went on: "They can, however, be informed that they will be required to obey the laws of the land. And they can be disarmed as a condition precedent to their assuming the appeal and habits of civilization." In making this argument, the *Graphic* was following a familiar editorial path, invoking the rule of law and demanding that offending Indians be neutralized and forced to practice the "habits of civilization." In this endeavor, the paper claimed, "There is no middle ground"—a black-or-white distinction that characterized Indians as either savage or civilized. The paper then identified some of the tribes that had made the leap from savagery to civilization—"Chippewas, Chocktaws [*sic*] [and] Winnebagoes." Significantly, the paper even identified "thousands of full-blooded Sioux" as examples of civilized Indians, a remarkable distinction given the national furor over that tribe's notoriety in the aftermath of the Little Bighorn. By recognizing both good and bad bands of Sioux, the *Graphic* again broke from the rampant and overarching anti-Sioux sentiment of 1876, an ideology that dominated much of the popular press in the last half of that year.

In the case of the *Daily Graphic,* this analysis shows that the Little Bighorn did change the nature of Indian cartoons. Before the battle, Indians appeared infrequently in the paper and when they did appear, they were not depicted as a national scourge. The most common cartoon image before the battle were as New England spirits, harmless and amusing ghosts who seemed to represent not savagery but a tie to aboriginal America. The Indian victory over Custer changed that image, at least for a time. Custer's fame and the public presumption of his invincibility ensured that this battle and his death would be a huge news story. The *Graphic,* like other mainstream papers, reacted to the news with outrage toward Sitting Bull and the Sioux. As a picture paper, the *Graphic* published several scathing anti-Indian cartoons. But the *Graphic,* unlike some other papers, soon moderated its hostility. Its editorials identified some good Indians, even among the hostile Sioux, and its anti-Indian cartoons disappeared. The paper's news illustrations reinforced this moderate tone, depicting Indians in more neutral terms. In the final analysis, the *Graphic* published some of the most racist and hateful anti-Indian cartoons, but it also retreated quickly from that extreme position and assumed a more moderate tone. None of this is to say that the paper was a pro-Indian journal, but it does suggest that the rabid tone of its most infamous cartoons was an extreme position, one the *Graphic* did not wish to sustain.

CHAPTER 7

Remington's Indian Illustrations

Race, Realism, and Pictorial Journalism

In May 2006, the *Fort Worth Star-Telegram* asked its readers to vote for the city's favorite artwork. At the request of the newspaper, Forth Worth's three major museums—the classical Kimball Art Museum, the avant-garde Modern Art Museum, and the Western-themed Amon Carter Museum—each nominated three popular pieces, a list that included an Andy Warhol self-portrait and a colorful flower by Georgia O'Keeffe. The winner, however, was an older, more glorious American painting, Frederic Remington's *A Dash for the Timber,* an action-packed image of cowboys fleeing a band of attacking Apaches.

Star-Telegram art critic Gaile Robinson was not surprised. "Romanticized exploits of a nation's most colorful past seem to pull strongest at the heartstrings of later generations," Robinson wrote.[1] Indeed, *A Dash for the Timber* is one of Remington's most famous works largely because it celebrates a triumphant national past, a time of manly activity and Western adventure. *Star-Telegram* readers made similar points. "My great-grandfather founded our family ranch in Aledo in 1883, and so I have always admired how such artists as Remington and [Charles M.] Russell were able to capture the rapidly changing landscape of that golden era of expansion," one reader concluded.[2] Another reader cited Remington's work as a Fort Worth favorite because "it fits our heritage better than all the others."[3]

Robinson and her readers got it right: Remington's exciting 1889 image—animated horses with hooves flying, cowboys blasting the charging Indians—does represent the "golden" heritage celebrated by many citizens of Fort Worth. More generally, Remington's painting represents the popular heritage celebrated across the American West, a land where brave men conquered the wild land and its people. The painting succeeds, in fact, largely because it captures a powerful, mythical moment in the American historical imagination, a time the *Star-Telegram* reader called the "golden era of expansion." For more than a century, Americans have romanticized the taming of the West, preferring heroic images of glory and conquest to the more realistic—and depressing—depictions of frontier life. Remington's hard-riding cowboys are fleeing their attackers, of course, but few Americans even in the nincteenth century doubted that civilization would triumph over savagery or that American values—individualism, expansionism, capitalism, and social progress—would dominate the continent. No wonder, then, that the good citizens of Fort Worth selected *A Dash for the Timber* as the city's favorite artwork in 2006.

Yet the action and excitement in Remington's famous painting obscures a number of themes Fort Worth and the rest of America might not want to celebrate, such as the displacement and racial subjugation of Native Americans. *A Dash for the Timber* emphasizes the pounding action of the chase and the bravery of the frontiersmen, but minimizes and subtly subverts the Apache legitimacy to the land. Cowboys and their horses dominate the canvas. The Apache attackers, in contrast, are revealed only on the far right edge of the painting, literally a marginal presence in the scene. Moreover, the painting suggests no reason for the Apache aggression. They attack, perhaps, because they are savages and that is what savages do. Or perhaps they attack because they are defending their lands, though this fact is not suggested in Remington's image. Significantly, too, *A Dash for the Timber* portrays an imaginary scene, not an actual incident. In other words, Remington created a dramatic Western chase in which cowboys were the victims of Indian aggression, a scene that surely happened many times in the West but also one that reversed the more general story of American conquest. Despite thousands of Indian raids on white travelers and settlements as well as a few battlefield successes against the army, the ultimate outcome of the Indian-white contest was never in doubt. Indian "savagery" was doomed; civilization and progress were inevitable. By 1889, only a handful of Indians remained free of government control; most had been subdued, confined, and impoverished. Nevertheless, Remington created a seemingly realistic depiction of Western men in action, one that highlighted frontier excitement over actual events or the larger historical truth. In *A Dash for the Timber,* Remington created on canvas a wholly believable and dramatic Western myth, where valiant cowboys wrested control of the wilderness from a relentless and ruthless enemy. It was—and is—a useful and highly popular way of celebrating America's westward expansion, a story Americans have told and retold for more than a century.[4]

As suggested by his continuing popularity in Fort Worth, Remington has been considered one of the "primary visual mythmakers of the Old West" for more than a century.[5] Peter Hassrick, the leading Remington biographer and scholar, has summarized Remington's importance to Western imagery in sweeping language: "Of the many writers and artists who have glorified the Western experience, none has been more singularly devoted, more overwhelmingly prolific, or more enduring than [Remington]. For millions of Americans and Europeans, his name has become synonymous with the West."[6] Despite this Western identity, Remington was a New York native who studied art at Yale and lived most of his life near New York City. Although he died young—at age forty-eight—he was an enormously successful and energetic Western artist, completing more than 2,700 paintings and drawings, publishing illustrations in forty-one different magazines, and illustrating 142 books.[7] He also created a number of iconic Western sculptures, art so popular that reproductions of his sculptures sell steadily today. For all these reasons, Remington's Western illustrations, paintings, and sculptures—his cowboys, horses, soldiers, buffalo, and Indians—are among the most significant Western images ever created, images that have reinforced the glories of expansion and conquest for several generations of white Americans.

Given Remington's enormous significance in defining the American West, this chapter investigates the social, cultural, and ideological assumptions surrounding Remington's early career as a pictorial journalist, especially his illustrations of Indians and Indian life. Although these images have been largely overlooked by art historians and other scholars,[8] Remington's Indian drawings appeared in a variety of popular journals, including *Harper's Weekly, Outing, Century,* and *Scribner's.* Indeed, these and other popular illustrations made Remington a famous artist, which—ironically—gave him the chance to give up illustrated journalism in order to pursue a career as a serious painter. Moreover, Remington's work as an illustrator had a profound effect on his paintings, especially in their subject matter and themes. This chapter asks the following questions about Remington's Indian illustrations: What ideas influenced his illustrations and how did these ideas shape his Indian images? What methods did he use and what themes did he emphasize? Finally, why and how were Remington's Indian illustrations understood and what influences did they have on the reading public's immediate and long-term view of Indians? To answer these questions, the chapter describes and analyzes a number of Remington's newspaper illustrations in the context of Remington's personal history, ideology, and artistic motives. Building on this material, I examine a representative number of Remington's Indian illustrations and draw a number of specific as well as general conclusions about the ideology and meaning of Remington's Indian illustrations in the last years of the nineteenth century.

Beyond biography and professionalism, the chapter investigates the production and meaning of Remington's Indian illustrations from a broad cultural and ideological perspective. This analysis applies James Carey's "ritual view of communication," a view that suggests that all representations, including apparently "realistic" illustrations and photographs, incorporate a point of view as well as social and cultural assumptions, and thus involve some degree of imagination, distortion, and misrepresentation.[9] Concerning popular Native American representations, the ritual view holds that such images incorporate a set of ideas and assumptions or, in Carey's phrase, "the representation of shared beliefs." As we shall see, Remington's Indian illustrations were rich with shared assumptions about the nature and status of Indians in American life. Thus Remington's Indian imagery could be more or less accurate, but his images were always in service of a larger cultural mission, a mission tied to telling a specific kind of American story. In addition, the study argues that the viewers of Remington's Indian illustrations routinely interpreted those images against a background of Western tales and Indian clichés, stereotypes, myths, and other cultural information. Thus the purpose of this chapter is not to praise or criticize Remington's historical accuracy or details—a veritable cottage industry among some art critics and Western history buffs[10]—but to provide a deeper and more illuminating ideological and cultural understanding of Remington's Indian illustrations and to identify the major themes Remington used to create popular and "useful" Indian images, pictures that could enliven an illustrated newspaper and capture the mythic American West that the public longed to see and celebrate.

Colonel Remington's Boy

Frederic Remington was born in 1861 in Canton, New York, to Clara Sackrider Remington and Seth Pierpont Remington. His mother's family was prominent in Canton; his father was a dedicated Republican and the founder of a local newspaper, the *St. Lawrence Plaindealer*.[11] Thanks to his father, Fred's upbringing was shaped by military training and athletic experiences. Shortly after Frederic's birth, Seth Remington sold his newspaper in order to serve as a cavalry officer in the Civil War. Captain Remington served the Union army with distinction, retiring from the army as a major, though he was known thereafter as "Colonel." "Fred had every right to glow with the pride he felt in his dashing father," Hassrick has noted.[12] In fact, young Fred's boyhood seems to have been dominated by his active and heroic father. As a horseman and investor in horse racing, the senior Remington took Fred to fairs and racetracks, where the boy began his lifelong interest in horses. Remington also proved to be, in the words of another biographer, "a sturdy active boy, a swimmer, a rider, a fisher and a leader in all sports."[13] In 1876, Seth Remington thought his son needed a more disciplined education and shipped Fred off to the Highland Military Academy in Worcester, Massachusetts, where he studied military tactics, dreamed of battlefield glory, and, significantly, discovered a newfound artistic ability.[14] In his free time, Hassrick discovered, Remington discussed sketches with a fellow cadet, Julian Wilder. Wilder, in turn, led Remington to a friend in Maine, Scott Turner, whose drawings impressed young Fred. "You draw splendidly," Remington wrote to Turner. Foreshadowing his future career, Remington added, "Your favorite subject is soldiers. So is mine."[15] Remington's ability with a pencil impressed other cadets as well, and he entertained his classmates with caricatures of other students and teachers at the school.

In 1878, Remington enrolled in the School of Fine Arts at Yale, where he studied drawing with John Henry Niemeyer, a teacher who emphasized the power of the line, a skill that Remington honed as a popular illustrator. At Yale, Remington published his first illustration in a college newspaper, the *Courant*. But Remington chafed under Niemeyer's instruction, and his chief interest on campus was athletics. "Remington loved football," Hassrick concluded. "He was a natural athlete, displaying strength and skill which enabled him to excel in all sports, including boxing and horsemanship."[16] Remington was so gung-ho about Yale football, Hassrick reported, that he allegedly "dipped his jersey in blood at a local slaughterhouse 'to make it look more business-like.'"[17]

Remington's Yale career was cut short in 1879 when his father died. Remington's new guardian was his uncle, Lamartin Remington of Albany, who disapproved of Fred's interest in art. He persuaded Fred to leave school and take a series of government clerkships in Albany. According to Hassrick, Remington hated this work and spent much of his time sketching pictures of his fellow workers. In fall 1879, young Fred met an alluring young woman, Eva Caten, from Gloversville, New York. The couple soon fell in love, but when Remington asked Eva's father for her hand, he was refused. Remington took this refusal as a sign of his limited prospects as a clerk. Like many ambitious young men before him, Remington saw brighter prospects in the West. "It was a land he had dreamed and read of for years," Hassrick wrote, "and there would be no better chance to see it than now."[18] In August 1881, Remington traveled west for the first time, going as far as Montana, where he met—and drew—a variety of Western characters and scenes. A few weeks later, he began his pictorial art career in earnest, traveling to New York City with a portfolio full of Western drawings. He managed to sell one to George W. Curtis of *Harper's Weekly*. Curtis turned the drawing over to veteran illustrator William A. Rogers, who redrew it for publication. It appeared as a full-page illustration in February 1882, with Remington credited for the original sketch. Remington was thrilled. He could now see possibilities in the West, a place where his art could flourish and his prospects could rise, perhaps enough to impress Eva Caten's stubborn father.

Remington's big chance came in October 1882, when he turned twenty-one and was able to claim his inheritance. With the encouragement of an old Yale classmate who was raising sheep in eastern Kansas, Remington decided to try his luck as a rancher. In March 1883, he traveled west and bought a ranch near Peabody, Kansas. He hired ranch hands, bought sheep, and repaired buildings. By the fall, he had doubled his acreage and learned a great deal about the challenges of sheep ranching. Uncle Lamartin even traveled from New York to celebrate Remington's twenty-second birthday on the Kansas prairie. Remington's success as a sheep rancher proved enough for Eva's father. In May 1884, Remington sold the ranch and returned to New York. The couple married in September 1884 and began life together in Kansas City, where Remington had purchased a house. He invested in a saloon, which prospered initially. Remington spent his days playing pool at the saloon, boxing, and riding. He also continued sketching, which turned out to be useful after the saloon relocated, and, in some sort of financial sleight of hand, Remington lost his investment. Down on his luck and out of money, the young couple returned to New York in 1885. Eva moved back home, and Remington went to New York City again to sell his drawings. He sold a second sketch to *Harper's Weekly*, though it too was redrawn.[19] Realizing that his skills needed improvement, Remington took three classes at the Arts Student League in New York. The classes helped, but Remington was impatient and anxious to go west again. This time, however, he went west with press credentials. *Harper's Weekly* wanted illustrations of the Apache campaign in Arizona, especially its notorious leader, Geronimo.[20] Although the army could not find Geronimo or his band, the *Harper's* assignment was a turning point for the young illustrator. Remington returned to New York with colorful frontier experiences, adventures he fully absorbed and re-created on the page. By 1886, Remington's artistic skill had improved and his confidence blossomed. He was well on his way to becoming a leading chronicler of Western life.

A brave father, a love of horses, athleticism, a military education, sheep ranching, and adventures in the West—all these experiences shaped Frederic Remington's life as an adult and his career as an artist. As Colonel Remington's son, Remington was a "man's man," tough, robust, and vital. This background proved ideal for Remington's self-discovery in the West, a vast and sometimes treacherous place that Remington could re-create in his imagination and on the printed page. Yet Remington's experience in the West was more mundane than heroic. Despite his travels in Montana and his months as a Kansas sheep rancher, Remington's life in the West was tedious, hardly the stuff of Western myth. Remington was not an experienced cowboy, for instance, even though this notion became a part of his popular identity.[21] Indeed, Remington encouraged the belief that he was an experienced Westerner because that idea helped bolster the perceived credibility of his drawings and paintings. To his credit, Remington did seek adventures in the West and he was able to observe Indians and cowboys in action. These observations—plus a dash of imagination and more than a little drama—helped Remington develop his "authentic" Western style—romantic, action-oriented cowboys, soldiers, and Indians. Such images fed the public appetite for exciting adventures in the West and helped Remington become the most famous artist of the American West.

Ideology, Indians, and Representation

Remington came of age as an artist in the last decades of the nineteenth century during an era dominated by social Darwinism, a philosophy that honored the heroic, self-made individual, people Remington called "men with the bark on."[22] Beyond his hypermasculine upbringing, Remington critic Alexander Nemerov has noted that Remington was a disciple of American philosopher John Fiske, who was in turn a follower of Herbert Spencer, the nineteenth-century British thinker who popularized social Darwinism and introduced, in Herbert Altschull's words, "the unfortunate phrase 'survival of the fittest.'"[23] Following that idea, Remington saw evidence for social evolution as he traveled in the American West. Pioneers and frontiersmen— that is, white, civilized Christians—were at the top of the evolutionary hierarchy, Remington believed, while Negroes and Indians, among others, were several rungs down the evolutionary ladder. Indians could be admired for their physical prowess, Remington thought, but they were in no way the intellectual equal of whites.

After visiting Apaches in Arizona, for instance, Remington described the "glaring incongruities" of the Apache mind. "I often think that he has no mental process, but is the creature of impulse," Remington wrote. "The searching of the ethnologist must not penetrate his thoughts too rapidly, or he will find that he is reasoning for the Indian not with him."[24] Remington's social Darwinism reflects a common nineteenth-century belief that Indians were primitive, instinctive creatures, more akin to animals than to civilized human beings. This idea also represents an explanatory motive for some of Remington's most interesting Indian illustrations, images that attempted to capture the mysteries of these "strange" and very different people. In Remington's mind, Indians were a worthy subject because they were a primitive and colorful ethnic "other," both physically and, as these quotes show, mentally.

Although he liked individual Indians and could be sympathetic to the plight of Indian peoples, Remington held fast to the hard realities of social evolution, in which the strong dominated the weak.[25] Nemerov has noted, for example, that Remington applied social Darwinism to his Western art. "[Remington's] writing and painting repeatedly refer to evolutionary processes that he hoped would eventually leave all but the Anglo-Saxon race extinct. He referred to Indians and so-called half-breeds, for example, as part of 'the scrap-heap of departing races.'"[26]

Given his interest in rugged, self-made men, it is no surprise that Remington's Western illustrations included many such characters—cowboys, soldiers, and Indians, three categories of Americans who could be admired for their masculine vitality. Remington particularly admired Indian men for their ferocity and toughness. After observing some Apache scouts, for example, Remington reported that the men were as "wild and savage as any race of men who ever lived." He continued: "The tales of their endurance in traveling are almost incredible. That they are cruel, one does not have to look a second time to guess."[27] Yet Remington was always more comfortable with soldiers and cowboys than with Indians, people he professed not to understand.[28] In fact, Remington never lived among Indian people for any extended period and, beyond his observations at army camps and Indian agencies, he had little experience with Indians.

Remington, then, was of two minds about Indians and Indian life. As a disciple of social evolution, he was a scientific racist who saw Indians as primitives from the low end of the social hierarchy. Yet Remington appreciated the power and dynamism of Indian life, aspects of Native American culture that he celebrated in his pictorial journalism. Indeed, effectively dramatizing Indians in a way the public could embrace was perhaps the most important element of his success as an illustrated journalist.[29]

Making "Realism" Real: Remington's Methods and Themes

Remington's "realistic" treatment of Western people and scenes was one of his most powerful strengths as a Western artist. From his first *Harper's* assignment in the West and throughout his career as a pictorial journalist, Remington focused on the people and activities of Western life, which he rendered in highly detailed and apparently realistic illustrations. Many of these drawings focused on the "Western" characteristics of the people he observed, especially their facial features, clothing, hats, weapons, and the like. Indeed, Remington produced hundreds of small but detailed drawings from the West, static images and informal portraits that represent one of his most prominent themes as a pictorial journalist.[30]

From the beginning of his career, Remington worked with both a sketchbook and a camera.[31] The camera, in fact, allowed Remington to produce detailed and apparently accurate illustrations. On his initial *Harper's* assignment, for instance, Remington took many photographs in southern Arizona and northern Mexico, some of which he worked into documentary images of campaign life for *Harper's*. These drawings included a two-page spread called "Mexican Troops in Sonora," which consisted of five images of soldiers.[32] Remington also produced a two-page spread of Indians called "Sketches among the Papagos of San Xavier, 1886–1887." These sketches focused mostly on the daily lives of the Papagos, as their individual titles indicate: "Home, Sweet Home," "Grinding [Corn]," and "Moving the Crops," as well as a profile portrait of an old Papago man, "Pehurreetar." Again, most of these drawings were realistic representations based on Remington's own photographs.[33]

Later in his career as an illustrator and artist, Remington relied more on models and Western artifacts to add accurate details to drawings and paintings produced in his New York studio. "Remington made numerous trips west throughout his career, [but] he always lived near Manhattan," Nemerov has noted. "If he wanted to sketch a buffalo, he went to the Bronx Zoo. If he wanted to portray a mounted soldier or Indian, he posed a model on a saddle display in his backyard in New Rochelle."[34] As he developed as a Western illustrator, Remington took increasing pride in the accuracy of his images and his studio was filled with cowboy and Indian clothing and artifacts that he used to make his drawings and paintings more realistic. In 1891, a *Harper's Weekly* writer, Julian Ralph, provided this description of Remington's studio:

> The trophies of his many visits and errands to the West hang all about the walls and litter the floors delightfully. Axes, clubs, saddles, spears, bow and arrows, shields, queer water-tight baskets, quaint rude rugs, gorgeous examples of beadwork, lariats, and hundreds of curios from the desert and wilderness complete a collection that has been a mine of profit and a well-sprung pleasure to him.[35]

These props surely helped Remington cultivate an air of realism and authenticity in his Western illustrations and paintings. But photographs, models, and props did not guarantee literal accuracy in Remington's Indian illustrations. As with famed Indian photographer Edward S. Curtis, Remington could use clothing and artifacts many times, blurring tribal distinctions and creating an inaccurate setting.[36] In other words, even detailed and superficially accurate drawings of clothing, weapons, and artifacts in Remington's Indian work provide no assurance that these items appeared on the correct subject or in the correct context. As we shall see, some of Remington's most acclaimed Indian illustrations were not based on props, photographs, or observed action in the West, but on his fertile imagination. As a pictorial journalist, Remington achieved his greatest success when he used his artistic license to create exciting and highly symbolic Indian scenes, an exercise that produced a type of realism that rang true in the mind of the public, regardless of its literal truth.

The Indian Type

Much of Remington's pictorial journalism focused on faces, including the faces of cowboys, soldiers, and Indians in the West. While these images appear realistic, Remington's social evolutionary ideas influenced some of his Indian portraits. This ideology also shaped his artistic interest in characteristic "types" of individuals, especially the masculine "types" he found in the West. In 1886, for example, Remington published a set of sketches of frontiersmen in *Harper's Weekly* with this telling title: "Types from Arizona."[37] In 1888, he published pictures of several "types" of Canadian Mounted Police[38] and sketches of "Old-Time Types."[39] Over the years, Remington illustrated many other Western "types" as well, including *A Texas Cowboy, A French Canadian Trapper, A Mounted Infantryman, An Apache Indian,* and many more.[40]

Remington found this categorization scheme useful because it helped crystallize his depiction of enduring Western figures, emphasizing particular characteristics of each "type" in ways the public could understand and appreciate. Indeed, the public did appreciate Remington's Western "types," which was one key to his early (and continuing) popularity. Remington's strong visual categorization, however, reduced the individualism of his sketches and portraits, reinforcing existing Western clichés and stereotypes. In this way, Remington's popular Western "types" worked against more personal or idiosyncratic representations of Western men—and Remington focused largely on men[41]—and toward familiar generalizations of these subjects.

Despite his keen interest in accuracy and ethnographic details, Remington's emphasis on Western and Indian "types" included a number of none-too-subtle racial signs. A series of drawings called "In the Lodges of the Blackfeet Indians" (figure 7.1) illustrates this point. In these drawings, Remington documented the particulars of native dress, hairstyles, lodging, and camp activity. Remington also drew several individuals, including a typical Blackfoot "Warrior," a "Squaw and Papoose," "A Family Group," a single man "In Winter Costume," and so on, all relatively straightforward documentation of scenes from the Indian frontier.[42]

One Blackfoot drawing in particular, however, seemed to go beyond simple documentation, displaying what historian Joshua Brown has called "physiognomic codes of race."[43] In this case, the subject was a warrior named Man-Shot, depicted in a

FIGURE 7.1. Frederic Remington's belief in social evolution shaped his creation of Indian "types," including the racially coded faces of Blackfeet Indians.

"Blackfoot Profile." Man-Shot's mouth is open, his brow is sloped, his expression is hard—details that are not an accident. That is, Remington's depiction of Man-Shot emphasized his "savage" facial features, a way of racially coding the worst characteristics of Blackfoot warriors. As noted earlier, Remington admired the vigor and toughness of Indian men. By depicting Man-Shot as dour and primitive, Remington was identifying him as a particular Indian "type" that he (and *Harper's* readers) had come to expect in the West. This was the Indian image that Remington went on to celebrate in his most popular pictorial journalism and paintings, the Indian warrior who could be rendered as a racially distinct enemy, a physically identifiable, exotic "other." Commenting on another Indian man he met, Remington made the characteristics of this racial representation perfectly clear: "Never was there a face so replete with human depravity, stolid, ferocious, arrogant, and all the rest."[44]

Remington's emphasis on distinct racial features is clear in other drawings as well. In an 1889 illustration published in *Century Magazine,* for example, Remington drew the face of an Apache soldier with a broad, pronounced nose and big lips. In fact, Remington's Apache man has distinctly simian features, an emblem of his primitive nature.[45] On occasion, Remington also rendered African American soldiers in a similar fashion, men with open mouths, large lips, and highly animated expressions.[46] Again, such depictions were racially coded and displayed the visual signs of social Darwinism, a hierarchy in which Indians and Negroes occupied the lower rungs.

Remington created a similarly primitive Indian in a painting published in *Harper's New Monthly Magazine* in 1892. This image, titled *The Courrier du Bois and the Savage,* depicted two archetypes of the wilderness experience, the French trapper and the American Indian.[47] The men meet on the shore of a northern lake, shaking hands in what Hassrick called "a fond gesture of greeting."[48] But the two men are portrayed in very different ways. The trapper is erect and fully clothed in fringed buckskin. He holds the barrel of his rifle in his left hand, a tomahawk in his belt. The Indian, whose tribe is unknown, is clothed only in a breechcloth and his back is slightly hunched. A quiver of arrows and a bow are strapped to his back. Unlike the trapper, the Indian's feet are bare. Remington emphasized the Indian's lean leg and arm muscles and gave the Indian an appropriately gaunt and "savage" chin, cheekbone, and nose. In all these ways, Remington's image illustrates the meeting of two worlds: the indigenous American savage—tough and elemental—and his rugged but more civilized companion, the French trapper.

This painting is yet another example of Remington's fascination with types and the symbolism of those types. There is no hint here of the names of these men because they were not men Remington saw in 1892 when he created the painting. To Remington, his editors, and his readers, a specific trapper shaking hands with a specific Indian was less important—and less meaningful—than this imaged scene that contained within it the symbolic power of frontier life. In this imagined West, French trappers and Indians met and shook hands as frontier brothers with a common goal: to gather furs and exploit the rich bounty of the wilderness. The painting was wholly imaginary but nonetheless "real" because it encompassed a national narrative that Americans wanted to believe.

The Indian Enemy

Remington's many sketches of Indian artifacts and Indian faces represent a significant part of his work as a pictorial journalist. But many of these illustrations were mundane, even ordinary. Many served more as visual documents of Indians and Indian life than as compelling visual narratives of the Western experience. To serve that larger purpose, and to tell that more exciting story, Remington also produced hundreds of more action-oriented Indian images. These representations pleased his editors in New York and became the basis for his growing reputation as the greatest artist of the American West.

To make these action-based drawings, Remington had to forgo the use of his camera. Nineteenth-century photographic equipment was too slow and too bulky to capture the Indian fighting the public longed to see. Remington was surely aware of this fact; even before he witnessed any Indian fighting, Remington created action drawings based on scenes he did not witness and could not photograph. His 1886 *Harper's Weekly* drawing of the wounded Corporal Scott, for instance, was based on a rescue story he heard from soldiers in Arizona.[49] Intrigued by the incident, Remington restaged the rescue in camp and took photographs of the soldiers to re-create their poses during the event.[50] The result was a secondhand but dramatic scene from the Indian frontier, an illustration that told a happy—and exciting—story of soldiers overcoming the Indian threat.

Notably, the Indians themselves were not always depicted in this early Remington Indian-fighting image. As it happens, Remington created a number of Indian-free battle scenes, drawings, and paintings in which soldiers were threatened by absent or nearly absent warriors. Another early *Harper's Weekly* drawing from Arizona, for instance, was called "The Apaches Are Coming."[51] It shows a rider coming to the door of an adobe home, warning the settlers of an Indian attack. No Apaches appear in the illustration. Similarly, Remington illustrated two Indian battles in which the soldiers are the central interest and the Indian attackers are assigned to the margins of the drawing. In a "Fight over a Water Hole," the artist locates himself near the water hole that two troopers are defending.[52] The Indians are barely visible on the horizon, their tribe unnamed but their threat unmistakable. The Indian threat is more prominent in Remington's 1879 drawing "Forsythe's Fight on the Republican River, 1868," but his perspective is similar: safely behind the army lines where he might have witnessed the fighting (though this battle took place when Remington was a boy, years before he became an illustrator).

In these examples, Indians themselves are absent or only marginally visible, but they are always threatening. This "Indian threat" theme supports both Remington's own social philosophy as well as his editor's desire for excitement from the Indian frontier. It also reinforces popular notions of Western conquest. In these images, Remington depicts Indians in one of their most obvious and notorious roles: as obstacles to Western expansion. By repeating and dramatizing this familiar theme, Remington was also contributing to its popularity, adding his own imagery to a long-standing visual trope about Indians in the West.

Another example of the enemy theme reveals how Remington moved from journalist to acclaimed painter and fine artist. One of Remington's most well-known illustrations, later re-created as an oil painting, was called "The Last Lull in the Fight" (figure 7.2) It depicts three tough frontiersmen at rest on a battlefield, encircled by the arrow-strewn bodies of their horses. The Indian attackers are absent, suggested only by the lethal projectiles surrounding the white fighters. It is a dramatic and newsworthy image, suitable for *Harper's Weekly* and, in its painted form, good enough to win a second-place medal in the 1889 Paris International Exposition.[53] This depiction and similar Remington illustrations reinforced the idea of Indians as enemies of civilization. By nineteenth-century standards, of course, the image was accurate enough; the Indian wars had been fought off and on for decades across the West. When this image was created, however, most Indians were confined to

FIGURE 7.2. Remington's work ennobled white resistance to Indian violence, focusing on heroic moments likely to catch the reader's eye, even when the details of such incidents were products of his vivid imagination.

reservations and the major Indian wars were over. Nevertheless, Remington and *Harper's Weekly* were keeping alive the adventure and romance of an earlier time, a time that had already fixed itself in the American mind.

In other action-oriented drawings, Remington moved the enemies of civilization to the center of his work. His illustration "Arrest of a Blackfeet Murderer" (figure 7.3) repeated the theme of the Indian as outlaw.[54] This engraving, published in *Harper's Weekly* in March 1888, was packed with drama. Two mounted cavalrymen ride alongside the accused Indian, pistols pointed at his head. The warrior frowns toward one of the soldiers, his left arm stretched up and outward, his left palm open to the sky. The mounts are in full gallop, hooves flying. It is an exciting example of Remington's most engaging pictorial journalism: men on powerful horses struggling for supremacy in the uncivilized West. As in other drawings, this image suggested the soldiers' duty and heroism. The savage, Remington seems to say, has committed the most serious crime—murder—and the forces of justice must be brought to bear. Finally, the illustration also provided *Harper's* with the action-packed West its readers wanted to see: the clash between the old ways of the Indians and the new realities of the wilderness tamed. Once again, Remington delivered the myth of the West in a way that was dramatic and easily understandable.

The Indian enemy theme was prominent even when Remington functioned more directly as a pictorial reporter, illustrating an Indian news event. In an illustration

FIGURE 7.3. The struggle for control of the West—all but over when Remington made this drawing in 1888—provided drama for the illustrated press and reinforced the idea of Indians as enemies of civilization.

called "The Turbulent Crows" (figure 7.4), Remington stressed the danger posed by the savages.[55] This image depicted the outcome of a power shift on the Crow reservation that Hassrick described as "the end of Crow passivity."[56] The Crows, Hassrick explained, had long been allies of the white in battles against their traditional enemies, the Sioux. But in October 1887, some reservation Crows became restless. A few of their warriors fell under the influence of some militant Indians, including Sword-Bearer, a chief who claimed his magic shirt was bulletproof. The local Indian agent, Henry E. Williamson, ordered the renegades arrested after they stole some horses from a Piegan band. The renegades responded by firing into the agency buildings. Although no one was injured, the event made news and led to a confrontation in which troops killed Sword-Bearer and subdued his men.

Harper's Weekly covered the initial violence in a story accompanied by a Remington illustration. The engraving emphasized the most common theme in nineteenth-century Indian news; namely, Indian violence against whites. Although no whites appear in the image, Remington focused on the angry warriors firing into Indian agency buildings. Remington, however, was not there to witness the event,

FIGURE 7.4. Although the Crows were often allies of the army during the Indian wars, Remington focused on Crow anger during a dispute at a Western agency in 1887.

although he had been to Montana and had some knowledge of Indians there. In other words, Remington created a group of representative Crow renegades shooting at an imaginary agency based on the details in the news story and his memory. At its best, Remington's illustration gave a general sense of what this event might have looked like. The agency buildings, the Indians, and their horses served as symbols of Crow violence, more of a representative illustration than a literal depiction of the scene. This was entirely effective for *Harper's* and its readers, providing a sense of Indian danger that was more "authentic"—and thus more useful—than a literal or more accurate drawing of the scene.

Meaning and Significance

Remington's Indian illustrations were clearly shaped by his belief in a racial hierarchy that placed whites atop the ladder of civilization. For Remington, Indians were a barbarous and inferior people doomed to disappear if they did not adopt civilized habits and beliefs.[57] But Remington was not absolute in his negative views of Indians. As noted earlier, Remington praised Indian men for their fierceness. He admired their bravery and masculine power. In short, Remington thought of Indian men as colorful, living symbols of a savage race and he was fascinated by their mysterious ways. Beyond his documentation of Indians and Indian artifacts, Remington routinely emphasized "savage" and "primitive" qualities of Indians in his most popular illustrations. Yet Remington's focus on Indians and Indian life was never comprehensive or fully sympathetic. His sketches, portraits, and battle scenes focused on the harsher aspects of Native American life, a focus that misrepresented the actual variety of individuals and tribes and their interactions with whites in the American West. Professional considerations also shaped Remington's Indian images. *Harper's Weekly* wanted pictures from the Indian frontier, the more action-packed and exciting the better. This gave Remington another incentive to go beyond the simple documentation of artifacts and Indian activities and to emphasize the savagery of Indians and the excitement of Indian fighting, even when he was far from the action and created the details from his own experience and imagination.

In a larger sense, it seems likely as well that both *Harper's Weekly* and Remington were interested in representing—and exploiting—Indians as cultural outsiders, as exotic "others." This was the time, after all, when Americans became increasingly interested in exotic cultures at home and abroad. The National Geographic Society, for instance, was founded in 1888, part of a new national interest in bringing the entire world to American parlors and living rooms. *National Geographic* magazine, also founded in 1888, published its first photographs in 1896.[58] Around the turn of the twentieth century, photographer Edward Curtis emphasized this theme in some Indian and non-Indian photographs. Curtis costumed and posed an African American woman as *A Desert Queen,* for instance, complete with props—necklace, tiara, and a sexualized low-cut garment. Curtis also photographed a Seattle judge's wife, Caroline McGilvra Burke, as *The Egyptian,* a photograph that included some of the "desert queen's" prop jewelry.[59] These examples show how popular visual imagery could be—and often was—created to conform to cultural trends. *Harper's Weekly,* a successful New York publication, and its most popular artist, Frederic Remington, were not immune to such trends. Indeed, they sought to capitalize on them so that their images would remain popular—and profitable.

The Indian representations of Remington and Edward Curtis are linked in a number of respects. In fact, Christopher Lyman has written about the popularity of Curtis's Indian photographs in terms that could easily be applied to some of Remington's Indian drawings and paintings. "The Curtis Indians," Lyman notes, "have come to occupy a particular place in the pantheon of cherished symbols that inform us about our American identity."[60] So too did Remington's Indians help define popular ideas about savagery and civilization on the frontier. In short, both men created powerful and visually effective Indian "types" for popular consumption. Both artists, however, deliberately manipulated their subjects to fit the myth.

Frederic Remington's Indian illustrations were well within the main currents of nineteenth-century American racial ideology, representing Indians as cultural outsiders, people opposed to the civilizing ideology of American life. Remington's imagery was not unusual or highly original, but he was perhaps the most successful illustrator of Indians and Western scenes because of his blending of realistic details with larger themes of conquest and destiny. In his newspaper and magazine illustrations, Remington took advantage of an instant nostalgia for the Wild West, creating and reifying a romantic national fantasy. Remington found tremendous success representing the exciting illusion of Western reality, images that wrapped apparently accurate details in a powerful ideology of American glory. This combination resonated with the public on a mythic level, delivering a believable portrait of Western adventure and reinforcing the correctness of Manifest Destiny.

CHAPTER 8

Visualizing Race

*Native American and African
American Imagery in* Frank Leslie's
Illustrated Newspaper

The 1889 Christmas edition of *Frank Leslie's Illustrated News-paper* included a number of illustrations and articles devoted to the festivities surrounding the last Christmas of the decade. In between scenes of "Christmas at an Old Folks' Home" and Patience Stapleton's romantic tale "The Hant of Dayton's Hollow," *Leslie's* published three drawings of Christmas among outsiders, people unlikely to be regular readers of *Leslie's*. One illustration showed the interior of a rustic cabin. A frontiersman sits at the table, heavy with holiday fare, a cup in hand. His companion stands at the open door, greeting a stooped and weary Indian man wrapped in a blanket (figure 8.1). The scene illustrated Christmas charity, as the caption made clear: "A Trapper's Cabin in the Far West.—'This Is Christmas Eve; You Are Welcome.'"[1]

Another full-page holiday drawing showed a group of African Americans at the porch of a fine plantation house. A sheepish lad, backed up by two hunters and several other adults, presents a freshly killed turkey to the owner (figure 8.2). The caption explains the obvious: "Wid a Merry Christmas to Marster."[2] A third outsider illustration showed a Christmas celebration of two black families in the South. The hosts stand outside their modest cabin, decked out in their Sunday best, greeting the wagon of their guests. It's a typical scene of people greeting, except that several people seem overly excited. The host father has an odd grin—almost a sneer—on his face, while two of the children in the wagon are awestruck over a snarling dog. The caption explains the scene: "Christmas in Old Virginia.—A Coon Dinner.—Arrival of Guests."[3]

These three scenes employ obvious racial stereotypes: the helpless, hapless Indian in the first drawing, and deferential, emotional blacks in the other two.[4] But there is more to these images than obvious racial stereotypes. None of the three, for instance, seems to be based on an actual occurrence—no names or locations were mentioned, as was often the case when scenes were based on verbal descriptions.[5] As imaginary scenes, these illustrations represent larger racial themes. That is, the

A TRAPPER'S CABIN IN THE FAR WEST.—"THIS IS CHRISTMAS EVE; YOU ARE WELCOME."—DRAWN BY SMITH.

FIGURE 8.1. In the spirit of Christmas, *Leslie's* published a picture of Christian charity in 1889, an illustration that made plain the outsider status of Native Americans.

"WID A MERRY CHRISTMAS TO MARSTER."—DRAWN BY KEMBLE.

FIGURE 8.2. Like Native Americans, African Americans were identified as outsiders in the pages of *Leslie's,* their status marked by their deference to the "Marster."

"hungry Indian" in *Leslie's* drawing is not a particular person, but a representative of all Indians, disarmed and defeated people whose traditional way of life had ended and who now lived off the charity of whites. Indians might survive, the popular thinking went, but only if they adopted the ways of civilization—including, as *Leslie's* advocated, private ownership of land, fluency in English, and an industrial education for their children.[6]

Similarly, the genial plantation blacks and the overexcited Christmas celebrants in these African American illustrations can be seen as examples of typical Southern blacks, people who, despite their official status as citizens with equal rights, were in fact marginalized outsiders. These blacks were marked in *Leslie's* Christmas edition by their good-natured deference to whites and their emotional immaturity, visible signs of their inferiority. Even as they celebrated Christmas with gifts and dinners (like whites), they were shown to be different, mere pretenders to genteel traditions routinely portrayed in *Leslie's*. If Indians were now helpless and threatened with extinction by the march of progress, African Americans remained persistent, closer to civilization—and thus more threatening. This may be the reason that *Leslie's* portrayed these blacks as wide-eyed simpletons and the editors labeled them *coons*.

This chapter investigates the images of Indians and blacks in *Frank Leslie's Illustrated Newspaper* in the last years of the nineteenth century, decades after the Emancipation Proclamation, a time when the frontier was closing and the nation was looking toward the new, more enlightened century. More specifically, this chapter explores the creation, meaning, and social significance of Native American and African American illustrations in *Leslie's* in order to develop a deeper understanding of race and its meanings from the late 1880s to the 1890s. These illustrations are significant because they provide documentary evidence about the way popular journalism made sense of race for middle-class Americans during these years. This is the case, in part, because the racial images in the illustrated papers were less the product of actual or observed events than they were willful constructions of a particular kind of racial story, a story that *Leslie's* helped enact and sustain.[7] Put another way, the images of Indians and blacks in *Leslie's* were cultural productions, created by a system of popular journalism as it worked to define and manage the meanings assigned to race and the cultural "other" in a time of social change. As we shall see, these illustrations of Indians and blacks emphasized a narrow range of meanings, particular scenes, and moments that reinforced—and sometimes redefined—contemporary racial understandings. This analysis examines this meaning-making process in order to explain more fully the role of popular pictorial journalism in the creation of racial meanings in the last years of the nineteenth century.

History, Race, and Imagery

This chapter investigates race and its meanings in the pictorial press. Before the halftone process was perfected in the early 1890s, making it possible to publish photographs in the press, the illustrated papers were the cheapest and most popular way to bring images of news events, personalities, and distant places to a mass audience. But turning real people and news events into popular and informative illustrations was hardly a straightforward process. As noted previously, the creation of news illustrations involved the interpretation of events and it was subject to particular points of view. Although many news illustrations were based on direct observation, field sketches, or photographs, illustrators could—and did—manipulate scenes for artistic as well as editorial reasons.[8] In other cases, illustrators created imaginary scenes that represented a version of the "truth," even if no one at the paper actually witnessed such a scene. Even photography, a technological and cultural practice that once seemed to promise an exact reproduction of reality, is an interpretative act. Historian Alan Trachtenberg has pointed out that photographers have to decide "where to place the edge of the picture, what to exclude, [and] from what point of view to show the relations among the included details." According to Trachtenberg, photographers, like historians, "seek a balance between 'reproduction and construction,' between passive surrender to the facts and active reshaping of them into a coherent picture or story."[9] Following this logic, I argue that the racial images in *Leslie's* are cultural constructions, created by pictorial journalists operating under professional and social constraints for readers with particular worldviews—capitalism, Protestantism, and social progress, to name just three.[10] In other words, the illustrators, artists, and editors at *Leslie's* were not simply illustrating the racial realities of the day—a complex cultural task that no newspaper could fully or accurately accomplish—but creating images and shaping stories to create—or re-create—a popular form of American racial ideology.

This chapter builds on Joshua Brown's book, *Beyond the Lines: Pictorial Reporting, Everyday Life, and the Crisis of Gilded Age America*, which makes a compelling case for the social significance of *Leslie's* and the importance of its pictures of America and the world. As the first successful illustrated weekly in the nation, Brown argues that *Leslie's* "set the pattern for nineteenth-century illustrated journalism," a fact that underscores its importance.[11] Brown also explains the dynamic nature of the pictorial process. "Rather than being a rigid representational form, illustrated journalism was constituted by a complex interaction between the creation and viewing of images that changed over the course of the late nineteenth century," he writes.[12] More significantly, Brown argues that these changes were driven "by a continuous and largely unsuccessful effort to find equilibrium amid rapid social change, a persistent attempt to encompass the demands of a broad and diverse 'middle' readership that was increasingly characterized by different experiences and perceptions in Gilded Age America."[13]

These ideas are useful here because, like Brown, I want to identify and analyze the dynamics of imagery in *Leslie's*, especially the imagery of race and racial difference. By linking these representations to the social world of working- and middle-class readers for which they were produced, I argue that the images of Native Americans and African Americans in *Leslie's* in the last years of the nineteenth century offer important evidence about the fluctuating meaning of race and racial difference at a time when Americans were attempting to develop new racial understandings and overcome a long history of conquest, subjugation, slavery, and discrimination.

Illustrating Race: Old and New Themes

Frank Leslie's second wife, Miriam, took control of Leslie's publishing empire after her husband's death in 1880. Like her late husband, Miriam Leslie proved to be an enterprising publisher. She helped revive the weekly's readership in 1881 by scooping the competition with the first illustrations of the assassination of President James Garfield. Like Frank, Miriam believed in speed. Her motto was simple: "The public shall have the newest news."[14] Mrs. Leslie sold the weekly in 1889, giving the new owners a chance to restate the purpose of *Frank Leslie's Illustrated Newspaper*. Following the paper's long-established visual tradition, the new publishers vowed to make the publication "so instructive and attractive as to be a family necessity."[15] More importantly, the new owners argued for the primacy of images in understanding the world. *Leslie's,* they wrote, shall not only "present art at its best and highest forms, but also be the picture-gallery of the world." Moreover, they emphasized the power of the image. "The eye cannot wait to compass a column of description when, with a glance, it can traverse Africa in a picture, explore Egypt in another," they wrote.[16] This language was self-serving, of course, but it attests to the presumed virtues of pictorial journalism as well as the paper's continuing commitment to reveal the world through images. For ten cents a week, American readers could read about and see—thanks to woodblock and other engraving techniques—a wide variety of people and places they would never otherwise encounter.

This chapter identifies four major racial themes in pictorial press illustrations of Indians and blacks in the last years of the nineteenth century: (1) negative stereotyping, (2) social progress, (3) scientific exoticism, and (4) classic humanism. None of these categories was entirely new, nor were these categories stable or discrete. Indeed, ideas about race continued to evolve across the last half of the nineteenth century as Americans tried to develop new ways to understand this sometimes slippery concept, ways that recognized the political and social changes brought about by emancipation and the end of the Indian wars. As explained below, the shifting themes in *Leslie's* and *Harper's* illustrations demonstrate how illustrators and pictorial journalists visualized race during this era, using combinations of old and new ideas in ways that sometimes stretched but never subverted the prevailing racial order.

Negative Stereotyping

The first and most obvious racial theme in *Leslie's* illustrations was an old one: negative racial stereotyping.[17] For Native Americans, such stereotypes included not only the poor or deficient Indian but also the ever-popular Indian as brutal savage. Although this theme began to disappear as the Indian wars diminished in the 1880s, the Ghost Dance movement and its violent conclusion at Wounded Knee fostered a brief return of this image, even as some in the press expressed sympathy for the plight of the Sioux.[18] When the crisis came to a head in late 1890, *Leslie's* portrayed Sitting Bull as the "high priest of the Indian Messiah craze." A half-page drawing published in November showed a grim-faced Sitting Bull "Foment[ing] Disaffection among the Sioux Bucks."[19] In mid-December, *Leslie's* published four sketches by its artist on the scene, Jerome H. Smith. Atop a caption that read "The Recent Indian Excitement in the Northwest," Smith produced a chief speaking for peace in one sketch, another sketch showed ranchers protecting their cattle, and a third showed the "exodus of half-breeds and squaw-men."[20] The fourth sketch, which covered the bottom third of the page, was the most dramatic. It showed the Ghost Dance itself, a group of excited men whirling in apparent estasy.[21] *Leslie's* reported that "Indian troubles" had not yet occurred but were still possible; General Miles had made arrangments to "hold the hostiles in check." *Leslie's* story also confirmed the savagery of the Sioux: "Some of the more excitable redskins have deepened the war spirit by cutting themselves with spears and knives, and engaging in ceremonies likely to aggravate the existing frenzy."[22] These were not Noble Savages—these were "excitable redskins," visibly deluded by the promise of deliverance. In late December, *Leslie's* published two cover drawings revealing "The Indian Excitement in the Northwest." These drawings featured contrasting Indian images. One illustrated the "good" or civilized Indian; it showed an Indian policeman warning white settlers of "A Probable Uprising." The other drawing made the uprising less probable and more real, at least for one Indian family. It showed a smoldering log cabin after an attack, a band of "bad" Indians retreating in the distance. The caption explained: "Sioux Bucks Plundering the Houses of Friendly Indians."[23]

In early 1891, *Leslie's* enlarged the negative stereotype with a page of drawings said to represent "The Indian Troubles in the Northwest.—A Group of Character Sketches."[24] Artist E. W. Kemble presented seven sketches, some of women in domestic situations but others that reinforced the idea of native savagery and violence. One drawing showed the faces of three unidentified men, all with grim expressions and headdresses. Other than their unpleasant demeanor, the men were not threatening or violent. Yet the caption emphasized violence: "Fighting Men with War-Bonnets." Another drawing showed a crouching warrior girded by a cartridge belt, with a rifle by his side. The caption explained: "A Hostile Signal Courier on Duty." Perhaps the most telling image showed two boys pointing pistols toward an unseen enemy. Like the courier, they too were wearing cartridge belts. Neither this image nor its caption suggested friendly children: "Cheyenne Boys in Fighting Rig." In fact, every face in these seven sketches was stoic or unhappy—no smiles here. Given the sad and violent circumstances of the Wounded Knee massacre, it is little wonder that *Leslie's* presented these Indians as grim and hostile. It is notable, however, that *Leslie's* did not claim that Kemble was in South Dakota at this time or that these images were eyewitness accounts. Given their lack of specific reference to Wounded Knee, it seems more likely that they were stock images from the northern plains, used because they reinforced the news by confirming Indian savagery. This explanation explains the generic quality of these drawings and why none of the captions referred to the Wounded Knee massacre directly. Without fresh images from the scene, *Leslie's* was using what it had on file from the region—that is, generic examples of Indian life that could be made to appear savage—to tell this story. In this way, the illustrations told a story the paper needed to tell about recent Indian violence. This was not the first time, nor the last, that creative visual practices shaped the Indian image in the West in a stereotypical fashion.

The following week, *Leslie's* again illustrated the Ghost Dance. In contrast to Kemble's drawings, the paper said this scene was drawn by "D. Smith from Sketches Made on the Spot."[25] The full-page illustration was a moody night scene of dancers and bystanders around a fire. The scene was serious; the faces of some dancers were filled with emotion, obviously moved by the moment. Nothing about the image was overtly negative, yet the illustration confirmed Sioux superstition. The short story accompanying the illustration, in fact, reported on the Wounded Knee massacre of December 29, blaming Big Foot's band of hostiles for "bring[ing] on collision and bloodshed."[26] In the context of the dance itself—a dance that promised the end of whites, the return of native supremacy, and immunity from soldier's bullets—this illustration reinforced the idea of Indian barbarity, even violence. In contrast to *Leslie's* middle-class ethos, the Sioux Ghost Dance was evidence of another way of life, a life far outside the experience—and the cultural expectations—of *Leslie's* readers. The frontier was closing and the Indian wars seemed to be over, but this image reminded readers that Indians were sometimes hostile and always culturally distinct, far outside the mainstream of American life.

African Americans also turned up in *Leslie's* as different from normal—that is, white—readers. As noted earlier, blacks were sometimes depicted as kind but simple folks, sorely in need of some sophistication. As with Native Americans, such representations can be explained by the long history of racial inequality in American life. In the pages of *Leslie's,* however, a major source of negative stereotyping was produced by one particular pictorial journalist, William Ludwell Sheppard. Sheppard was a native Virginian and a former Confederate army officer who had a history of demeaning Southern blacks.[27] Following the Civil War, Sheppard was a regular contributor to *Leslie's,* and his illustrations of blacks often betrayed some level of condescension toward his subjects. In October 1889, for example, *Leslie's* published a full-page Sheppard engraving of a black preacher speaking to his flock from the back of a wagon (figure 8.3). The preacher and many in the crowd were animated, clearly moved by the preacher's message. One boy was on his knees, his hands clasped over his head. The preacher himself had his hands outstretched, his mouth wide. The caption for the drawing explains the scene: "A Negro Prophet in Florida.—'Prepar'

FIGURE 8.3. William Ludwell Sheppard's illustration of a religious revival emphasized the emotional nature of Southern blacks, a sign of difference between "normal" Americans and unsophisticated blacks.

for de Day of Wrath.'" Not surprisingly, the accompanying story also stressed the emotional nature of black religious life in the South. "The negroes of the South are peculiarly susceptible of religious emotions, and they not infrequently give way to extravagant demonstrations which border upon hysteria, if not insanity," it noted.[28]

Sheppard was not the only artist to depict African American religious life in the South. *Leslie's* published a page of twelve sketches of an outdoor revival or camp meeting by one of its regular artists, E. W. Kemble, in August 1889. In contrast to the finely detailed engravings—like Sheppard's—Kemble's drawings were rough field sketches, more crude caricatures than individualized portraits. Most of the figures were indistinct in their features, but some of them had obvious ape-like qualities.[29] As before, these drawings emphasized the emotion and drama of the camp-meeting experience, including images of gaudily dressed worshippers. The captions highlighted the peculiar nature of this event. All were written in dialect and the words stressed the high spirits of the occasion. One image showed a man in a long coat and a top hat, his arm extended above his head. "An' We'll Poun' Ole Satan 'Til He Screeches," the man says.

The accompanying story continued this emotional emphasis. The camp meeting was dying out in the North, the writer noted, but it flourished "in its glory" in the

South. The article continued: "Here may be seen all of those features which have struck unemotional spectators as grotesque." Nevertheless, the writer insisted that this religious observance was not as ridiculous as it might appear: "Their religious fervor is sincere," he concluded.

Such representations of Southern black life demonstrate the distance between blacks and whites, including *Leslie's* illustrators and correspondents. The camp meeting was presented as a relic of the antebellum South and the worshippers were portrayed as simpleminded. "The southern colored man is very emotional," the article concluded, "and when his feelings are worked upon skillfully by one who knows how to deal with them, he says and does things which, however ridiculous they may appear, are the genuine outcome of his nature." This theme reinforced a presumed difference between blacks and whites: whites were logical and rational, while blacks were spontaneous and emotional. In *Leslie's*, scenes of black worship in the South revealed this difference, reinforcing the idea of African Americans as a step or two down the social ladder, less civilized and more flamboyant than "ordinary" whites, including the readers of *Leslie's*.

Beyond black religion, politics was another "racialized" topic in *Leslie's* depiction of African Americans. In September 1888, for instance, *Leslie's* ran a full-page illustration and a short article on "Colored Campaigners," African American men involved in a colorful political demonstration in the South. Perhaps because of their unwelcome role in politics, the black campaigners were treated as a political novelty, an amusing sideshow of political campaigns. The drawing showed two groups of elaborately costumed men, each marching in support of an unidentified candidate. One group wore "Roman" helmets, decorated with stars and stripes; the other wore plumed fezzes. Their expressions made clear their animus toward the other side, while the caption made plain the colorful nature of the event: "The Humors of the Presidential Canvass at the South.—Rival Political Organizations Marching."[30]

The story explaining the illustration provided more evidence about the character of this event. Several New York costume houses, the paper said, can transform the plain processionist into "a howling 'plumed knight' or a rocky—'old Roman'—according to his political leanings." The article continued:

> These gorgeous trappings are universally employed to give color, so to speak,
> to the campaign; and nowhere are they such an unfailing source of pride and
> delight as in the colored districts. The Darktown politicians rig out their rival
> Falstaffian armies in uniforms before the most pronounced lawn-tennis blazer
> would appear pale and unobtrusive; then, crowned with the mighty helmets of
> silver *papier-mâché,* they march against each other in some "doubtful ward,"
> to the intense excitement of the populace. It is not unheard-of for one of these
> panoplied Ethiopian knights to turn up at the police-court on the morning
> after the battle, when his woful [*sic*] quixotic look usually renders the justice
> speechless, and enlivens the sad grind of justice.[31]

Such written and visual images use black political activity as a source of comic relief. African Americans in such imagery are represented as participants in political life—a recognition of their emancipation—but ridiculed for their transgressions of political decorum and personal conduct. In short, *Leslie's* words and pictures separated African Americans from the political mainstream and, once more, marked their inferior status.

The Progress of the Races

The last years of the nineteenth century were marked by periodic waves of optimism concerning Native Americans and African Americans. The post–Civil War era promised an era of social progress, industrial growth, and technological advancement that was supposed to improve the lives of many working- and middle-class Americans, an idea that *Leslie's* documented in every edition.[32] Occasionally, *Leslie's* attached this optimistic vision to Indians and blacks, using engravings, editorials, and reporting to support this idea. In 1891, for instance, the paper published an image based on a photograph of Sioux students outside their school building—called "Sitting Bull's Indian School-House"—at Pine Ridge, a sign of native education and a tacit endorsement of the idea of Indian education.[33] This endorsement was made more forcefully in an editorial published in the same issue. In response to the tragedy at Wounded Knee, *Leslie's* called for education and training for Indian children as a way of improving the future of native people. "Industrial schools should be provided for all Indian children," editorialist John B. Riley argued. This sort of vocational education called for boys to be taught "farming, gardening, the care of stock, the use of tools, and . . . the mechanical trades. The girls should be taught all kinds of household work."[34] Indian progress was the solution to the long-standing Indian problem, a position *Leslie's* illustrated consistently during this period.

One of the most significant examples of Native American progress was documented by George Foster, an amateur artist-correspondent who published a long, illustrated story on Indian Territory in *Leslie's* in 1888. "Those who visit Indian Territory with the expectation of finding it a land of tomahawks, bow-and-arrows, and wigwams, will return disappointed," Foster wrote.[35] *Leslie's* published eight Foster drawings of Indian Territory, images that emphasized progress. For example, he drew a bird's-eye view of the village of "Tulsu" (now the city of Tulsa), a train passing through a scattering of frame buildings, including a church. Other Foster illustrations depicted new buildings, including the impressive stone council house constructed for the Creeks (figure 8.4), the Cherokee Orphanage, and the "Indian University at Muskogee" (now Bacone College). Foster also drew "before" and "after" images of the Choctaw council house, the former a simple log structure, the latter an ornate, two-story stone building. Foster's focus on territorial buildings puts Native American progress in concrete terms. Based on these drawings, a casual reader could reasonably conclude that these Indians were building schools, enacting

A JOURNEY THROUGH THE INDIAN TERRITORY.
FROM SKETCHES BY GEORGE E. FOSTER.

FIGURE 8.4. The social progress of Indians—a topic not often covered in the illustrated papers—was featured in George Foster's report from Indian Territory in 1888.

legislation, and moving toward mainstream ideals of self-sufficiency and prosperity. This was good news, indeed, because such conclusions confirmed the rightness of assimilation, the government's policy designed to solve the "Indian problem." More than most other tribes, the five so-called civilized tribes of Indian Territory were evidence of successful assimilation, a goal that many Americans wanted for native peoples.

Only one of Foster's drawings depicted the old, uncivilized Indian. In "A Pawnee Indian's House," Foster produced images of traditional native life. Three figures appeared in the drawing, all in traditional clothing, a small tepee and a primitive cooking shelter in the background. This image tempered the idea of Indian advancement, but it was only one of eight sketches, the other seven of which documented progress.

Like his drawings, Foster's story reported Indian progress. "All over the Territory the Indian has donned the garb of civilization, and the fact is being proved that if the Government had spent half the money in educating Indians that it has in fighting them, the Indian question would long ago have been settled." Such a conclusion was highly optimistic, of course, though it neatly summarized one aspect of the Indian problem at the close of the frontier. With most tribes subdued and confined to reservations, *Leslie's* readers could take comfort in a new reality for Indian peoples, a reality that took advantage of education and opportunity to bring Indians from savagery to civilization.

Leslie's featured far fewer examples of African American advancement. Nevertheless, education and progress were endorsed as ways for blacks to improve their lot, as a *Leslie* editorial noted in September 1891. Edwin A. Curley, who identified himself as a "Northern Democrat," wrote about his ten-week journey through the South. His tour had convinced him that blacks were making progress in the South. As for education, Curley admitted that blacks had "poor facilities," but he concluded that "the colored race is making very substantial progress in education."[36]

African American progress also appeared on occasion in *Leslie's* illustrations. One prominent example during this era was a report on the turpentine industry in North Carolina, an industry that employed many blacks. In December 1891, the paper ran a page of illustrations based on photographs from the turpentine belt.[37] Several images showed black men at sawmills and other worksites in the distance. One drawing, labeled "Uncle Abe's Cabin," showed a plain board house with a family posed in front. Another image portrayed a black man tending a barbecue pit.

Notably, there were no images here of frivolity; this was a serious report on blacks at work. The area's Negroes, the article said, were scattered about the country, some having gone North while others worked locally. A few were doing nothing, the writer said, "happy in their ignorance of a better life." Despite this aside, the writer asked and answered a question about black advancement: "Are they improving? Yes. . . . The intelligent and business-like appearance of colored men met with on the cars, at the hotels, and in various occupations attests to the progress already made." In addition, "The South is also giving them better advantages in the line of education."

Southern blacks were shown here to be progressive and apparently "normal" people. Though poor, these Southern blacks, like middle-class whites, were represented as stable, hardworking, and capable of self-improvement through education. Such images were refreshingly free of the visual clichés and overt bias of many other illustrations during this era. Like the progressive Native Americans of Indian Territory, these North Carolina blacks were advancing, climbing the ladder of civilization.

Discovering the Other

A more "modern" way of presenting Native Americans and African Americans to *Leslie's* middle-class readership was to emphasize the picturesque and exotic, to show Indians and blacks as colorful people worthy of public curiosity and the attention of rising sciences such as ethnology and anthropology.[38] In the case of Native Americans, this theme was demonstrated most consistently during this era in a stream of images and stories from Alaska, including many from *Leslie's* own northern expedition. Most of these engravings presented native Alaskans, called "Esquimaux" in *Leslie's,* as exotic others. In September 1888, for example, *Leslie's* published five illustrations and a story that described people and places along the Alaska coast. The tone of these representations was ethnographic. One engraving showed a man's face, emphasizing his chin ornaments; another showed two individuals atop an underground house. A third illustration was labeled "Method of Burial" and showed a raised platform holding a wrapped corpse. The story was equally descriptive. Concerning a somewhat diffident image of "A Belle," the story said she "represents a type of the better-looking native women. The coarse, black and well-beaded hair, the greasy features, the almond eyes and flat forehead and nose, the worn teeth (caused by using them for bending and working wood, iron, and the tough hide used in making boats), and the tattooed chin, are characteristics of Alaska Esquimau[x] women."[39] These words and images revealed Alaska natives to be different from most Americans but, in contrast to the Ghost Dancers or other apparently dangerous U.S. Indians, also colorful and harmless. This was not a difficult case to make, since these people were distinctive in appearance and manners, and they posed no threat to America or Americans. Yet these representations did not reveal Alaska natives as the equal of whites—their tattoos, body ornaments, and customs were evidence of that. In representing the exotic other, *Leslie's* was also maintaining the existing racial hierarchy, a hierarchy in which the Alaska Esquimaux were a curious but clearly subordinate group.

The exotic other theme was also applied to some U.S. Indians, especially the peoples of the Southwest. In early 1888, *Leslie's* published an engraving of two native women in traditional dress. Over the caption "Two Maricopa Squaws," the image showed the women posing with large clay pots on their heads.[40] The picture offered a kind of tourist "snapshot" of Southwestern Indian life, providing—like a postcard—a colorful glimpse of the native people of the Southwest. The same page also included a tourist-type illustration of a Yuma chief. As with the Maricopa women, the image offered readers an exotic other, a man in a ragged army coat, wearing a low-crowned hat, staring stone-faced at the camera. It was not a happy image, but it presented the man as an object of interest to curious readers.

Even the Apaches, once the most feared of the Southwestern Indians, could be represented as safe and exotic, as *Leslie's* demonstrated in 1891. The paper ran three drawings of a White Mountain Apache ceremony, "The Devil's Dance," pictures that focused on the picturesque.[41] The illustrations showed the tribe's elaborate masks and headdresses, a theme picked up in the article. "The head-gear, which is a mask covering the entire head, is made of black cloth, with almost imperceptible slits for the eyes and mouth, [and] is drawn down under the chin and tied with a string," the article explained.[42] The story was free of anti-Apache bias, emphasizing instead the spectacle and the color of the dance. Such details rendered the White Mountain Apaches as safe and attractive Indians, far removed from the Ghost Dancers of the northern plains. In so doing, *Leslie's* artists and editors were transforming the Apaches from savages to anthropological objects, native people whose differences could be observed and appreciated by readers anxious to learn more about Indian life in the Southwest.

Leslie's rarely portrayed African Americans as the exotic other. Nevertheless, there were hints at this kind of representation, especially in depictions of African life. As noted previously, *Leslie's* saw its mission as making the distant world accessible—and visible—to American readers. This mission included occasional illustrations of Africa taken from the foreign press, most of which emphasized the picturesque or the unusual. One example appeared in April 1888, when *Leslie's* published an engraving with the caption "Western Africa.—Mode of Traveling in Sierra Leone."[43] The image showed four Africans carrying a white explorer in a covered hammock, an illustration that highlighted the exotic African while also reinforcing the existing racial order.

Although *Leslie's* rarely imagined blacks as fully exotic, it sometimes came close. A full-page Kemble drawing published in September 1889, for example, showed an apron-clad black "auntie" or "mammy" standing before a cobbler on a New Orleans street. The cobbler was examining the woman's old shoe. The caption explained the image: "Is It Worth Mending?—A Street Scene Near the French Market in New Orleans."[44] The picture was not particularly exotic, yet it did present a benign image of black life in the South. In that sense, the picture was ethnographic, presenting northern readers with a glimpse of New Orleans street life. The image also helped reinforce the "mammy" stereotype: the black woman as fat, good-natured, subservient.[45] Like the Apaches discussed earlier, such blacks were portrayed as colorful and nonthreatening, qualities that made them acceptable for popular consumption.

Erasing Race

On rare occasions, *Leslie's* images attempted to overcome race—or to downplay its existence—and to represent Native Americans and African Americans simply as humans, without explicit reference to race or racial difference. This relatively modern theme, sometimes called *classic humanism*,[46] was one method *Leslie's* illustrators could use to promote racial harmony and depict Indians and blacks as similar to whites. A significant instance of this theme was a remarkable illustration and story—perhaps a fable—about Rain-In-The-Face, once a feared Sioux (Lakota) chief. The headline summarized the theme of the piece: "A Story of Indian Affection."[47] Writer J. M. Quinn spun a long, romantic tale explaining how Rain-In-The-Face was—despite his savagery—a father who, like all fathers, grieved over a lost child. Quinn began his story by attacking the belief that Indians were brutes: "It sometimes seems that love and tenderness are strangers to the fierce and warlike characters of the world who have acquired their fame through most bloody and heartless deeds." Continuing this theme, Quinn wrote:

> Yet those who have studied the lives of these grim and savage warriors—who have stripped the better being of its coarse and hardened exterior—have found the fires of affection warm aglow. In every human being is an instinct which, although dormant, alas! too much of the time, is admirable and noble when aroused.[48]

The story went on to explain how Rain-In-The-Face had found true love with a woman from a neighboring tribe. In time, however, the marriage failed and the woman returned to her tribe and took their son, Koska, with her. Rain-In-The-Face was heartbroken. To overcome his loneliness, he and a white friend plotted to take the boy back. On the appointed night, Rain-In-The-Face entered his wife's lodge to find the boy missing. His wife explained that Koska died only hours earlier; his body was now resting on a burial platform in a nearby tree. A shocked and grieving Rain-In-The-Face went to the tree to see his son. Quinn summed up the chief's reaction: "He [Koska] was not in the tree, but had gone to the happy hunting-grounds where sorrow is unknown, where he could become far greater than on earth, and where, when once they meet, there will be no separation. So thought Rain-In-The-Face."[49]

The story was illustrated by a romantic, full-page drawing, said to be based on a photo by David F. Barry, a well-known Bismarck photographer. The engraving showed a mounted Rain-In-The-Face grieving at the foot of his son's tree. The caption asked and answered a question: "Is the Indian Capable of Affection?—The Sioux Chief Rain-In-The-Face Mourning His Dead Child."[50] The scene was dark, the moon rising in the distance. Rain-In-The-Face was dark too, his features and clothing indistinct in the dim light. He was shown facing his son's body, his left arm extending toward the sky. The image is dramatic, so carefully composed and serene that it appears posed. Indeed, it purports to be a rendering of a photograph of a private moment, a scene that could be captured only if photographer Barry had accompanied Rain-In-The-Face to find his child, which seems unlikely, or if it was reenacted by the chief, which is possible but also unlikely. Whatever its veracity, this image, and the story it illustrates, presented a once-savage Sioux chief as a caring parent, every bit as human as any other parent. This idea—the universal nature of all human beings—is the very definition of classic humanism and demonstrates one way that *Leslie's* could soften racial differences and represent an Indian as a "normal" individual.

Leslie's also used humanism on occasion to portray African Americans. In 1891, for example, *Leslie's* published a photographic portrait of a teenage black boy, an image published as part of an amateur photo contest. The photo, taken by Clarence Moore of Philadelphia, showed a smiling lad clad in a worn shirt and hat, his tongue tucked beneath his upper teeth. The image is friendly and open, an interpretation the caption emphasized: "An Open Countenance."[51] The portrait failed to give the boy's name, but it appeared without comment in the middle of a page devoted to photographic techniques. As such, it could be read as a sign of photography's power to capture "truth," at least for a moment. That is, by presenting a happy, nonthreatening black child in an apparently realistic photograph, *Leslie's* was removing, temporarily at least, the most obvious signs of racial ordering.[52] The young man was obviously an African American, but he was presented here without overt racial bias. Nevertheless, the lad's hat and shirt cast him as poor, a member of the lower class. In this way, the boy's smile, a sign of his humanity, was undercut by his apparent poverty, a mark of his lower-class status. In any case, middle-class readers of the paper were unlikely to identify fully with this boy no matter how pleasant his demeanor. In this way, even *Leslie's* idealized, humanistic depiction of a black child could not fully escape the hierarchy of race and class.

Conclusion

The racial imagery in *Frank Leslie's Illustrated Newspaper* was not balanced or evenly distributed in the years under review in this chapter. As documented previously, Native Americans were usually portrayed more sympathetically than African Americans. Indians were also depicted as more progressive than blacks. Several factors may explain these differences in representation. First, as suggested earlier (and in spite of Wounded Knee), Indians in the early 1890s were seen predominately as nonthreatening, both militarily and culturally. After all, most native people were located on reservations far outside U.S. population centers, a fact that made them more remote and easier to romanticize. The tribes of the Southwest, for example, were easy to depict in documentary-style ethnographic illustrations precisely because they were both colorfully bizarre and safely distant. Indians were so culturally benign, in fact, that in 1891 *Leslie's* could publish a portrait of a white woman,

Elaine Goodale, alongside a portrait of her mixed-race Sioux husband, Dr. Charles Alexander Eastman. The article explained, in neutral terms, that Dr. Eastman was the grandson of Captain Charles Eastman of the U.S. Army and a graduate of Dartmouth College.[53]

African Americans, by contrast, were closer and more familiar to whites and often perceived as less interesting to illustrators and more threatening to the status quo. More significantly, perhaps, and unlike Indians, blacks were citizens who had rights, and their efforts to exercise those rights were contested by whites in many cities and states. The fact that African Americans had been enslaved in America also meant that blacks were automatically assigned a low social status, a position the illustrators often reproduced in *Leslie's*. All of these factors shaped the work of artists such as Sheppard and Kemble, whose drawings presented Southern black religious life as overwrought and ridiculous. Unlike Indians, whose apparent strangeness could be presented as exotic, black strangeness was ridiculed. And unlike the mixed-race marriage of Elaine Goodale and Dr. Eastman, no black-white married couples were pictured in the newspaper.

Notwithstanding these differences, this chapter shows that racial ideology became more complex in the final years of the nineteenth century. As noted previously, *Leslie's* illustrators often relied on the racism of earlier decades to portray these groups, repeating the old stereotypes of savage Indians and ignorant blacks. But the old stereotypes did not fit the social and political circumstances of the late nineteenth century, an era that offered new (and often illusive) opportunities for freed blacks and assimilated Indians. These new conditions meant these groups could sometimes be recognized in the illustrated press for their efforts at education and self-improvement, recognition that undermined the old stereotypes. In addition, the camera and the visual power of the pictorial press combined with the emerging sciences of ethnology and anthropology to promote the portrayal of native peoples and, more rarely, blacks as outsiders sometimes worthy of journalistic interest and popular attention. Finally, realistic illustrations and photography helped foster the popular notions of universal humanity—the idea that all humans are alike under the skin—providing a "modern" way to represent the other and smooth over racial divisions.

From its founding in 1855, *Frank Leslie's Illustrated Newspaper* became one of the most important journals of the last half of the nineteenth century. One of its principal editorial goals was to make the distant world visible and known for an audience of working- and middle-class readers. To fulfill this mission, *Leslie's* artists and editors represented Native Americans and African Americans through a multifaceted lens, one that could be focused on different aspects of race as the political and social climate shifted. With the specific exception of Sheppard's biased drawings from the South, the changing image of race in *Leslie's* was not a deliberate process of racial misrepresentation, but the result of a popular system of journalistic image making that drew upon the complex but highly functional interaction between the newspaper and its readers. When Indians or blacks appeared threatening, as in the Ghost Dance or in election campaigns, the illustrations were demeaning, hostile, or racist. In less threatening times, the long-anticipated progress of Native Americans and African Americans could be reported and illustrated. Indians and blacks could even be celebrated as colorful and interesting—as long as they posed no apparent threat to the status quo. On occasion, individuals from these groups could be recognized as ordinary human beings, a humanism that was a marked improvement from a legacy of negative stereotypes.

These shifts in emphasis and ideology were useful for *Leslie's* and its readers, providing racial categories that stretched racial definitions without directly challenging the existing order, which remained largely unexamined. With the small but notable exception of the Goodale-Eastman marriage portraits, the artists and editors at *Leslie's* never represented Indians or blacks in ways that were politically or socially equal to whites. To do so would have violated the tacit understanding that *Leslie's* had with its readers: an understanding to explore and illustrate the world in ways that affirmed the status quo and its underlying ideology. In visualizing race in nineteenth-century America, *Leslie's* offered clichés, social progress, realism, exoticism, and other ideas, but it also supported a white-dominated world where Indians and blacks could be recognized for their progress and acknowledged for their humanity, yet never accepted as full and equal members of American social or political structure. For this kind of representation and racial recognition, blacks and Indians would have to wait many more decades, long after the end of the illustrated press and the demise of *Frank Leslie's Illustrated Newspaper*.

Conclusion

Illustrating Race, Demonstrating Difference

One of the most shocking Indian illustrations ever published in the pictorial press appeared at the bottom of an inside page in *Harper's Weekly* in April 1870.[1] Over a mild caption ("An Indian Peace Offering"), the half-page engraving showed a Piegan Indian warrior at a table, presenting a gruesome gift to General Philippe Regis de Trobriand, who was recoiling in horror at the sight (figure 9.1). The offering—the severed head of an Indian man—was indeed sensational. Yet *Harper's* explained the scene in understated language, referring to "a very curious incident that took place recently at Fort Shaw, Montana." The story explained that the head belonged to "Pete," an Indian who had murdered many white settlers in the region. According to *Harper's,* the Piegans were suing for peace and had presented Pete's head to the general "as a pledge of their sincerity." The head of the dead "brave"—a word the editors put in quotation marks—was "deeply pitted with small-pox and scarred with wounds," the editors said, and a "ghastly spectacle." Yet "as a token of their desire to cultivate more friendly relations with the whites," *Harper's* concluded, the head "was more eloquent than words."[2] In other words, the Piegans in this image were "good" Indians, first impressions to the contrary.

This disturbing illustration and the story that explained it raise a number of questions about Indians and the problem of racial representation in the pictorial press. Why was this scene illustrated? Was it newsworthy simply for its shock value? If so, why did the paper run the image on an inside page and tone down its explanation? The answers to these questions reveal some of the problems and contradictions of illustrated Indians in the last half of the nineteenth century. On its face, this illustration was another example of Indian difference, a vivid reminder that Indians were barbaric and deficient creatures sorely in need of moral instruction. The story, however, suggests a more complicated interpretation of this encounter, explaining that an Indian murderer (if indeed he was a murderer), Pete, had been killed by some "good" Indians in the interest of a greater peace with whites. Perhaps the promise of peace explains why *Harper's* found this gruesome incident "more eloquent than words."

AN INDIAN PEACE-OFFERING.

FIGURE 9.1. The scene was shocking but *Harper's Weekly* explained the circumstances in understated terms, noting the peaceful intentions of the Piegans, who delivered the head as a "pledge of their sincerity."

At this remove, it is hard to know exactly what this image might have meant to middle-class, white readers who discovered it in the pages of *Harper's Weekly*. Yet this sensational illustration suggests some of the social and cultural forces at play in the production of Indian illustrations in the pictorial press. As we have seen, the representation of Indians in the pictorial press was a complex ideological and cultural process, so much so that even mundane illustrations of Indians and Indian life were not as straightforward as they appeared. In other words, the production and meaning of most Indian illustrations was complicated, fraught with ambiguous and sometimes contradictory racial ideas. Moreover, such pictures were powerful in the last decades of the nineteenth century. In the same way that photographs made the West more vivid and real for nineteenth-century Americans,[3] illustrated Indians provided American readers with a set of influential and useful visual tropes that signaled racial and cultural differences and, in a great many cases, reinforced ideas of Indian inferiority. In short, Indian illustrations in *Leslie's, Harper's Weekly,* and other illustrated papers did more than merely depict newsworthy Indians; these images made Indians vivid and "real" in the American popular imagination.

The Meanings of Indian Illustrations

As detailed in the preceding chapters, Indians were portrayed in a number of ways across the last decades of the nineteenth century, most of them following familiar stereotypes and patterns of visual and linguistic representation. In general, the pictorial press represented Indians as racial outsiders and cultural curiosities, usually in an "us versus them" manner where Euro-American standards and values were the norm and Indian standards and values were abnormal and thus deviant. This was a journalistic form of racial simplification and cultural "othering" that almost always separated Indians from whites. This separation, in turn, was the inevitable result of nineteenth-century ideas about race and racial difference and it played out in the pictorial press in Indian images that made Indians nearly always appear "Indian" to one degree or another. In other words, the ordinary practices of pictorial journalism meant that Indians had to look "Indian"—their faces, hair, clothes, and other characteristics clearly distinguished from characteristics that might undermine the illustration's "Indianness." That is, the editorial process of representing Indians in the illustrated press required artists, illustrators, and editors to produce visual distinctions based on presumed racial characteristics that emphasized—and sometimes overemphasized—the differences between Euro-Americans and Native Americans. As practiced by the pictorial press, this racial simplification was both convenient and routine; it was apparently "natural" too, a reflection of the prevailing nineteenth-century ideas about Indians that placed them well below Europeans in the racial hierarchy. For readers of the illustrated papers, Indian images were racially useful—Indians were easily distinguished from "normal" Americans. Not coincidentally, this simplified racial representation almost always reinforced the dominant American ideologies of the last half of the nineteenth century, including the supremacy of Euro-American civilization and culture, the inevitability of social progress, and the righteousness of Manifest Destiny.

Illustrating Indians in this way made it easy to represent Indians as types, generic figures without names or individual identities or tribes. Although some exceptional Indians warranted an individual identity and thus a name in the press, many Indians pictured in the illustrated papers were unidentified, lumped together in a broad category known simply as *Indians.* As we have seen, this sort of representation was a way of dehumanizing individual Indians and their cultures, reducing them to types and stripping them of their personalities. In addition, tribal distinctions—important in the lived experience of actual Indians and the whites who interacted with them—were frequently erased or diminished in the pictorial press. These illustrated Indians, no matter the visual and cultural differences between tribes, were simply *Indians.* Again, this was a convenient simplification for illustrated journalists, allowing them to produce and publish a small range of Indian pictures, captions, and stories that their readers would recognize and understand.

This research also documents the fundamental ambiguities in American popular thought that shaped the image of the Indian in the pictorial press. As noted previously, the Indian was both celebrated and vilified in the illustrated press in pictures that followed the ebb and flow of popular opinion. Thus W. M. Cary could depict a proud warrior battling an eagle for the creature's prized feathers, "an act of bravado" that *Harper's Weekly* saw fit to publish on its cover in 1878. On the other hand, Indians were killers, as *Leslie's* revealed in 1873 in a dramatic cover illustration of an Indian attack on a pioneer family, vivid evidence of Indian savagery on the frontier.[4] Not surprisingly, the Sioux and Cheyenne victory over Custer's Seventh Cavalry in 1876 generated a number of anti-Indian illustrations, including a *Daily Graphic* cartoon that advocated extermination. Yet, as documented in chapters 6 and 7, hostile Indian illustrations largely disappeared a few months after the Little Bighorn. Even Sitting Bull—sometimes demonized as Custer's killer and one of the worst Indians alive—was presented in relatively innocuous pictures after the battle, eventually becoming an Indian celebrity who toured with Buffalo Bill's Wild West show and attracted curious and admiring crowds.[5] These shifts in the tone and nature of Indian imagery can be explained by the enduring and complicated relationship between Indians and Euro-Americans, a relationship exemplified by the persistence of "good" Indian and "bad" Indian stereotypes in American life. The good Indian, of course, was the Noble Savage, an idealized figure that never completely fell out of favor in American popular culture. Even during the violence of the Indian wars, the idea of the Noble Savage helped redeem the Indian as an American symbol for many Euro-Americans. Although Indians were violent and evil, as the pictorial press made clear, the illustrated papers presented some Indians who could be admired, even as their differences and deficiencies were recognized and documented. Once the fighting stopped, it seems, the American public was quick to forgive hostile Indians; the public did not seem to carry a grudge, at least not for long. Thus the popular idea of the Indian in late nineteenth-century America was often unstable, shifting from good to bad and back as Indian-white relations changed. This finding supports historian Philip Deloria's argument that "Indianness has always been about contradictions."[6] Indeed, contradictions were a hallmark of the illustrated Indian, who was sometimes good, sometimes bad—but was always different, always Indian.

This journalistic process—turning living Indian people into words and images for popular consumption—was a task with important symbolic and real-world consequences. One consequence of the illustrated Indian was the cumulative power of these representations to maintain and reinforce the existing order. That is, Indian images in the nineteenth-century press reinforced the dominant forces of nineteenth-century American life, supporting and confirming, in James Carey's words, a set of "shared beliefs" and "a particular view of the world."[7] In other words, Indian illustrations worked at a broad cultural level in ways that supported the status quo—Euro-American views about the organization of society, politics, race, religion, work, clothing, weaponry, and the like—and identified Native Americans and Native American life as different from "normal" ideas and practices of American life. In the pictorial press, illustrated Indians were routinely positioned on the "wrong" side of history and progress; their images marked by signs of racial difference and, in a great many cases, deficiency.

At a more practical level, the very process of creating Indian images and representing them in the pictorial press involved journalistic choices that operated within the bounds of the dominant society. Indian illustrations were always constructed artifacts, as Michael Schudson puts it, products of journalistic frames, choices, and shadings that constructed particular versions of social reality. Schudson notes, too, that readers and viewers take these constructed versions of reality to be real, and respond to them as if they were.[8] In the case of illustrated Indians, the process of producing Indian images involved a series of journalistic decisions and choices, professional—but also ethnocentric—practices that routinely reaffirmed Indian inferiority in the last half of the nineteenth century. Visual Indian stereotypes—repeated in one form or another by the illustrated press for several decades—had a significant impact on the American imagination. Evidence for this point can be found in Devon Mihesuah's catalog of Indian stereotypes published in 1996.[9] Mihesuah's list includes the following stereotypes, all of which appeared in one form or another in the illustrated papers:

- Indians are all alike
- Indians were conquered because they were inferior
- Indians had no civilization until Europeans brought it to them
- Indians were warlike and treacherous
- Indians did not value or empower women
- Indians . . . live in tipis, wear braids and ride horses
- Indians are stoic and have no sense of humor[10]

These and other Indian ideas, produced and repeated in the pictorial press, took on a life of their own in American popular culture—nineteenth-century dime novels and Hollywood Westerns of the 1940s and 1950s are the most obvious examples—and shaped the idea of the Indian even into the twenty-first century.

One final illustration demonstrates the powerful ideology that shaped the creation of the illustrated Indian. In 1868, as violence between Indians and whites continued in the American West, *Harper's Weekly* published a showcase set of nine Indian scenes on a single page[11] (figure 9.2). These scenes, drawn by W. M. Cary, purported to show "The Life of an Indian." In broad strokes, that's exactly what Cary's pictures showed, starting with "Infancy" and ending with a "Funeral Ceremony." Other important stages of Indian life were also portrayed, including "Boyhood," which showed a boy practice-hunting with his bow and arrow, and "Manhood," which showed an actual buffalo hunt. The next stages were a sun dance (a "Trial

FIGURE 9.2. W. M. Cary's "The Life of an Indian" simplified Native American life and reinforced the idea that all American Indians were Plains Indians.

of Endurance"), followed by courtship ("The Tender Passion"). In the center of the page—the largest and most dramatic picture—Cary imagined the young warrior gloating "with savage pride" over his "First Scalp," a key feature of the American Indian's warrior society.[12] The next scene continued the warrior theme; it showed a celebratory "Scalp Dance." The final scenes on the page depicted illness and death, including the warrior being treated in the "Medicine Lodge" and ending in the funeral. These stages of life weren't exactly wrong, but they were presented in *Harper's Weekly* as if they applied to all Indians, regardless of tribe or region. This was, as the caption put it, the life of "*an* Indian," as if all Indians lived in tepees and hunted buffalo. By presenting Indians in this way, *Harper's* was simplifying Indians and Indian life for the casual reader. As a matter of storytelling, this was effective visual journalism. The editors explained as much on *Harper's* cover page, declaring that Cary's illustrations served "the treble purpose of sketching strange manners and customs, giving a not uninteresting narrative of the real life of a living, though fast perishing race, and displaying a work of no little artistic merit." These "handsome vignettes," the editors continued, "illustrate scenes which occur in the career of every red man."[13] Cary's pictures kept complicated tribal differences out of the picture, rendering the Indian experience on the plains—where all Indians appeared to live—easy to follow and appealing. No whites appeared here; Cary showed no fights with settlers or soldiers. There were scalps on display—a handy reminder of Indian savagery—but these were Indian scalps. In short, this was Indian life reduced to its most significant moments and then made safe for public consumption, a journalistic image of Indians that swept individual and tribal differences aside in the race for compelling imagery and racial simplicity. If these pictures reduced Indians to a single stereotype, readers understood and expected that stereotype in 1868. In post–Civil War America, Indians were simply Indians—more alike than different—yet distinctly different from ordinary Euro-Americans.

Cary's vignettes suggest that the Indians that Americans wanted to see in the last half of the nineteenth century were interesting but universalized savages of American West, proud yet still dangerous warriors in full feather, muscles rippling. Over and over again in the pictorial press, Indian men who fit this model were presented as "the Indian," one great, iconic warrior who could represent all American Indians. That was the case in 1868 when Cary created "The Life of an Indian" for *Harper's Weekly*. There were many other possibilities for illustrating Indians, pictures representing other Indian stories and themes, but the illustrated press celebrated—and American readers embraced—the magnificent Plains Indian warrior most of all.

Notes

Introduction

1. *Harper's Weekly* (hereafter HW), December 7, 1878, 965.

2. Ibid., 970.

3. William de la Montagne Cary and other illustrators sometimes needed a fertile imagination in order to produce the kinds of exciting illustrations that editors wanted. For example, Cary biographer Mildred Ladner notes that the artist "was not above inventing when his sketchbook failed to meet his needs"; see Mildred D. Ladner, *William de la Montagne Cary: Artist on the Missouri River* (Norman: University of Oklahoma Press, 1984), 99.

4. Joshua Brown, *Beyond the Lines: Pictorial Reporting, Everyday Life, and the Crisis of Gilded Age America* (Berkeley: University of California Press, 2002), 22.

5. Robert F. Berkhofer Jr., *The White Man's Indian: Images of the American Indian from Columbus to the Present* (New York: Vintage Books, 1978), 28.

6. Ibid., 3; italics in original.

7. Selene G. Phillips, "'Indians on Our Warpath': World War II Images of American Indians in *Life* Magazine, 1937–1949," in *American Indians and the Mass Media,* ed. Meta G. Carstarphen and John P. Sanchez (Norman: University of Oklahoma Press, 2012), 34.

8. Devon A. Mihesuah, *American Indians: Stereotypes and Realities* (Atlanta, GA: Clarity Press, 1996), 9.

9. Ibid., 10.

10. James W. Carey, *Communication as Culture: Essays on Media and Society* (Boston: Unwin Hyman, 1989), 18.

11. Ibid., 20.

12. Michael Schudson, *The Sociology of News,* 2nd ed. (New York: Norton, 2011), xvii.

13. Ibid., xiv.

14. Ibid., xvi–xvii.

15. Juan Gonzalez and Joseph Torres, *News for All the People: The Epic Story of Race and the American Media* (London: Verso, 2011), 3. Also see John M. Coward, *The Newspaper Indian: Native American Identity in the Press, 1820–90* (Urbana: University of Illinois Press, 1999), 19.

16. Gonzalez and Torres, *News for All the People,* 2.

17. Ibid.

18. Coward, *Newspaper Indian,* 10.

19. Robert Taft, *Artists and Illustrators of the Old West, 1850–1900* (New York: Charles Scribner's Sons, 1953), 249.

20. Louis P. Masur, "'Pictures Have Now Become a Necessity': The Use of Images in American History Textbooks," *Journal of American History* (March 1998): 1409.

21. Ibid., 1409–10.

22. Brown, *Beyond the Lines,* 3.

23. Quoted in Michael Griffin, "The Great War Photographs," in *Picturing the Past: Media, History, and Photography,* ed. Bonnie Brennan and Hanno Hardt (Urbana: University of Illinois Press, 1999), 147.

24. Taft, *Artists and Illustrators,* xvi.

25. Ibid.

26. Quoted in Brown, *Beyond the Lines,* 8.

27. Frederic Hudson, *Journalism in the United States, from 1690 to 1872* (New York: Harper and Brothers, 1873), 705.

28. Kevin G. Barnhurst and John Nerone, "Civil Picturing vs. Realist Photojournalism: The Regime of Illustrated News, 1865–1901," *Design Issues* 16, no. 1 (Spring 2000): 61–64.

29. Quoted in William E. Huntzicker, "Picturing the News: Frank Leslie and the Origins of American Pictorial Journalism," in *The Civil War and the Press,* ed. David B. Sachsman, S. Kittrell Rushing, and Debra Reddin van Tuyll (Piscataway, NJ: Transaction Publishers, 2000), 312–13. In the inaugural issue, Leslie wrote that he wished to impart "to the journal all the rapidity and freshness essential to the efficiency of a newspaper." To that end, he continued, "we have completed an organization of artist agencies throughout most parts of the American continent. By their aid we shall have pictorial delineations of every remarkable event that occurs over its vast extent"; see *Frank Leslie's Illustrated Newspaper,* December 15, 1855, 6.

30. *Frank Leslie's Illustrated Newspaper* (hereafter FLIN), January 3, 1857, 74.

31. Richard Samuel West, *Satire on Stone: The Political Cartoons of Joseph Keppler* (Urbana: University of Illinois Press, 1988), 75.

32. Frank Luther Mott, *A History of American Magazines, 1850–1865* (Cambridge, MA: Harvard University Press, 1938), 454.

33. Ibid., 473.

34. Robert Taft, *Photography and the American Scene* (New York: Macmillan, 1938), 446.

35. Brown, *Beyond the Lines,* 14–15, and Taft, *Photography and the American Scene,* 419.

36. Brown, *Beyond the Lines,* 18.

37. Ibid., 40–46. Importantly, Leslie saw his weekly as a newspaper and emphasized breaking news. See Barnhurst and Nerone, "Civic Picturing vs. Realist Photojournalism," 61.

38. Brown, *Beyond the Lines,* 25–31. Also see West, *Satire on Stone,* 65.

39. FLIN, December 15, 1855, 6.

40. Madeline B. Stern, *Purple Passage: The Life of Mrs. Frank Leslie,* quoted in Ladner, *William de la Montagne Cary,* 154.

41. This account draws on a detailed technical explanation found in Brown, *Beyond the Lines,* 34–40, as well as Huntzicker, "Picturing the News," 313.

42. Mott, *History of American Magazines,* 453.

43. Andrea G. Pearson, "*Frank Leslie's Illustrated Newspaper* and *Harper's Weekly*: In-

novation and Imitation in Nineteenth-Century American Pictorial Reporting," *Journal of Popular Culture* 23, no. 4 (Spring 1990): 83.

44. Ibid., 81–82.

45. Ibid., 88.

46. Brown, *Beyond the Lines,* 41–43. See also Barnhurst and Nerone, "Civil Picturing vs. Realist Photojournalism," 61.

47. Mott, *History of American Magazines,* 470–71.

48. Fiona Deans Halloran, *Thomas Nast: The Father of Modern Political Cartoons* (Chapel Hill: University of North Carolina Press, 2012), 85.

49. J. Henry Harper, quoted in Mott, *History of American Magazines,* 469.

50. Mott, *History of American Magazines,* 474, 478–80. Also see Halloran's work on Curtis in *Thomas Nast,* 2012. Commenting on *Harper's Weekly* in 1873, Frederic Hudson wrote that Curtis's editorials were "distinguished by breadth of view, evident sincerity of opinion, force and clearness of style, and strict and unvarying attention to the amenities of journalism." Concerning Nast, Hudson added, "Nast is a genius. He can not be compared with any other cartoonist, living or dead"; see Hudson, *Journalism in the United States,* 707.

51. Mott, *History of American Magazines,* 471.

52. Pearson, "Innovation and Imitation," 88.

53. Ibid., 88. Also see Peter Johnson, *Front Line Artists* (London: Cassell, 1978), 6. Johnson declares, "Nothing sold a picture newspaper like a good war."

54. West, *Satire on Stone,* 65.

55. Mott, *History of American Magazines,* 475–76.

56. *FLIN*, December 10, 1864, 178. Also see Huntzicker, "Picturing the News," 318.

57. Huntzicker, "Picturing the News," 321. On Waud's life and work, see Frederic E. Ray, *Alfred R. Waud: Civil War Artist* (New York: Viking, 1974).

58. Michael L. Carlebach, *The Origins of Photojournalism in America* (Washington, DC: Smithsonian Institution Press, 1992), 67.

59. Commenting on the Western illustrations of W. M. Cary, Fred Myers, then director of Tulsa's Gilcrease Museum, noted the rising interest in the West following the Civil War: "As more settlers moved out onto the plains (the transcontinental railroad was completed in 1869), as the Indian Wars progressed along their inevitable course, as the cowboy galloped into his role as hero for the nation, the eastern publishers of magazines and newspapers created an industry that supplied exciting, illustrated information about the developing region"; see Myers's "Foreword" in Ladner, *William de la Montagne Cary,* xiii.

60. Theodore Davis, "A Summer on the Plains," *Harper's New Monthly Magazine,* February 1868, 292.

61. Woodblock and other engraving processes predate the development of the pictorial press in America by many decades, although the illustrated papers made news and feature pictures available to a mass audience on a weekly basis. Joshua Brown notes that pictures were scarce in colonial America, although during the revolutionary era "woodcuts and copperplates appeared on Patriot broadsides, almanacs, and newspapers published in northern seaboard cities"; see Brown, *Beyond the Lines,* 9.

62. Quoted in Brown, *Beyond the Lines,* 19.

63. FLIN, December 15, 1855, 4.

64. HW, October 31, 1863, 693.

65. Taft, *Photography and the American Scene,* 420.

66. Brown, *Beyond the Lines,* 34.

67. Carlebach, *Origins of Photojournalism,* 63.

68. Taft, *Photography and the American Scene,* 420.

69. This passage is based on a thorough description of the production process in Brown, *Beyond the Lines,* 34–40.

70. Martha A. Sandweiss, *Print the Legend: Photography and the American West* (New Haven, CT: Yale University Press), 148.

71. The original photograph, by Julian Vannerson, shows Och-Lochta Micco posed in elaborate ceremonial clothing. The unattributed lithograph shows an almost identical Och-Lochta Micco, but holding "a rifle for added effect"; see Carlebach, *Origins of Photojournalism,* 45.

72. Sandweiss notes that most nineteenth-century Indian photography "came to serve the needs of their non-Indian makers and publishers." Moreover, most of these images "quickly found their place within a single overarching narrative story—the inevitable decline of the nation's native cultures, the determinist tale of a 'vanishing race'"; see Sandweiss, *Print the Legend,* 217.

73. Carlebach, *Origins of Photojournalism,* 65.

74. Carlebach and other scholars have pointed out that Civil War photographers were not above altering reality in the interest of a more dramatic photograph. Carlebach cites the case of a Gettysburg photograph called *Home of the Rebel Sharpshooter* by Timothy O'Sullivan and Alexander Gardner. The photographers arranged the soldier's body and his rifle to improve the composition of the photograph; see Carlebach, *Origins of Photojournalism,* 82. For a lively, somewhat quirky discussion of truth and deception in early war photography, see Errol Morris, *Believing Is Seeing: Observations on the Mysteries of Photography* (New York: Penguin Press, 2011), 3–71.

75. Carlebach, *Origins of Photojournalism,* 48–49. Also see Estelle Jussim, *Frederic Remington, the Camera and the Old West* (Fort Worth: Amon Carter Museum, 1983), 7.

76. Brown, *Beyond the Lines,* 34.

77. Sandweiss, *Print the Legend,* 171.

78. Coward, *Newspaper Indian,* 27. This idea is drawn from Wayne Franklin, *Discoverers, Explorers, Settlers: The Diligent Writers of Early America* (Chicago: University of Chicago Press, 1979), 5.

79. Quoted in Coward, *Newspaper Indian,* 25.

80. Ibid., 30. For a more extensive discussion of the representation of Indians in *Publick Occurrences,* see John P. Sanchez, "America Indian News Frames in America's First Newspaper, *Publick Occurences Both Foreign and Domestick,*" in *American Indians and the Mass Media,* ed. Meta G. Carstarphen and John P. Sanchez (Norman: University of Oklahoma Press, 2012), 9–17.

81. Coward, *Newspaper Indian,* 30.

82. James Fenimore Cooper, in his introduction to the revised edition of *The Last of the Mohicans* (1850), quoted in Roy Harvey Pearce, *Savagism and Civilization: A Study of the Indian and the American Mind* (Berkeley: University of California Press, 1988), 203. Also see Berkhofer, *White Man's Indian,* 93–95.

83. Berkhofer, *White Man's Indian*, 90.

84. *Western Weekly Review* (Franklin, TN), June 20, 1834, 1. Quoted in Coward, *Newspaper Indian*, 49.

85. Coward, *Newspaper Indian*, 49.

86. *Washington Telegraph* story reprinted in the *Western Weekly Review* (Franklin, TN), February 16, 1838, quoted in Coward, *Newspaper Indian*, 50.

87. Reproduced in Berkhofer, *White Man's Indian*, illustration 2, following 138.

88. Reproduced in W. Graham Arader III, *Native Grace: Prints of the New World, 1590–1876* (Charlottesville, VA: Thomasson-Grant, 1988), 24. De Bry's illustration was based on a drawing by English artist John White.

89. Woodcuts from seventeenth- and eighteenth-century editions of the Rowlandson narrative are in the public domain and can be found online. Also see Berkhofer, *White Man's Indian*, 84, and Pearce, *Savagism and Civilization*, 23.

90. George Catlin, *Letters and Notes on the Manners, Customs, and Conditions of the North American Indians*, vol. 1 (New York: Dover Publications, 1973), 3.

91. Alan Trachtenberg, *Shades of Hiawatha: Staging Indians, Making Americans, 1880–1930* (New York: Hill and Wang, 2004), 14.

92. Carol Clark, *Charles Deas and 1840s America* (Norman: University of Oklahoma Press, 2009), 101.

93. See Mott, *History of American Magazines*, 409–12.

94. Gonzalez and Torres, *News for All the People*, 3.

Chapter 1. Posing the Indian

1. *Frank Leslie's Illustrated Newspaper* (hereafter FLIN), September 10, 1881, 24. Bell established a photographic studio on Pennsylvania Avenue in Washington, DC, and was a favorite of federal officials. See Frank H. Goodyear III, *Red Cloud: Photographs of a Lakota Chief* (Lincoln: University of Nebraska Press, 2003), 4, 51–55.

2. FLIN, September 10, 1881, 26.

3. Ibid.

4. These portraits were located through a series of keyword searches in electronic editions of *Leslie's* and *Harper's Weekly*. This analysis focuses on posed individual and group studio portraits, which were more common than Indian portraits made in makeshift studios in the field.

5. See, for example, Paul Andrew Hutton, ed., *The Custer Reader* (Lincoln: University of Nebraska Press, 1992), esp. the "Photographic Essay," 549–60; John M. Coward, "Making Images on the Indian Frontier: The Adventures of Special Artist Theodore Davis," *Journalism History* 36, no. 3 (Fall 2010): 150–59; and William E. Huntzicker, "Custer's Pictorial Images: Heroism and Racism in the Illustrated Press," in *Speaking About Custer*, ed. Sandy Barnard (Terre Haute, IN: AST Press, 1991), 23–49. One study that examines Indian portraits in the pictorial press is Mindy Duncan, "Finding Focus in the Early Illustrated Press in the United States: Images of Native Americans in *Frank Leslie's Illustrated* and *Harper's Weekly*, 1860–1890," *Atlanta Review of Journalism History* 2 (2001): 14–17.

6. Stuart Hall, "The Spectacle of the 'Other,'" in *Representation: Cultural Representations and Signifying Practices*, ed. Stuart Hall (London: Sage, 1997), 235–36. In a discussion of

"difference" and its significance, Hall points out that meaning is made in simple but powerful "binary oppositions"—black/white and masculine/feminine, for example, or, in this case, Indian/white. These oppositions are rarely neutral, however—they describe a dominant power and a subordinate one. In this sense, racial meanings are created through the marking of difference, through the representation of "us" (whites) and "them" (Indians).

7. Goodyear, *Red Cloud*, 1. Also see Julie Schimmel, "Inventing 'the Indian,'" in *The West as America: Reinterpreting Images of the Frontier, 1820–1920*, ed. William H. Truettner (Washington, DC: Smithsonian Institution Press, 1991), 149–89. Robert Hughes, *American Visions: The Epic Story of Art in America* (New York: Alfred A. Knopf, 1997), 175–85.

8. George Catlin, *Letters and Notes on the Manners, Customs, and Conditions of the North American Indians*, vol. 1 (New York: Dover Publications, 1973), 3.

9. Lee Clark Mitchell, "The Photograph and the American Indian," in *The Photograph and the American Indian*, ed. Alfred L. Bush and Lee Clark Mitchell (Princeton, NJ: Princeton University Press, 1994), xvi.

10. Joshua Brown, *Beyond the Lines: Pictorial Reporting, Everyday Life, and the Crisis of Gilded Age America* (Berkeley: University of California Press, 2002), 74.

11. David Park, "Picturing the War: Visual Genres in Civil War News," *Communication Review* 3, no. 4 (1999): 301. Also see Catherine A. Lutz and Jane L. Collins, *Reading National Geographic* (Chicago: University of Chicago Press, 1993), 96.

12. Goodyear, *Red Cloud*, 4.

13. Martha A. Sandweiss, *Print the Legend: Photography and the American West* (New Haven, CT: Yale University Press, 2002), 210–15.

14. Goodyear, *Red Cloud*, 52. Anthropologist James Faris has also documented the ways that photographers manipulated their Indian subjects in the studio, pointing out that "delegation photographers frequently added their own notions of what [clothing] was appropriate to the circumstance." See James C. Faris, *Navajo and Photography* (Albuquerque: University of New Mexico Press, 1996), 74.

15. Goodyear, *Red Cloud*, 52.

16. Ibid.

17. Sandweiss, *Print the Legend*, 7–8.

18. Mitchell, "Photograph and the American Indian," xiii.

19. Ibid., xi.

20. Joanna Cohan Scherer, "You Can't Believe Your Eyes: Inaccuracies in Photographs of North American Indians," *Studies in the Anthropology of Visual Communication* 2, no. 2 (1975): 67–79. Scherer not only documents many egregious examples of inaccuracies in ethnographic Indian photographs, but also notes that most of the photos she examined were accurate as historical records. "The value of revealing these inaccuracies is to caution the researcher about the complexity of picture research and to make them aware that the visual record cannot be taken at face value but must be studied and analyzed, perhaps even more than the written source," she concludes (77).

21. Scherer, "You Can't Believe Your Eyes," 68.

22. Kevin G. Barnhurst and John Nerone, "Civil Picturing vs. Realist Photojournalism: The Regime of Illustrated News, 1856–1901," *Design Issues* 16, no. 1 (Spring 2000): 72.

23. Mitchell, "Photograph and the American Indian," xvii.

24. Ibid.

25. Richard White, "The West Is Rarely What It Seems," in *Faces of the Frontier: Photographic Portraits from the American West, 1845–1924,* Frank H. Goodyear III (Norman: University of Oklahoma Press, 2009), 23.

26. Sandweiss, *Print the Legend,* 215–17.

27. Goodyear, *Red Cloud,* 1.

28. Ibid., 4.

29. Ibid., 5.

30. Ibid.

31. In his book on photography of Navajo people, Faris cites instances of Indian resistance to the camera, Navajo who covered themselves or turned their heads to avoid the photographer. I have found no illustrations of this resistance in the pictorial press, perhaps because illustrations based on such photographs would draw attention to the intrusiveness of the camera. See Faris, *Navajo and Photography,* 33–34, 46–47.

32. Brady published *The Gallery of Illustrious Americans* in 1850. It featured twelve lithographs made from his daguerreotypes and featured three former presidents, four senators, and three generals, as well as several other prominent men, including artist John James Audubon. See Alan Trachtenberg, *Reading American Photographs: Images as History, Mathew Brady to Walker Evans* (New York: Hill and Wang, 1989), 45–46.

33. A useful discussion of the engraving process is in Brown, *Beyond the Lines,* 34–40.

34. FLIN, June 1, 1867, 169.

35. FLIN, September 7, 1867, 392.

36. See, for example, three judicial portraits in FLIN, December 5, 1868, 188.

37. See, for example, the illustration of Mission Indian women making baskets and ropes in *Harper's Weekly,* October 20, 1877, 821. This subject matter—Indian women at work in a domestic setting—was relatively unusual in the illustrated press, as were portraits of individual Indian women. Portraits of Indian children were even more unusual. When the Ute Indians became violent in 1887, *Leslie's* published a front-page portrait of Ute chief Colorow alongside a Ute woman with a baby. They were identified only as "Ute Squaw and Papoose." On the other side of Colorow, *Leslie's* published another portrait of unidentified Utes above the caption "Ute Brave and Squaws"; see FLIN, September, 3, 1887, 33.

38. Quoted in Trachtenberg, *Reading American Photographs,* 27.

39. Trachtenberg, *Reading American Photographs,* 27.

40. Barnhurst and Nerone, "Civil Picturing vs. Realist Photojournalism," 72. Also see the discussion of portraits in Lutz and Collins, *Reading National Geographic,* 96–98.

41. FLIN, June 24, 1871, 243. The three portraits appear on 233.

42. Sandweiss, *Print the Legend,* 216.

43. Ibid., 215.

44. Mitchell, "Photograph and the American Indian," xvii.

45. Ibid., xviii. The photograph itself is reproduced on 27.

46. *Gleason's Pictorial,* October 23, 1852.

47. Ibid.

48. Ibid.

49. *Ballou's Pictorial,* January 19, 1856.

50. Ibid.

51. HW, January 27, 1866, 49.

52. Ibid.

53. Ibid., 50.

54. Ibid.

55. Ibid.

56. HW, October 20, 1877, 821.

57. Brady's original photograph is reproduced in Goodyear, *Red Cloud,* 36.

58. Bird identifies stoicism as "a central stereotype of American Indians," linking this idea to early American anthropology and its search for "untainted primitivism." See S. Elizabeth Bird, "Gendered Construction of the American Indian in Popular Media," *Journal of Communication* 49, no. 3 (Summer 1999): 63.

59. HW, October 20, 1877, 821.

60. See, for instance, *Leslie's* illustration of the Fetterman massacre, January 19, 1867, 281, a highly fictionalized drawing that included warriors stabbing soldiers with lances and chopping soldiers with tomahawks, as well as two warriors scalping soldiers with knives and holding their bloody trophies aloft.

61. See, for example, Roger A. Fischer, *Them Damned Pictures: Explorations in American Political Cartoon Art* (North Haven, CT: Archon Books, 1995). Also see John M. Coward, "Making Sense of Savagery: Native American Cartoons in *The Daily Graphic,*" *Visual Communication Quarterly* 19, no. 4 (October–December 2012): 200–215.

62. HW, June 12, 1858, 377.

63. Ibid.

64. The other illustration on the page is a non-Indian man identified as "Ben Bruno, Negro Slave and Favorite."

65. HW, June 12, 1858, 377.

66. FLIN, January 31, 1863, 300.

67. Although it is unclear who took the original portrait of Little Crow, the *Leslie's* portrait of him appears to be the same image as the portrait appearing on a cabinet card in the 1890s. This card, which can be found online, was produced by J. H. Gravenslund of Hutchinson, Minnesota. The cabinet card photograph shows Little Crow's torso wrapped in a blanket, which does not appear in the *Leslie's* image.

68. FLIN, July 12, 1873, 277.

69. See, for example, the *New York Times,* April 13, 1873, and the *San Francisco Daily Examiner,* April 14, 1873. The *Times* editorial of April 13, 1873, began with this sentence: "By a crime of unparalleled atrocity, the United States Army has lost one of its most valued officers in the murder of Gen. CANBY, and the Modoc Chief, Capt. JACK, has gained enduring infamy as the most treacherous and bloodthirsty of savages."

70. *Leslie's* credited the photos to C. F. Watkins, the owner of a photo gallery in San Francisco. Bush and Mitchell note that Heller took the original Modoc photographs, which were later "appropriated and produced" by Watkins. See Alfred L. Bush and Lee Clark Mitchell, eds., *The Photograph and the American Indian* (Princeton, NJ: Princeton University Press, 1994), 301.

71. Prints of Heller's Modoc mug shots were published on cards with authentication by Captain C. B. Throckmorton, who certified that Heller "has this day taken the Photographs of the above Modoc Indian prisoner under my charge"; see Bush and Mitchell, *Photograph and the American Indian,* 47–48.

72. FLIN, July 12, 1873, 287.

73. Ibid.

74. FLIN, November 22, 1890, 280.

75. The original photograph is reproduced in Joanna Cohan Scherer, *Indians: The Great Photographs That Reveal North American Indian Life, 1847–1929* (New York: Bonanza Books, 1982), 29.

76. Ibid., 28.

77. See, for example, the crazed and howling savages in Thomas Nast's anti-Tammany cartoon in *Harper's Weekly,* July 17, 1886, 460, or the hideous half-Indian, half-buck creature published in the *Daily Graphic,* August 15, 1876. The *Graphic* cartoon showed the Indian-animal in death above this caption: "The Right Way to Dispose of Sitting Bull and His Braves." Also see the dark and unflattering drawing of Sitting Bull in the Nast cartoon in the *Harper's Weekly* of March 22, 1879, 232. Nast's Indian cartoons are described in Arlene M. Halley, "Thomas Nast's Indian Imagery," *Journal of the Thomas Nast Society* 8, no. 4 (1994): 1–29.

78. HW, September 18, 1886, 601.

79. Commenting on the power of this photo in the popular imagination, one scholar wrote, "This is the face that launched a hundred articles, stories, and novels"; see C. L. Sonnichsen, "From Savage to Saint: A New Image for Geronimo," in *Geronimo and the End of the Apache Wars,* ed. C. L. Sonnichsen (Lincoln: University of Nebraska Press, 1968), 14. More recently, William M. Clements has written that Geronimo's face "represented the quintessence of recalcitrant savagism, the most adamant and frustratingly final obstacle to civilization's progress"; see William M. Clements, *Imagining Geronimo: An Apache Icon in Popular Culture* (Albuquerque: University of New Mexico Press, 2013), 155.

80. Robert M. Utley, *The Indian Frontier of the American West, 1846–1890* (Albuquerque: University of New Mexico Press, 1984), 198. This place and time is corroborated by Clements, *Imagining Geronimo,* 156.

81. See, for instance, Goodyear, *Faces of the Frontier*, 120, which lists the photograph as "c. 1887." Also see Tim Johnson, ed., *Spirit Capture: Photographs from the National Museum of the American Indian* (Washington, DC: Smithsonian Institution Press, 1998), 79.

82. It appears on the front page of the *St. Louis Globe-Democrat,* June 3, 1885.

83. Clements, *Imagining Geronimo,* 160.

84. Randall produced a well-known portrait of Mangus, son of Mangus Coloradas, which was published in *Harper's Weekly,* April 17, 1886. Several of these portraits, including the famous Geronimo portrait, are published in Edwin F. Sweeney, *From Cochise to Geronimo: The Chiricahua Apaches, 1874–1886* (Norman: University of Oklahoma Press, 2010), 259–66, although without attribution to Randall. Also, some of these Apache portraits are attributed to Ben Wittick, who was a partner with Randall at one time. Other photographers capitalized on souvenir portraits of Indians in the last decades of the nineteenth century, including David F. Barry, who worked on the northern plains.

85. Sandweiss, *Print the Legend,* 235.

86. Trachtenberg, *Reading American Photographs,* 127.

Chapter 2. Illustrating Indian Lives

1. Mildred D. Ladner, *William de la Montagne Cary: Artist on the Missouri River* (Norman: University of Oklahoma Press, 1984), 3. Also see Robert Taft, *Artists and Illustrators of the Old West, 1850–1900* (New York: Charles Scribner's Sons, 1953), 52, 292.

2. Taft, *Artists and Illustrators,* 52.

3. Ibid., 52–53. Also see Ladner, *William de la Montagne Cary,* esp. ch. 3–7.

4. Taft, *Artists and Illustrators,* 292.

5. *Harper's Weekly* (hereafter HW), April 1, 1876, 267.

6. Ibid.

7. Ladner, *William de la Montagne Cary,* 151.

8. HW, April 1, 1876, 267.

9. Another example of generic Indian life was a set of Cary pictures published as a full page in *Harper's Weekly* in 1868. This page, captioned "The Life of an Indian," consisted of nine scenes, starting with "Infancy," passing into "Manhood," and ending in "Funeral Ceremony." The largest and most dramatic scene was in the center of the page. It showed a warrior astride his horse, celebrating the taking of "The First Scalp." See HW, June 20, 1868, 392.

10. Quoted in Anthony Grafton, *New Worlds, Ancient Texts: The Power of Tradition and the Shock of Discovery* (Cambridge, MA: Belknap Press of Harvard University Press, 1992), 76. A reproduction of the broadside is also in Grafton, *New Worlds, Ancient Texts,* 76.

11. W. Graham Arader III, *Native Grace: Prints of the New World, 1590–1876* (Charlottesville, VA: Thomasson-Grant, 1988), 24.

12. Ibid., 24, 26.

13. Wendy Shadwell, "Introduction," in ibid., 17.

14. Julie Schimmel, "Inventing 'the Indian,'" in *The West as America: Reinterpreting Images of the Frontier, 1820–1920,* ed. William H. Truettner (Washington, DC: Smithsonian Institution Press, 1991), 151.

15. Schimmel, "Inventing 'the Indian,'" 153–54.

16. George Catlin, *Letters and Notes on the Manners, Customs, and Conditions of the North American Indians,* vol. 1 (New York: Dover, 1973), 3.

17. Mandan village life is discussed in Catlin, *Letters and Notes,* "Letter No. 11." Funeral customs are discussed in "Letter No. 12."

18. Schimmel, "Inventing 'the Indian,'" 149–50. As I have argued previously, the press tended to emphasize those "facts" about Indians that confirmed native differences "in cosmology, language, religion, food, dress, and the like"; see John M. Coward, *The Newspaper Indian: Native American Identity in the Press, 1820–90* (Urbana: University of Illinois Press, 1999), 19.

19. Robert F. Berkhofer Jr., *The White Man's Indian: Images of the American Indian from Columbus to the Present* (New York: Vintage Books, 1979), 26.

20. Joshua Brown, *Beyond the Lines: Pictorial Reporting, Everyday Life, and the Crisis of Gilded Age America* (Berkeley: University of California Press, 2002), 7. Also see Fiona Deans Halloran, *Thomas Nast: The Father of Modern Political Cartoons* (Chapel Hill: University of North Carolina Press, 2012), 206.

21. Alan Trachtenberg, *Shades of Hiawatha: Staging Indians, Making Americans, 1880–1930* (New York: Hill and Wang, 2004), 170.

22. Writing about the earliest film depictions of Native Americans, film historian Alison Griffiths cites the power of film to reduce cultural rituals to "ethnographic spectacle." See Alison Griffiths, "Science and Spectacle: Native American Representation in Early Cinema," in *Dressing in Feathers: The Construction of the Indian in American Popular Culture,* ed. S. Elizabeth Bird (Boulder, CO: Westview Press, 1996), 79–95. Some pictorial press illustrations follow this pattern, though in less dramatic form.

23. HW, April 23, 1864, 260. "Bierstadt" appears to be a reference to Albert Bierstadt, the German-born American painter who traveled to the West to paint landscapes as well as Indians in 1859 and again in 1863.

24. HW, April 23, 1864, 260.

25. *Frank Leslie's Illustrated Newspaper* (hereafter FLIN), February 10, 1866, 324.

26. Ibid.

27. Ibid.

28. Ibid.

29. HW, September 19, 1874, 773.

30. Ibid., 782.

31. HW, January 2, 1875, 8–9. Although the engraving is signed "Jules Tavernier & Frenzeny," Claudine Chalmers writes that the scene was sketched by Tavernier, who witnessed the sun dance near the Red Cloud agency in June 1874. See Claudine Chalmers, *Chronicling the West for 'Harper's': Coast to Coast with Frenzeny and Tavernier in 1873–1874* (Norman: University of Oklahoma Press, 2013), 167.

32. HW, January 2, 1875, 10.

33. Beyond America, Chalmers writes that Europeans, especially the French, were fascinated by stories and pictures of Noble Savages. See Chalmers, *Chronicling the West,* 161.

34. FLIN, April 8, 1882, 102. Cushing's role as a pioneering ethnologist, participant-observer, and adventurer among the Zuni is detailed in Eliza McFeely, *Zuni and the American Imagination* (New York: Hill and Wang, 2001), esp. ch. 4, "A Place of Grace: Frank Hamilton Cushing."

35. FLIN, April 8, 1882, 102.

36. Ibid., 97.

37. This group is identified in other texts as the Priesthood of the Bow, as McFeely explains it, "the society responsible for protecting the Zuni from its enemies both physically, as warriors, and metaphysically, as priests"; see McFeely, *Zuni and the American Imagination,* 98.

38. HW, March 6, 1869, 152.

39. Ibid., 157.

40. HW, June 20, 1874, 512.

41. Ibid., 513.

42. HW, July 26, 1884, 480–81.

43. Ibid., 479.

44. HW, June 7, 1879, 445.

45. Ibid., 447.

46. Ibid.

47. HW, April 30, 1870, 284.

48. Ibid.

49. Ibid.

50. HW, August 12, 1876, 665.

51. Ibid., 668.

52. Ibid.

53. Ladner, *William de la Montagne Cary*, 155.

54. HW, May 2, 1874, 377.

55. Ibid., 381.

56. HW, May 1, 1858, 281.

57. HW, May 16, 1874, 420.

58. Ibid., 421.

59. Ibid., 422.

60. HW, June 4, 1870, 353.

61. Ibid.

62. Chalmers, *Chronicling the West,* 180.

63. HW, July 3, 1875, 537. Chalmers attributes this drawing to Tavernier, whose Utah scenes, she writes, "display more boisterous irony than Frenzeny's"; see Chalmers, *Chronicling the West,* 180.

64. Chalmers identifies this object as a cane. I interpreted it as the barrel of a rifle, as suggested by the story. See Chalmers, *Chronicling the West,* 180.

65. HW, October 20, 1877, 821.

66. Ibid.

67. Ibid.

68. FLIN, May 5, 1883, 176.

69. Ibid., 174.

70. HW, March 26, 1870, 197. This engraving was reversed or "flopped" in the production process; thus Cary's signature appears backward in the lower right corner of the drawing.

71. HW, March 26, 1870, 197.

72. See Glenda Riley, *Confronting Race: Women and Indians on the Frontier, 1815–1915* (Albuquerque: University of New Mexico Press, 2004), 95–106. Also see Lillian Schlissel, *Women's Diaries of the Westward Journey* (New York: Schocken Books, 1982), 15, and "Tables," following 231. Schlissel reviewed diaries from ninety-six women, only seven of whom reported Indian attacks or threats. Women's diaries, Schlissel notes, "correct the historical record" regarding Indian-white relations in western journeys.

73. HW, June 20, 1874, 512.

74. Ibid., 513.

75. FLIN, January 9, 1875, 296.

76. Ibid., 295.

Chapter 3. The Princess and the Squaw

1. *Harper's Weekly* (hereafter HW), June 29, 1907, 958.

2. Ibid.

3. Ibid.

4. Ibid.

5. Glenda Riley, *Confronting Race: Women and Indians on the Frontier, 1815–1915* (Albuquerque: University of New Mexico Press, 2004), 41.

6. J. Frederick Fauz, "Pocahontas (Matoaka)," in *Encyclopedia of North American Indians,* ed. Frederick E. Hoxie (Boston: Houghton Mifflin, 1996), 490–91. In her essay on Pocahontas and Indian women, Rayna Green cites earlier European legends very similar to the Pocahontas-Smith rescue story. See Green, "The Pocahontas Perplex: The Image of Indian Women in American Culture," *Massachusetts Review* 16, no. 4 (Autumn 1975): 698–700.

7. Robert S. Tilton, *Pocahontas: The Evolution of an American Narrative* (Cambridge: Cambridge University Press, 1994), 110. The actual identity of this woman and child is unknown; Tilton cites Philip Barbour, who writes that the portrait may represent "an 18th-century Iroquois woman and child"; see Philip L. Barbour, *Pocahontas and Her World* (Boston: Houghton Mifflin, 1970), 235.

8. Green writes that the "Pocahontas perplex emerged as a controlling metaphor in the American experience"; see Green, "Pocahontas Perplex," 703.

9. Alan Trachtenberg, *Shades of Hiawatha: Staging Indians, Making Americans, 1880–1930* (New York: Hill and Wang, 2004), 23.

10. Tilton, *Pocahontas,* 131.

11. This study focuses on news and feature illustrations in *Frank Leslie's Illustrated Newspaper* and *Harper's Weekly.* It does not include cartoons or advertising imagery that depicted Indian women. Indian imagery in nineteenth-century advertising, male and female, is examined by Jeffery Steele, "Reduced to Images: American Indians in Nineteenth-Century Advertising," in *Dressing in Feathers: The Construction of the Indian in American Popular Culture,* ed. S. Elizabeth Bird (Boulder, CO: Westview Press, 1996), 45–64.

12. Bird writes that the "popular imagery of American Indians has tended to focus on males." See S. Elizabeth Bird, "Gendered Construction of the American Indian in Popular Media," *Journal of Communication* 49, no. 3 (Summer 1999): 72. Also see, for example, John M. Coward, *The Newspaper Indian: Native American Identity in the Press, 1820–90* (Urbana: University of Illinois Press, 1999), and William E. Huntzicker, "Picturing American Indians: Newspaper Pictures and Native Americans in the 1860s and 1870s," in *Seeking a Voice: Images of Race and Gender in the 19th-Century Press,* ed. David B. Sachsman, S. Kittrell Rushing and Roy Morris Jr. (West Lafayette, IN: Purdue University Press, 2009), 45–55.

13. Stuart Hall, "The Spectacle of the 'Other,'" in *Representation: Cultural Representations and Signifying Practices,* ed. Stuart Hall (London: Sage, 1997), 234–35. Hall writes that meaning depends on the difference between opposites; in this case, white/Indian and male/female. These "binary oppositions," Hall argues, are subject to oversimplification, "swallowing up all distinctions in their rather two-part structure." Moreover, one pole is usually dominant, subordinating its opposite within its "field of operations." Thus racial meanings are created through the marking or identification of difference, a process that includes the subordinate "Other."

14. The images and stories in this study were located through keyword searches in electronic databases of *Frank Leslie's Illustrated Newspaper* and *Harper's Weekly.* These searches yielded several dozen illustrations.

15. See, for example, the cover of *Leslie's* on July 12, 1873, which featured eleven portraits of Indians at war with the army in Northern California. Ten of the portraits are men; the eleventh was identified as "One-Eyed Dixie, the Squaw Interpreter."

16. The word *squaw* has a controversial history and has been associated with a long list of derogatory terms for Indian women. These terms include *vagina, prostitute, harlot,* and similar words. I use the term here because it was used in the pictorial press to describe some Indian women, especially women who were old, seemingly poor, or who appeared dirty or unkempt. A thoughtful discussion of the word and its history is in Stacey J. T. Hust and Debra Merskin, "The 'S'-Word: Activist Texts and Media Coverage Related to the Movement to Eradicate 'Squaw,'" in *American Indians and the Mass Media,* ed. Meta Carstarphen and John P. Sanchez (Norman: University of Oklahoma Press, 2012), 128–49.

17. Carolyn Kitch has argued persuasively that illustrations in early twentieth-century popular magazines helped define ideas about "femininity, masculinity, class status, and Americanness"; see Kitch, *The Girl on the Magazine Cover: The Origins of Visual Stereotypes in American Mass Media* (Chapel Hill: University of North Carolina Press, 2001), 4.

18. Historian Anthony Grafton has pointed out that Roman writer Pliny the Elder drew on ancient legends to compile his *Natural History* (AD 77–79), describing far-off places inhabited by "monstrous races . . . men with the heads of dogs, men with one large foot under whose head they rested in the desert sun"; see Grafton, *New Worlds, Ancient Texts: The Power of Tradition and the Shock of Discovery* (Cambridge, MA: Belknap Press, 1992), 35, 37.

19. E. McClung Fleming, "The American Image as Indian Princess, 1765–1783," *Winterthur Portfolio* 2 (1965): 65–81. Also see Green, "Pocahontas Perplex," 701–3, and Trachtenberg, *Shades of Hiawatha,* 23.

20. The illustration is by Theodore Galle, after Jan vander Stradt. See Philip J. Deloria, *Playing Indian* (New Haven, CT: Yale University Press, 1998), 29. Also see Margarita Zamora, *Reading Columbus* (Berkeley: University of California Press, 1993), 152–54.

21. Deloria, *Playing Indian,* 29. The Indian woman as an allegorical symbol of America took several forms beginning in the sixteenth century. Many of these are discussed in Fleming, "American Image as Indian Princess."

22. *Frank Leslie's Illustrated Newspaper* (hereafter FLIN), June 28, 1856, 36.

23. Ibid., 35.

24. FLIN, February 17, 1866, 348.

25. Ibid.

26. HW, June 19, 1909, 18–19.

27. Women's magazines were particularly active in promoting activities in the domestic sphere, the so-called cult of true womanhood. See, for example, Sarah Mitchell, "A Wonderful Duty: A Study of Motherhood in *Godey's* Magazine," in *Seeking a Voice: Images of Race and Gender in the 19th-Century Press,* ed. David B. Sachsman, S. Kittrell Rushing, and Roy Morris Jr. (West Lafayette, IN: Purdue University Press, 2009), 171–78. Also see Glenda Riley's discussion of "American discourse on white womanhood" in *Confronting Race,* 11–32.

28. Joshua Brown, *Beyond the Lines: Pictorial Reporting, Everyday Life, and the Crisis of Gilded Age America,* 2, 107–8. Also see Kate Roberts Edenborg and Hazel Dicken-Garcia, "The Darlings Come Out to See the Volunteers: Depictions of Women in *Harper's Weekly*

during the Civil War," in *Seeking a Voice: Images of Race and Gender in the 19th-Century Press,* ed. David B. Sachsman, S. Kittrell Rushing, and Roy Morris Jr. (West Lafayette, IN: Purdue University Press, 2009), 205–14. See, for instance, idealized "ladies" in maternal roles in FLIN, January 17, 1891, 453, and February 21, 1891, 43.

29. HW, August 22, 1857, 532.

30. FLIN, January 17, 1857, 104.

31. HW, March 2, 1872, 173.

32. FLIN, July 3, 1875, 289.

33. The "poor Indian" theme in Indian illustrations is documented by Mindy Duncan, "Finding Focus in the Early Illustrated Press in the United States: Images of Native Americans in *Frank Leslie's Illustrated* and *Harper's Weekly*," 1860–1890," *Atlanta Review of Journalism History* 2 (Spring 2001): 42–46.

34. FLIN, February 27, 1875, 413.

35. FLIN, January 3, 1891, 409.

36. Riley notes that these ideas originated in European descriptions of Indian life and, over time, "were repeated so often that they became truisms"; see Riley, *Confronting Race,* 89.

37. HW, March 20, 1875, 240.

38. Ibid., 242.

39. HW, June 14, 1873, 520.

40. Ibid., 518.

41. Riley, *Confronting Race,* 91–92.

42. HW, March 18, 1876, 233.

43. Ibid., 234.

44. HW, June 21, 1884, 393. Although he is often overshadowed as a Western illustrator and painter by Frederic Remington and others, Henry Farny produced many Indian portraits and camp scenes, some of which rival his more famous contemporaries. See Denny Carter, *Henry Farny* (New York: Watson-Guptill, 1978).

45. HW, June 21, 1884, 395.

46. FLIN, April 30, 1870, 97.

47. Ibid., 99.

48. FLIN, June 18, 1870, 209.

49. Ibid., 211.

50. HW, September 15, 1866, 580.

51. Ibid.

52. The developing field of anthropology, Lutz and Collins write, emphasized colorful cultural difference, an exoticism that "involves the creations of an other who is strange but—at least as important—beautiful"; see Catherine A. Lutz and Jane L. Collins, *Reading National Geographic* (Chicago: University of Chicago Press, 1993), 91–92.

53. See, for example, Coward, *Newspaper Indian,* ch. 4–5.

54. HW, September 7, 1889, 730–31.

55. Southwestern pottery became a symbol of "authentic" Indian craftwork for twentieth-century collectors. See Leah Dilworth, *Imagining Indians in the Southwest* (Washington, DC: Smithsonian Institution Press, 1996), esp. ch. 3, "The Spectacle of Indian Artisanal Labor." Also see John M. Coward, "Selling the Southwestern Indian: Ideology and Image in *Arizona Highways,* 1925–1940," *American Journalism* 20, no. 2 (Spring 2003): 22–24.

56. Not surprisingly, photographers were also drawn to Indian women carrying water pots on their heads. See, for example, Edward Curtis, who photographed two blanketed women in *Zuni Water Carriers,* and posed a woman named Flower Morning (Povi-Tamu) in *Girl and Jar—San Ildefonso.* These photographs are reproduced in Christopher M. Lyman, *The Vanishing Race and Other Illusions: Photographs of Indians by Edward S. Curtis* (Washington, DC: Smithsonian Institution Press, 1982), 58, 133. Also see the work of an unidentified photographer who took a group photo of women at the Tesuque Pueblo in Alfred L. Bush and Lee Clark Mitchell, *The Photograph and the American Indian* (Princeton, NJ: Princeton University Press, 1994), 175.

57. HW, September 7, 1889, 732.

58. Ibid.

59. Lutz and Collins, *Reading National Geographic,* 90–91.

60. HW, June 7, 1890, 445.

61. Ibid., 447.

62. HW, October 14, 1893, 891. Sharp went on to become one of the leading artists in Taos, New Mexico, where he was well known for his Indian paintings. See Arrell Morgan Gibson, *The Santa Fe and Taos Colonies: Age of the Muses, 1900–1942* (Norman: University of Oklahoma Press, 1983), and Laura M. Bickerstaff, *Pioneer Artists of Taos,* rev. and expanded ed. (Denver: Old West, 1983). For a more critical perspective, see Sherry Clayton Taggett and Ted Schwartz, *Paintbrushes and Pistols: How the Taos Artists Sold the West* (Santa Fe, NM: John Muir Publications, 1990).

63. HW, October 14, 1893, 892.

64. FLIN, January 3, 1880, 317. In 1887, *Leslie's* emphasized the civilizing process when it published side-by-side portraits of two young—but very different—Indians. One picture showed "Miss Kitty Ross," the smiling, well-dressed daughter of a Cherokee leader, alongside another Indian, the blanket-wrapped, stone-faced boy Crow Foot, son of the Lakota leader Sitting Bull. The caption explained that this was "A Suggestive Contrast—The Indian in the Wild and in the Civilized State"; see FLIN, March 26, 1887, 85.

65. FLIN, January 3, 1880, 317.

66. Kenny A. Franks, "La Flesche Family," in *Encyclopedia of North American Indians,* ed. Frederick E. Hoxie (New York: Houghton Mifflin, 1996), 324–25.

67. FLIN, January 3, 1880, 317.

68. The highly sexualized "darkened Other" became a popular female type in the last decades of the nineteenth century, as did the exotic colonial woman, both appealing to white male fantasies. See Katherine H. Adams, Michael L. Keene, and Jennifer C. Koella, *Seeing the American Woman, 1880–1920: The Social Impact of the Visual Media Explosion* (Jefferson, NC: McFarland, 2012), esp. ch. 6–7.

69. Robert F. Berkhofer Jr., *The White Man's Indian: Images of the American Indian from Columbus to the Present* (New York: Vintage Books, 1979), 51. Also see Cynthia Eagle Russett, *Darwin in America: The Intellectual Response, 1865–1912* (San Francisco: W. H. Freeman, 1976), 50–51.

Chapter 4. Making Images on the Indian Frontier

1. Theodore Davis, "A Summer on the Plains," *Harper's New Monthly Magazine,* February 1868, 292.

2. Robert Taft, *Artists and Illustrators of the Old West, 1850–1900* (New York: Charles Scribner's Sons, 1953), 64.

3. Taft, *Artists and Illustrators,* 70. Also see George C. Groce and David H. Wallace, *The New-York Historical Society's Dictionary of Artists in America, 1564–1860* (New Haven, CT: Yale University Press, 1957), 168. Both Taft and Groce and Wallace are uncertain of Davis's actual training. Groce and Wallace write: "[Davis] is said to have had some training in drawing from one Herrick, possibly Henry W. Herrick, wood engraver and designer, who was living in Brooklyn in 1856."

4. Taft, *Artists and Illustrators,* 70–71.

5. This account is drawn from Peter Hastings Falk, ed., *Who Was Who in American Art, 1564–1975* (Madison, CT: Sound View Press, 1999), 846.

6. In 1867, *Harper's* reported that Davis was a witness to numerous Civil War battles, including the famous battle between the *Monitor* and *Merrimac* at Hampton Roads in Virginia and the Battle of Shiloh in Tennessee, both in early 1862. If so, it is curious that Davis did not get any credit for correspondence or drawings concerning these battles. See *Harper's,* April 22, 1862, which featured drawings of the ironclad battle, but no mention of Davis. The following week, in fact, *Harper's* published a Davis drawing of Fort Clinch in northern Florida, which suggests that Davis may have been elsewhere during the ironclad battle. Drawings of Shiloh in April and May 1862 are credited to Henry Mosler; nothing in *Harper's* suggests that Davis was at that engagement either. The 1867 report also put Davis at Vicksburg, Antietam, and on Sherman's infamous march to the sea, all of which are supported by drawings in the newspaper.

7. A Davis illustration of Sherman's march appeared on the cover of *Harper's Weekly* on March 4, 1865, 129.

8. Davis's service to the military was noted in his obituary in *Harper's Weekly,* November 26, 1894, 1114.

9. Letter from Caroline D. Pennypacker to Robert Taft, December 30, 1939, Theodore Davis file, box 20, Taft Papers, Kansas State Historical Society, Topeka.

10. Falk, *Who Was Who in American Art,* 846. Also see Doris Ostrander Dandy, *Artists of the American West: A Biographical Dictionary* (Chicago: Sage Books, 1974), 63.

11. The *Harper's* obituary reported that "it was largely for the benefit of his health that he settled fourteen years ago at Asbury."

12. *Weekly Rocky Mountain News,* December 1, 1865, 1.

13. Ibid.

14. Ibid. The Dr. Whipple who accompanied Davis on this trip should not be confused with Bishop Henry Benjamin Whipple, an Episcopalian leader in Minnesota known for his advocacy on behalf of Indians.

15. *Weekly Rocky Mountain News,* December 6, 1865, 2.

16. Ibid.

17. Ibid.

18. Ibid.

19. *Harper's Weekly* (hereafter HW), January 27, 1866, 57–58.

20. Ibid., 58.

21. *Harper's New Monthly Magazine,* July 1867, 142.

22. Ibid., 144.

23. Ibid., 149.

24. Ibid., 147.

25. Ron Tyler, *Prints of the West* (Golden, CO: Fulcrum Press, 1994), 119.

26. Ibid.

27. Ibid.

28. L. G. Moses, *Wild West Shows and the Images of American Indians, 1883–1993* (Albuquerque: University of New Mexico Press, 1996), 22.

29. Jon Tuska, *The American West in Film: Critical Approaches in the Western* (Lincoln: University of Nebraska Press, 1988).

30. This paragraph follows arguments advanced in John M. Coward, *The Newspaper Indian: Native American Identity in the Press, 1820–90* (Urbana: University of Illinois Press, 1999), 128.

31. Oliver Knight, *Following the Indian Wars: The Story of the Newspaper Correspondents among the Indian Campaigners* (Norman: University of Oklahoma Press, 1960), 62.

32. Ibid., 63.

33. Elmo Scott Watson, "History in the News," undated newspaper clipping, Theodore Davis file, box 20, Taft Papers, Kansas State Historical Society, Topeka.

34. William E. Huntzicker, "Custer's Pictorial Images: Heroism and Racism in the Illustrated Press," in *Speaking About Custer,* ed. Sandy Barnard (Terre Haute: IN: AST Press, 1991), 38.

35. HW, August 17, 1867, 513.

36. Ibid.

37. Edgar A. Howell, "A Special Artist in the Indian Wars," *Montana* 15, no. 2 (Spring 1965): 20–21. Howell notes that an illustration of the bodies of the Kidder party published in Custer's memoir, *My Life on the Plains,* is substantially more gruesome. It shows mutilated flesh, not bare bones, and appears more accurate than Davis's original illustration.

38. A side-by-side comparison of William A. Bell's photograph and the *Harper's Weekly* engraving of Sergeant Wyllyams's body is in Michael L. Carlebach, *The Origins of Photojournalism in America* (Washington, DC: Smithsonian Institution Press, 1992), 124.

39. Knight, *Following the Indian Wars,* 72.

40. See ibid., 93–103; Knight notes that the battle became controversial almost immediately for another reason: the fate of Major Joel Elliott and his party of eighteen men, all killed when they split off from the main force. For years afterward, many observers blamed Custer for abandoning Elliott and his men, another disputed aspect of Custer's legacy.

41. HW, December 19, 1868, 802.

42. Ibid.

43. Ibid., 804.

44. Ibid.

45. HW, December 26, 1868, 825.

46. Central City (CO) *Daily Miners' Register,* December 19, 1865, 3, typescript article in Theodore Davis file, box 20, Taft Papers, Kansas State Historical Society, Topeka.

Chapter 5. Illustrating the Indian Wars

1. *Illustrated Police News,* July 13, 1876. This illustration is reproduced in Paul Andrew Hutton, ed., *The Custer Reader* (Lincoln: University of Nebraska Press, 1992), 549.

2. Mark Kellogg, a reporter from Bismarck, North Dakota, who was with Custer at the Last Stand, died in the battle, along with all of Custer's immediate command. For more on Kellogg at the Little Bighorn, see Oliver Knight, *Following the Indian Wars: The Story of the Newspaper Correspondents among the Indian Campaigners* (Norman: University of Oklahoma Press, 1960), 194–219.

3. *Daily Graphic*, July 19, 1876, 122.

4. Ibid., 120.

5. Writing in 1968, Barbara Tyler, curator of history at the Amon Carter Museum, identified more than 800 illustrations of Custer's Last Stand. See Don Russell, *Custer's Last* (Fort Worth, TX: Amon Carter Museum of Western Art, 1968), 1. Also see Hutton, *Custer Reader,* 549, who refers to over 1,500 Last Stand renderings.

6. Robert F. Berkhofer Jr., *The White Man's Indian* (New York: Vintage Books, 1978), 84.

7. Robert Hughes, *American Vision: The Epic Story of Art in America* (New York: Alfred A. Knopf, 1997), 182–84.

8. Michael L. Carlebach, *The Origins of Photojournalism in America* (Washington, DC: Smithsonian Institution Press, 1992), 65, and Andrea G. Peterson, "*Frank Leslie's Illustrated Newspaper* and *Harper's Weekly*: Innovation and Imitation in Nineteenth-Century American Pictorial Reporting," *Journal of Popular Culture* 23, no. 4 (Spring 1990): 81.

9. Robert L. Craig, "Fact, Public Opinion, and Persuasion: The Rise of the Visual in Journalism and Advertising," in *Picturing the Past: Media, History, and Photography,* ed. Bonnie Brennen and Hanno Hardt (Urbana: University of Illinois Press, 1999), 46.

10. Robert Taft, *Artists and Illustrators of the Old West, 1850–1900* (New York: Charles Scribner's Sons, 1953), 58–71.

11. *Harper's Weekly* was aimed at a more elite audience than *Leslie's* and in its early years published more genteel illustrations and fewer action-oriented images. This changed during the war, however, as *Harper's* sought to show more action and hired a number of illustrators from *Leslie's.* See David Park, "Picturing the News: Visual Genres in Civil War News," *Communication Review* 3, no. 4 (1999): 290, 294.

12. Walter Lippmann, *Public Opinion,* quoted in Eliot King and Jane L. Chapman, ed., *Key Readings in Journalism* (New York: Routledge, 2012), 343.

13. Recalling his experiences sketching Civil War battles, Theodore Davis wrote that it would have been convenient if every battlefield had "some elevated spot" from which to sketch the action. Instead, Davis wrote, the artist was "obliged to visit every accessible point which seems likely to be an important one, and there make a sufficient memorandum . . . as will enable him to decide at the close of the action precisely what were its most interesting features." This was probably easier to do in the Civil War than in Indian battles, which were usually shorter than Civil War engagements. Davis also wrote of the dangers of battlefield sketching, noting that to sketch a battle "one must accept the most dangerous situations." See Theodore R. Davis, "How a Battle Is Sketched," *St. Nicholas* 16 (July 1889): 661–68.

14. For example, camp scenes were a prominent feature of Custer's 1867 campaign in Kansas. See *Harper's Weekly* (hereafter HW), June 29, 1867, 405. The Modoc war was also illustrated with numerous camp scenes and posed images of soldiers and their Indian allies. See HW, June 14, 1873, 497, 500; also HW, June 21, 1873, 533. Similar camp scenes were used to illustrate the Sioux campaign of 1876. See HW, July 22, 1876, 592. *Frank Leslie's*

Illustrated Newspaper (hereafter FLIN) also relied on camp scenes in its illustrations of the Indian wars. See, for example, its front-page illustrations of the post–Little Bighorn Sioux campaign August 12, 1876, 369, and inside the issue, 377.

15. A sketch by one "Mr. Herman" of St. Paul was published in HW, January 17, 1863, 39. Also see FLIN, January 24, 1863, 285. The *Leslie's* full-page sketch, attributed to W. H. Childs, shows a large crowd of soldiers and civilians gathered around a massive gallows in Mankato, Minnesota. It documents the hanging of thirty-eight warriors connected to the Sioux uprising in Minnesota, an event Judith Nies called "the largest public hanging in American history"; see Nies, *Native American History: A Chronology of a Culture's Vast Achievements and Their Links to World Events* (New York: Ballantine Books, 1996), 268.

16. Park, "Picturing the News," 318–19.

17. HW, for example, claimed that its drawing of Indians attacking a wagon train in 1868 was "a graphic, truthful, and timely illustration of one of these desperate encounters now so frequent on the plains." See HW, September 19, 1868, 606.

18. HW, July 16, 1870, 449.

19. HW, October 31, 1863, 693. The Battle of White Stone Hill was part of a series of conflicts on the northern plains that grew out of the Minnesota Sioux uprising of 1862. Details on White Stone Hill (or Whitestone Hill) are in Gregory F. Michno, *Encyclopedia of Indian Wars: Western Battles and Skirmishes, 1850–1890* (Missoula, MT: Mountain Press, 2003), 124–25.

20. FLIN, December 6, 1879, 245.

21. Ibid., 239.

22. HW, September 12, 1863, 577.

23. The Sioux uprising was sparked by incompetent and corrupt Indian agents who refused to release rations to the tribe in June 1862. A brief account of the uprising is in Nies, *Native American History*, 267–68. Also see Michno, *Encyclopedia of Indian Wars*, which reports on numerous conflicts between the Sioux and whites in Minnesota and the Dakotas from 1862 through 1864.

24. HW, September 12, 1863, 587.

25. Hughes, *American Vision*, 182–87. Hughes traces the origin of the Demonic Indian in fine art to John Vanderlyn's 1804 painting, *Murder of Jane McCrea*. Other pictorial press examples of the violent Indian trope include HW, October 10, 1868, 653, which depicts an Indian attack on a "bull-train" near Sheridan, Kansas; HW, July 16, 1870, 457, an illustration that shows settlers fighting unseen Indians who have attacked their cabin; FLIN, September 12, 1868, 408, which shows the capture of a Union Pacific freight train by the Sioux; and the dramatic cover illustration on FLIN, May 14, 1873, 149, which shows Indians breaking down a cabin door as the settlers desperately fight for their survival.

26. An account of the newspaper coverage of the Fetterman fight is in John M. Coward, *The Newspaper Indian: Native American Identity in the Press, 1820–90* (Urbana: University of Illinois Press, 1999), 125–58.

27. *Chicago Tribune*, December 27, 1866, 4; Coward, *Newspaper Indian*, 136.

28. FLIN, January 19, 1867, 280.

29. Ibid., 281.

30. HW, March 23, 1867, 180.

31. Coward, *Newspaper Indian*, 135–36.

32. Russell, *Custer's Last,* 15.

33. FLIN, March 19, 1864, 401, and HW, March 19, 1864, 177. Also see William E. Huntz-icker, "Custer's Pictorial Images: Heroism and Racism in the Illustrated Press," in *Speaking About Custer,* ed. Sandy Barnard (Terre Haute, IN: AST Press, 1991), 23–49.

34. Don Russell opens his book *Custer's Last* with this proclamation: "No single event in United States history, or perhaps in world history, has been the subject of more bad art and erroneous story than Custer's Last Stand at the Battle of the Little Big Horn on June 25, 1876"; see Russell, *Custer's Last,* 3. Also see Brian W. Dippie, *Custer's Last Stand: The Anatomy of an American Myth* (Lincoln: University of Nebraska Press, 1976), and Bruce A. Rosenberg, "Custer: The Legend of the Martyred Hero in America," in *The Custer Reader,* ed. Paul A. Hutton (Lincoln: University of Nebraska Press, 1992), 527.

35. FLIN, July 22, 1876, 335.

36. Park, "Picturing the News," 301.

37. FLIN, July 29, 1876, 349.

38. Ibid., 347.

39. Ibid.

40. HW, July 29, 1876, 617.

41. Ibid., 618.

42. Ibid.

43. Ibid.

44. It is significant that all the pictorial press illustrations of Custer and the Little Bighorn are positive. Although Custer had many detractors and some of them were publicly criti-cal of his actions at the Little Bighorn, I have found no pictorial press images of Custer as a coward or a fool. Given the shock of the Sioux and Cheyenne victory and anti-Indian feelings of the day, it was probably impossible to publish a critical picture of Custer in the weeks following his death. To do so would have surely met with a popular backlash, a wave of criticism no artist or editor would welcome. The safest visual response—the only one, really—was unabashed heroism and glory on the battlefield, or as *Harper's Weekly* showed, patriotic sentimentality and mourning.

45. HW, January 13, 1866, 20.

46. HW, May 2, 1868, 281.

47. Ibid., 282.

48. Ibid.

49. HW, September 14, 1867, 584.

50. HW, September 16, 1876, 766–67.

51. Ibid.

52. Ibid.

53. Ibid.

54. FLIN, October 14, 1871, 65.

55. Ibid., 72.

56. FLIN, December 26, 1868, 233.

57. For a thoughtful discussion of the nature of and subsequent debate about the Washita campaign, see Michael A. Elliott, *Custerology: The Enduring Legacy of the Indian Wars and George Armstrong Custer* (Chicago: University of Chicago Press, 2007), 132–41.

58. FLIN, December 26, 1868, 235.

59. Ibid.

60. S. Elizabeth Bird, *Dressing in Feathers: The Construction of the Indian in American Popular Culture* (Boulder, CO: Westview Press, 1996), 3. Also see Berkhofer, *White Man's Indian*, 119.

61. Hughes, *American Vision*, 177–80.

62. Ibid., 187. Also see Carol Clark, *Charles Deas and 1840s America* (Norman: University of Oklahoma Press, 2009), 101.

63. Hughes, *American Vision*, 175.

Chapter 6. Making Sense of Savagery

1. *Daily Graphic* (hereafter DG), August 3, 1876, 223.

2. Thomas Milton Kemnitz, "The Cartoon as a Historical Source," *Journal of Interdisciplinary History* 4, no. 1 (Summer 1973): 82.

3. *Cartoons* are defined here as drawings or caricatures of invented scenes created in the newsroom to meet the editorial and story needs of the newspaper. News illustrations, in contrast, are defined as sketches, drawings, and other renderings that purport to represent actual events, often events witnessed by the artist or photographer in the field. For a more complete discussion of the "modes of illustration" in the illustrated press, see Kevin G. Barnhurst and John Nerone, "Civic Picturing vs. Realist Photojournalism: The Regime of Illustrated News, 1865–1901," *Design Issues* 16, no. 1 (Spring 2000): 65.

4. This research is based on a page-by-page examination of the *Daily Graphic* from late 1874 until late 1876, a period that starts well before the Little Bighorn and extends several months after the battle.

5. Roger A. Fischer, *Them Damned Pictures: Explorations in American Political Cartoon Art* (North Haven, CT: Archon Books, 1996). Fischer's chapter 5 is called "Better Dead Than Red," 101–20.

6. S. H. Horgan, "The Origin and End of the 'New York Daily Graphic,'" *Inland Printer*, November 1906, 361.

7. Rebecca Zurier, "Picturing the City: New York in the Press and the Art of the Ashcan School," PhD diss., Yale University, 1988, 91.

8. Ibid., 93, citing a *Graphic* article published May 6, 1873.

9. Quoted in ibid., 92.

10. Ibid., 93.

11. Ibid. Twain's letter was published in the *Graphic* on March 14, 1873.

12. DG, March 4, 1875, 25.

13. Ibid.

14. DG, March 4, 1876, 36.

15. George Juergens, *Joseph Pulitzer and the New York World* (Princeton, NJ: Princeton University Press, 1966), 94.

16. Ibid., 105.

17. Horgan, "Origin and End of the 'New York Daily Graphic,'" 360.

18. See Hopkins, Livingston, entry at the National Library of Australia's Federation Gateway, http://www.nla.gov.au/guides/federation/people/hopkins.html, accessed November 5, 2010.

19. DG, November 4, 1874, 17.

20. DG, December 18, 1874, 347.

21. Don Russell, *Custer's Last* (Fort Worth, TX: Amon Carter Museum of Western Art, 1968), 17.

22. DG, July 19, 1876, 122.

23. Russell notes that Cary "was peculiarly qualified to become the first Custer fight artist." Cary had sketched Indians along the Missouri as early as 1861, and had traveled with Major Marcus Reno on a survey expedition in 1874. Cary, Russell writes, "should have known what a 7th Cavalry trooper looked like in the field"; see Russell, *Custer's Last,* 15.

24. Russell, *Custer's Last,* 15.

25. Ibid.

26. DG, November 10, 1874, 65.

27. DG, November 24, 1874, 179.

28. Joseph A. Citro, *Green Mountain Ghosts, Ghouls and Unsolved Mysteries* (New York: Houghton Mifflin, 1994), 28.

29. Ibid., 27.

30. DG, December 7, 1874, 263.

31. DG, March 11, 1876, 92.

32. DG, March 12, 1875, 87.

33. Ibid., 89.

34. DG, April 24, 1873, 1.

35. The paper's editorials were equally hostile. In an editorial published July 6, 1876, for example, the paper explained the Indian victory as a triumph of Indian "cunning," "stealth," and "trickery." The following day, the paper published several columns on the policy changes needed to defeat the Indians, including a condemnation of the Little Bighorn Indians: "The Sioux are the perfection of Nature's wild men. . . . [T]he Sioux infancy is spent listening to the delectabilities of war till the child precociously weeps to take a scalp." The commentary continued: "Eating only meat, often raw, the wild Sioux have become jackals, and no Indian nation since our first settlement has been so wicked, so powerful, and so untamable"; see DG, July 6, 1876, 30, and July 7, 1876, 38.

36. DG, August 15, 1876, 303.

37. Cartoonist Hopkins, a regular contributor to the *Daily Graphic* in the mid-1870s, was an Ohio native who went on to draw for *Puck, Harper's Weekly,* and a number of other New York publications before immigrating to Australia in 1883. Hopkins created a number of cartoon Indians, including some for his satirical book, *A Comic History of the United States.* See Hopkins, Livingston, entry at the National Library of Australia's Federation Gateway, http://www.nla.gov.au/guides/federation/people/hopkins.html, accessed November 5, 2010.

38. DG, July 26, 1876, 167.

39. Ibid.

40. DG, July 26, 1876, 169.

41. DG, July 28, 1876, 183.

42. DG, October 11, 1876, 644.

43. DG, October 14, 1876, 722.

44. DG, October 30, 1876, 827.

45. DG, August 7, 1876, 218.

Chapter 7. Remington's Indian Illustrations

1. Gaile Robinson, "The West Has Won," *Fort Worth Star-Telegram,* May 22, 2006, 1E. Robinson noted too that in 2005 Britons participating in a BBC contest to name Britain's greatest painting selected an equally heroic work, *The Fighting Temeraire,* a maritime painting by J. M. W. Turner.

2. Robinson, "West Has Won," 2006, 1E.

3. Ibid., 8E.

4. The triumphal vision of Western expansion is so ingrained in the popular consciousness that attempts to revise or challenge the vision quickly become controversial. An example was the 1991 controversy over the Smithsonian museum exhibit *The West as America: Reinterpreting Images of the Frontier, 1820–1920,* which was criticized by traditional historians, conservative cultural critics, and many members of the public as, in the words of the *Wall Street Journal,* "an entirely hostile ideological assault on the nation's founding and history" ("Pilgrims and Other Imperialists," May 17, 1991). An overview of the controversy surrounding the exhibit is Andrew Gulliford, "The West as America," *Journal of American History* 79, no. 1 (June 1992): 199–208.

5. William H. Goetzmann and William N. Goetzmann, *The West of the Imagination* (New York: W. W. Norton, 1986), 237.

6. Peter H. Hassrick, *Frederic Remington* (New York: Harry N. Abrams, 1973), 15.

7. Melissa J. Webster, "The Frederic Remington Catalogue Raisonne," in *Frederic Remington: A Catalogue Raisonne of Paintings, Watercolors and Drawings,* vol. 1, ed. Peter H. Hassrick and Melissa J. Webster (Cody, WY: Buffalo Bill Historical Center, 1996), 32, and Frank Dobie, "Titans of Western Art," *American Scene* 5 (1964): 5.

8. Robert Taft, one of the few historians to examine Remington's career as an illustrator, focused largely on Remington's life as a sheep rancher in Kansas. See Taft, *Artists and Illustrators of the Old West, 1850–1900* (New York: Charles Scribner's Sons, 1953), 194–211.

9. James W. Carey, "A Cultural Approach to Communication," in *Communication as Culture: Essays on Media and Society* (Boston: Unwin Hyman, 1989), 18.

10. See, for example, Peter H. Hassrick, "Frederic Remington the Painter: A Historiographical Sketch," in *Frederic Remington: A Catalogue Raisonne of Paintings, Watercolors and Drawings,* vol. I, ed. Peter H. Hassrick and Melissa J. Webster (Cody, WY: Buffalo Bill Historical Center, 1996), 43, 51.

11. This biographical summary is drawn from Hassrick, *Frederic Remington.*

12. Hassrick, *Frederic Remington,* 15.

13. Henry C. Pitz, *Frederic Remington: 173 Drawings and Illustrations* (New York: Dover, 1972), vi.

14. Estelle Jussim, *Frederic Remington, the Camera and the Old West* (Fort Worth, TX: Amon Carter Museum, 1983), 4.

15. Quoted in Hassrick, *Frederic Remington,* 18. A reproduction of one early Remington drawing of soldiers appears in Pitz, *Frederic Remington: 173 Drawings,* vi.

16. Hassrick, *Frederic Remington,* 19.

17. Quoted in Hassrick, *Frederic Remington,* 19.

18. Hassrick, *Frederic Remington,* 19.

19. This drawing, "Ejecting an Oklahoma Boomer," was redrawn by the well-known *Harper's* illustrator Thure de Thulstrup. See Hassrick, *Frederic Remington*, 22.

20. Popular interest in the West rose during the 1880s. According to Robert Taft, *Harper's Weekly* and other pictorial papers promoted the West by publishing an increasing number of illustrations during the decade, including Remington and Charles M. Russell. See Taft, *Artists and Illustrators*, 176. Concerning the Geronimo campaign, Jussim notes that *Harper's* jumped at his Arizona sketches because they were "just the thing for an audience eager for news about Geronimo and whose interest in Indians was suddenly revived by that journal's sensationalist treatment"; see Jussim, *Frederic Remington, the Camera and the Old West*, 19.

21. Hassrick, "Frederic Remington the Painter," 42.

22. Quoted in Goetzmann and Goetzmann, *West of the Imagination*, 238.

23. Alexander Nemerov, *Frederic Remington and Turn-of-the-Century America* (New Haven, CT: Yale University Press, 1995); J. Herbert Altschull, *From Milton to McLuhan: The Ideas behind American Journalism* (New York: Longman, 1990), 201.

24. Frederic Remington, "On the Indian Reservations," *Century* 38, no. 3 (July 1889): 400.

25. In his July 1889 piece for *Century*, "On the Indian Reservations," Remington expressed admiration for some Apaches, writing that "these Indians have a natural dignity" (397). Later in the article, he describes Comanches as "a jolly, round-faced people" (401). Remington also admired the testing ordeals that young Indian men endured because, in Jussim's words, they were "the finest male virtues"; see Jussim, *Frederic Remington, the Camera and the Old West*, 26.

26. Nemerov, *Frederic Remington and Turn-of-the-Century America*, 9.

27. Frederic Remington, "Soldiering in the Southwest" in *Frederic Remington's Own West*, ed. Harold McCracken (New York: Dial Press, 1960), 20.

28. Remington, "On the Indian Reservations," 400.

29. Art historian Joan Troccoli has noted the connection between Remington's career as an illustrator and his success in capturing symbolic action in his later paintings. His *Harper's* experience, she writes, "had taught him how to select the most illuminating moment in a story, as well as a pictorial economy that would enable the viewer to get the point at a glance"; see Joan Carpenter Troccoli, *Painters and the American West: The Anschutz Collection* (Denver, CO: Denver Art Museum/New Haven, CT: Yale University Press, 2000), 113.

30. See, for example, Hassrick and Webster, *Frederic Remington: A Catalogue Raisonne*, which is brimming with such illustrations.

31. Hassrick, *Frederic Remington*, 24.

32. *Harper's Weekly* (hereafter HW), August 7, 1886, 509. Remington's Southwestern photos are discussed in Hassrick, "Frederic Remington the Painter," 25–26.

33. Hassrick, "Frederic Remington the Painter," 25–26.

34. Nemerov, *Frederic Remington and Turn-of-the-Century America*, 8. Also see Jussim, *Frederic Remington, the Camera and the Old West*, 24.

35. Quoted in Hassrick, *Frederic Remington*, 31.

36. Christopher M. Lyman, *The Vanishing Race and Other Illusions: Photographs of Indians by Edward S. Curtis* (Washington, DC: Smithsonian Institution Press, 1982), 90, 110.

37. HW, August 21, 1886, 532.

38. HW, October 13, 1888, 780.

39. In *Picturesque California,* ed. John Muir (San Francisco: J. Dewing, 1888), 238.

40. Goetzmann and Goetzmann, *West of the Imagination,* 242. Also see Jessica Hodge, *Remington* (London: Saturn Books, 1997), 10. Multiple examples of Remington's illustrated types are reproduced in Hassrick and Webster, *Frederic Remington: A Catalogue Raisonne.*

41. See Hassrick, "Frederic Remington the Painter," 48–49, 54, 59. Hassrick cites several scholars who are critical of Remington's dedication to a nineteenth-century "cult of masculinity." Hassrick notes, however, that Remington did include women in many paintings, countering the assertion that he erased women from the Western scene.

42. HW, July 23, 1887, 521.

43. Joshua Brown, *Beyond the Lines: Pictorial Reporting, Everyday Life, and the Crisis of Gilded Age America* (Berkeley: University of California Press, 2002), 57.

44. Brian W. Dippie, *Remington and Russell,* rev. ed. (Austin: University of Texas Press, 1994), 18, 44.

45. "Apache Soldier, or Scout," *Century Magazine,* July 1889, 394. Remington's use of exaggerated facial features follows a pattern used by other pictorial journalists of the era. The "harsh physiognomic codes" applied to African Americans are documented in Brown, *Beyond the Lines,* 212.

46. See, for example, "Indians Were Seen to Fall and Be Dragged out of Fire," *Outing,* February 1887, 430. The two African American soldiers in the drawing are highly exaggerated, especially when compared to the white officer in the image.

47. *Harper's Monthly,* February 1892, 393.

48. Hassrick, *Frederic Remington,* 94.

49. HW, August 21, 1886, 529.

50. Webster, "Frederic Remington Catalogue Raisonne," 26.

51. HW, January 30, 1886, 76.

52. *Collier's,* December 5, 1903, 24–25.

53. HW, March 30, 1889, 244–45. Also see Hodge, *Remington,* 14.

54. HW, March 31, 1888, 233.

55. HW, November 5, 1887, 800.

56. Hassrick, *Frederic Remington,* 62.

57. Nemerov, *Frederic Remington and Turn-of-the-Century America,* 9. For a more benign reading of Remington's Indian attitudes, see Roscoe L. Buckland, *Frederic Remington: The Writer* (New York: Twain, 2000), 32–47.

58. Catherine A. Lutz and Jane L. Collins *Reading National Geographic* (Chicago: University of Chicago Press, 1993), 27.

59. Lyman, *Vanishing Race,* 46–47.

60. Ibid., 13.

Chapter 8. Visualizing Race

1. Christmas edition, *Frank Leslie's Illustrated Newspaper* (hereafter FLIN), December 7, 1889, 9.

2. Ibid., 4.

3. Ibid., 16.

4. These African American qualities are part of a larger list of negative stereotypes identified by scholars. Marilyn Kern-Foxworth, for example, cites a list of nineteen basic stereotypes applied to blacks, including "the happy slave" and "the devoted servant." See Kern-Foxworth, *Aunt Jemima, Uncle Ben, and Rastus: Blacks in Advertising, Yesterday, Today, and Tomorrow* (Westport, CT: Greenwood Press, 1994), 79.

5. Joshua Brown, *Beyond the Lines: Pictorial Reporting, Everyday Life, and the Crisis of Gilded Age America* (Berkeley: University of California Press, 2002), 33.

6. These goals were advocated in a *Leslie's* editorial titled "How to Solve the Indian Problem," March 7, 1891, 78.

7. Brown, *Beyond the Lines,* 33–34. Artists were dispatched to cover predictable news events, Brown notes, but "it is safe to say that most of the artist-reporters' work—including that of the broad network of corresponding artists who mailed in their sketches of distant news—occurred after the event, requiring them to reconstruct the news through verbal testimonials and visual transcriptions of the details of place and circumstance."

8. Several side-by-side comparisons of photographs and illustrations based on the photos can be found in Michael L. Carlebach, *The Origins of Photojournalism in America* (Washington, DC: Smithsonian Institution Press, 1992), esp. ch. 4. One comparison shows a portrait of the Apache man Mangus with only minor changes. Other comparisons, however, show significant editorial changes in emphasis and detail.

9. Alan Trachtenberg, *Reading American Photographs: Images as History, Mathew Brady to Walker Evans* (New York: Hill and Wang, 1989), xiv. Also see similar arguments in Bonnie Brennen and Hanno Hardt, *Picturing the Past: Media, History, and Photography* (Urbana: University of Illinois Press, 1999), 6.

10. John M. Coward, *The Newspaper Indian: Native American Identity in the Press, 1820–90* (Urbana: University of Illinois Press, 1999), 20.

11. Brown, *Beyond the Lines,* 4.

12. Ibid.

13. Ibid., 4–5.

14. Quoted in William E. Huntzicker, "Frank Leslie (Henry Carter)," in *American Magazine Journalists,* ed. Sam Riley, vol. 79 of *Dictionary of Literary Biography* (Detroit: Gale Research, 1989), 220.

15. FLIN, May 11, 1889, 222.

16. Ibid.

17. An overview of Native American stereotypes in the press can be found in Coward, *Newspaper Indian.* For an overview of African America stereotypes, see Jannette L. Dates and William Barlow, *Split Image: African Americans in the Mass Media,* 2nd ed. (Washington, DC: Howard University Press, 1993).

18. The illustrated press coverage of the Ghost Dance movement and Wounded Knee is well documented in William E. Huntzicker, "The 'Sioux Outbreak,' in the Illustrated Press," *South Dakota History* 20, no. 4 (Winter 1990): 299–322. Huntzicker describes the coverage in *Harper's Weekly* in some detail, incuding the illustations by its star artist, Frederic Remington. Huntzicker also notes that *Harper's* published an editorial sympathizing

with the Sioux in November 1890, not only blaming political patronage for incompetent or dishonest Indian agents, but also supporting the government's takeover of seventeen million acres of "surplus" Indian land.

19. FLIN, November 22, 1890, 280.

20. FLIN, December 13, 1890, 354.

21. Smith's sketch of the Sioux Ghost Dancers shows them highly agitated and threatening, unlike the more artfully rendered Ghost Dancers painted by Frederic Remington for *Harper's Weekly*. See *Harper's Weekly*, December 6, 1890, 960–61.

22. FLIN, December 13, 1890, 351.

23. FLIN, December 27, 1890, 385.

24. FLIN, January 3, 1891, 409.

25. FLIN, January 10, 1891, 437.

26. Ibid., 432.

27. Brown, *Beyond the Lines*, 122.

28. FLIN, October 19, 1889, 201.

29. FLIN, August 10, 1889, 5.

30. FLIN, September 15, 1888, 73.

31. Ibid.

32. Despite such journalistic optimism, the actual conditions of the postbellum era were sometimes chaotic. For example, in *Beyond the Lines*, Brown documents the many labor disputes in the Pennsylvania coalfields as well as the Great Upheaval of 1877, a violent national railroad strike that disrupted the nation's economic system.

33. FLIN, March 7, 1891, 89.

34. Ibid., 78.

35. FLIN, August 11, 1888, 410.

36. FLIN, September 5, 1891, 66.

37. FLIN, December 19, 1891, 345.

38. This theme was not new in the illustrated press, which had published many documentary-style images of Indians in its pages, especially Indians in the American Southwest. This theme became more significant in the last years of the nineteenth century as ethnography and anthroplogy became more popular and important. The National Geographic Society was founded in 1888, only one manifestation of the growing interest in knowing and ordering the world through science and photography. See Catherine A. Lutz and Jane L. Collins, *Reading National Geographic* (Chicago: University of Chicago Press, 1993), 15–31.

39. FLIN, September 22, 1888, 92.

40. FLIN, March 24, 1888, 85.

41. FLIN, May 23, 1891, 267.

42. Ibid., 272.

43. FLIN, April 28, 1888, 164.

44. FLIN, September 21, 1889, 108.

45. The "mammy" stereotype is extensively discussed in Kern-Foxworth, *Aunt Jemima, Uncle Ben, and Rastus,* esp. ch. 4, "Aunt Jemima: The Most Battered Woman in America Rises to the Top."

46. This term and its implications are discussed in Lutz and Collins, *Reading National Geographic,* 61, 161–64.

47. FLIN, December 29, 1888, 334.

48. Ibid.

49. Ibid.

50. Ibid., 337.

51. FLIN, October 31, 1891, 203.

52. See Lutz and Collins, *Reading National Geographic,* 96, which offers a useful discussion of the meaning of the smile in photographs of the ethnic other. Lutz and Collins write, for example, that the smile "is a key way of achieving idealization of the other, permitting the projection of the ideal of the happy life."

53. FLIN, June 27, 1891, 352. The untroubled presentation of this marriage can be contrasted with the very different public response to the marriage of two Cherokees, John Ridge and Elias Boudinot, to white women in the 1820s. Boudinot's marriage to Harriet Gold in 1826 was so controversial that it forced the closing of the Foreign Mission School in Cornwall, Connecticut, later that year.

Conclusion

1. *Harper's Weekly* (hereafter HW), April 30, 1870, 284.

2. Ibid., 285.

3. Martha Sandweiss, *Print the Legend: Photography and the American West* (New Haven, CT: Yale University Press, 2002), 3.

4. HW, December 7, 1878, 965; *Frank Leslie's Illustrated Newspaper,* May 17, 1873, 149.

5. Robert M. Utley, *The Lance and the Shield: The Life and Times of Sitting Bull* (New York: Ballantine Books, 1993), 260–67.

6. Philip J. Deloria, *Playing Indian* (New Haven, CT: Yale University Press, 1998), 167.

7. James W. Carey, *Communication as Culture: Essays on Media and Society* (Boston: Unwin Hyman, 1989), 18, 20.

8. Michael Schudson, *The Sociology of News,* 2nd ed. (New York: W. W. Norton, 2011), xiv.

9. Devon A. Mihesuah, *American Indians: Stereotypes and Realities* (Atlanta, GA: Clarity Press, 1996).

10. Ibid., 3–4.

11. HW, June 20, 1868, 392.

12. Ibid, 385.

13. Ibid.

Index

91–92, 164–65, 178; feminized male grooming, 57–60, *59*; "good" vs. "bad" Indians and, 16; *Leslie's* sensationalism and, 49–50, *50*; "normal" ideas as basis for, 187–88; outsider Indians, 166, *167*; racial otherness, 186; Southwest Indian exoticism, 90–91, 178–79, 218n38; touristic other, 88–90, 92, 178–79, 218n38; wife swapping, 57, *58*. *See also* racism; stereotypes

Outing, 151

painting: defense of painted portraiture, 26; Indian chief portraits, 23; Remington paintings, 149–51, 159–61; wagon train attacks, 99–100

Papago, 156

Pawnee, 47, *176*, 177

Peale, Rembrandt, 26

Pearson, Andrea, 10–11

performances: Centennial Exhibition in Philadelphia, 146; Cushing performances, 52–53, *53*; fairs and festivals, 48–49; marksmanship contest tourist entertainment, 68–69; stage attack reenactments, 100; Wild West shows, 48, 100

Perrin, L. K., 97–98

Phillips, Selene, 4

Phillips, Wendell, 142–45, *143*, *145*

photography: amateur photography, 181; Civil War photography, 194n74; ethnographic photography, 195n20; halftone invention, 9, 168–69; illustrations relationship with, 7, 14; illustrious Americans portraiture, 25–26, 197n32; as imaginative art, 24; Indian portrait photography, 23–25; Indian resistance to, 195n31; mute/pacified Indian image and, 41; photographers as illustration subjects, 21–22, *22*; realism and, 14; Remington as photographer, 156; rise of commercial photography, 27; sick Indian photograph cure, 84–86, *85*; still-subject vs. action photography, 14

pictorial journalism: overview, 3; "double-mindedness" towards Indians, 42; early development of, 8–9; engraving and block printing, 9–10, 109–10, 170, 193n61; Gilded Age middle readership, 169–70; journalism as secondhand material, 110–11; popular ethnography and, 70; "special artist" illustrator role, 7; subject matter in, 9, 10, 14; "understanding gap" of Native Americans, 18–19. *See also* deception; ethnography; illustrations; media; newspapers; political journalism; travel journalism

Piegan, 184–85, *186*

Pocahontas: in American popular culture, 4–5; depoliticized women and, 78–79; domestic/familial representation of, 75; European legend rescue legends and, 203n6; "good" Indian story cycle and, 16; *Harper's* "Princess Pocahontas" illustration, 71–73, *72*; narrative development of, 75

political journalism: African American political campaigns and, 174–75, 183; Bright Eyes Ponca advocacy, 91; criticism of Black Hills Indian dealings,

140–41, *140*; *Daily Graphic* anti-Indian cartoons, 139–48, *142–43*; Indian rights activism and, 112, 123–25, *124*, 130–31; *Leslie's* swill milk campaign, 10–11; political cartoons, 134; racial progress discourse and, 175–76; Tweed corruption exposé, 11; women's rights and, 79. *See also* pictorial journalism; progressivism and Indian rights

Ponca, 21–22, *22*, 91

portraiture: overview of Indian portraits, 17, 23–24; Apache portraiture, 39–40, *40*, 199n84; Billy Bowlegs portrait deception, 13; delegation portraiture, 27, *28*; illustrious Americans portraiture, 25–26, 197n32; Indian chief portraiture, 23, 25, 41; Indian princess portraiture, 91–92; Louis Heller portraiture style, *37*, 38–39; peaceful Indian subjects of, 34–35, *35*, 132–33, *133*; as study subject, 22–23. *See also* posing

posing, 14, 23–24, 194n74. *See also* portraiture

potlatch, 146

Powhatan, 75

presentism, 17

progressivism and Indian rights: classic humanism approach, 180–81; corruption of Indian agents and, 217n18; criticism of government policies, 65–66, *65*, 82–84, 123–25, *124*, 140–41, *140*; eastern Indian rights activism, 112; Indian education movement, 175–76; land rights activism, 217n18; Noble Savage image and, 130–31. *See also* political journalism

Pueblo, 87–91

Pulitzer, Joseph, 135

Quinn, J. M., 180–81

racism: African American deferential outsiders stereotype, 166–67, *167*; classic humanism approach to, 180–81; deracialized Indian women, 75–77; first families of Virginia (FFVs), 75; Gilded Age racial meanings, 168–69; Indian portraiture and, 24–26, 41; *Leslie's* racial representation, 18, 168–71, 181–83; media racial representation, 6, 73, 75; mixed-race marriage, 181–82, 219n53; racial otherness, 186; Remington racial hierarchy, 155–59, *158*, 163–64; social Darwinism and, 154–55, 158–59; "soft" prejudice, 138; of Western settlers, 42; wooden Indian figures and, 63–64, *63*. *See also* anti-Indian sentiment; otherness

Rain-In-The-Face, 180–81

Ralph, Julian, 156

Randall, A. Frank, 40–41, 199n84

realism. *See* domestic and ceremonial activities; representation

Red Cloud, 24–25, 32–34, *33*

Reinhart, C. S., 118–20, *119*, 144–45, *145*

Remington, Frederic: action pictures of, 160–63, 215n29; biographical sketch, 152–54; character typology and, 155–59, *158*; enduring popularity of, 149–50; exotic otherness in, 164–65, 215n25; gen-

JOHN M. COWARD is an associate professor of communication
at the University of Tulsa. He is the author of *The Newspaper
Indian: Native American Identity in the Press, 1820–90.*

THE HISTORY OF COMMUNICATION

The University of Illinois Press
is a founding member of the
Association of American University Presses.

Designed by Jim Proefrock
Composed in 11.5/14 Bulmer
with Historical Fell Type display
at the University of Illinois Press

Manufactured by Sheridan Books, Inc.
University of Illinois Press
1325 South Oak Street
Champaign, IL 61820-6903
www.press.uillinois.edu